OXFORD HISTORICAL MON(

The Bismarck Myth

Weimar Germany and the Legacy of the Iron Chancellor

ROBERT GERWARTH

OXFORD

UNIVERSITY PRESS

OXFORD
UNIVERSITY PRESS

Great Clarendon Street, Oxford OX2 6DP

Oxford University Press is a department of the University of Oxford.
It furthers the University's objective of excellence in research, scholarship,
and education by publishing worldwide in

Oxford New York

Auckland Cape Town Dar es Salaam Hong Kong Karachi
Kuala Lumpur Madrid Melbourne Mexico City Nairobi
New Delhi Shanghai Taipei Toronto

With offices in

Argentina Austria Brazil Chile Czech Republic France Greece
Guatemala Hungary Italy Japan Poland Portugal Singapore
South Korea Switzerland Thailand Turkey Ukraine Vietnam

Published in the United States
by Oxford University Press Inc., New York

British Library Cataloguing in Publication Data

Data available

Library of Congress Cataloging in Publication Data

Data available

ISBN 978-0-19-928184-8 (Hbk.) 978-0-19-923689-3 (Pbk.)

1 3 5 7 9 10 8 6 4 2

Typeset by Laserwords Private Limited, Chennai, India
Printed in Great Britain
on acid-free paper by
Biddles Ltd.,
King's Lynn, Norfolk.

To my parents

ACKNOWLEDGEMENTS

My interest in Bismarck's popular image and his mystification after 1890 goes back many years. In this time I have received much support from others and it is a pleasure to record my gratitude and indebtedness to them.

Various libraries and archives, listed in the bibliography, have opened their facilities to me and offered me assistance and advice, for which I thank them. In particular I would like to express my gratitude to Prince Ferdinand von Bismarck, who has kindly invited me to undertake research in the family archive in Friedrichsruh and who granted me access to the private papers of his father, Otto von Bismarck. I would also like to thank the following individuals and institutions for permission to reproduce published and unpublished material: the Bundesarchiv (Koblenz and Berlin), Christoph & Friends—Das Fotoarchiv, the Otto-von-Bismarck-Stiftung, Christoph Bellin (Bildarchiv Hamburg), the Deutsches Historisches Museum (Berlin), Klaus Kirchner (Erlangen), and the Staatsbibliothek Berlin / Bildarchiv Preußischer Kulturbesitz.

My doctoral supervisor, Hartmut Pogge von Strandmann, first taught me in 1997, then encouraged me to return to Oxford in 2000, and has since supported me in many friendly ways. This study would not be the same without his keen interest and critical judgement.

Many other great scholars have contributed to this book's completion in one way or another. My former academic supervisor, Heinrich August Winkler, first introduced me to the world of Weimar Germany and has remained a source of inspiration ever since my undergraduate years at Berlin's Humboldt Universität. I am also greatly indebted to Niall Ferguson and Sir Ian Kershaw, who examined the doctoral thesis on which this book is based. Their suggestions have helped me greatly to revise the manuscript for publication.

I would also like to thank Chris Burrows, Porscha Fermanis, Ailish Johnson, Lothar Machtan, Anna Menge, Leslie Mitchell, Anthony Nicholls, John Röhl, Nick Stargardt, and Jonathan Wright for commenting on parts of my work in draft and for making many inspiring suggestions. These friends and colleagues have provided personal support and scholarly encouragement over the past four years. It goes without saying that in the end, I alone am responsible for any shortcomings in this study.

Two scholarship organizations, the Konrad Adenauer Foundation and the German Academic Exchange Service (DAAD), provided generous financial aids in 2000–1 and 2001–2 respectively. In 2002–3 I was fortunate to be the holder of Oxford University's Bryce Research Studentship in Modern History. Without this financial support I could not have undertaken and concluded my research on the Bismarck myth. Furthermore I would like to thank the British Academy for electing me to a Postdoctoral Fellowship, the Fellows of Corpus Christi College, Oxford, for appointing me as a Research Fellow, and the Wiener Library for awarding this book the 2004 Fraenkel Prize in Contemporary History.

Those to whom I owe most of all come last. Porscha Fermanis has lived with this book for the last two years and I want to thank her for making countless crucial improvements to the manuscript. My final and greatest debt of gratitude is to my parents. As a necessarily inadequate acknowledgement of their support, this book is dedicated to them.

Robert Gerwarth
Oxford, June 2004

CONTENTS

LIST OF ILLUSTRATIONS

LIST OF ABBREVIATIONS

ADAP	Akten zur Deutschen Auswärtigen Politik
BA	Bundesarchiv
CDU	Christlich Demokratische Union Deutschlands (German Christian Democratic Union)
BVP	Bayerische Volkspartei (Bavarian People's Party)
DDP	Deutsche Demokratische Partei (German Democratic Party)
DNVP	Deutschnationale Volkspartei (German Nationalist People's Party)
DVP	Deutsche Volkspartei (German People's Party)
FDP	Freie Demokratische Partei Deutschlands (German Free Democratic Party)
HZ	*Historische Zeitschrift*
KPD	Kommunistische Partei Deutschlands (German Communist Party)
MSPD	Mehrheitssozialdemokratische Partei Deutschlands (German Majority Social Democratic Party)
NKFD	Nationalkomitee Freies Deutschland (National Committee of Free Germany)
NPL	*Neue Politische Literatur*
NSDAP	Nationalsozialistische Deutsche Arbeiterpartei (National Socialist German Workers' Party)
NV	Nationalversammlung, Stenographische Berichte der Verfassunggebenden Deutschen Nationalversammlung
PAH	Preußisches Abgeordnetenhaus (Prussian Lower House)
PP	*Past and Present*
RT	Akten des Reichstages, Stenographische Berichte
SA	Sturmabteilung
SPD	Sozialdemokratische Partei Deutschlands (German Social Democratic Party)
USPD	Unabhängige Sozialdemokratische Partei Deutschlands (Independent German Social Democratic Party)

1. The Bismarck Memorial in Hamburg, 1923.

I

Introduction

In early 1921, little more than two years after the end of the Great War and the outbreak of the German revolution of 1918–19, the left-liberal periodical *Weltbühne* devoted a two-page article to a cultural phenomenon which it referred to as the 'Bismarck legend'. What the author of the article, the distinguished journalist Richard Lewinsohn, described in his analysis was alarming: Bismarck—dead since 1898—had become 'a severe political danger' for the Republic of Weimar. The Republic, so Lewinsohn insisted, had to emerge from Bismarck's shadow if it was ever to become a state in its own historical right.[1] Lewinsohn was not the only democrat who perceived Bismarck's legacy and the way it was exploited by Weimar's right-wing circles as a threat to the Republic. In his book *Bismarcks Schatten*, a liberal professor of jurisprudence, Hermann Ulrich Kantorowicz, maintained that the consolidation of democracy in Germany could only emerge 'over the rubble of the Bismarck cult'.[2]

The right-wing opponents of democracy provided plenty of evidence for the validity of such arguments. In April 1919, during the negotiations for a new constitution in the city of Weimar, the conservative periodical *Tradition*—a weekly publication of the Patriotic Leagues or *Vaterländische Verbände*—suggested that the 'coup d'état' of 1918 was a conspiracy against Bismarck's legacy. The Social Democrats, Left Liberals, and Centre Catholics who had betrayed Bismarck 'just as Peter had once denied the Saviour' would eternally be stigmatized as 'wreckers of Bismarck's creation' and 'blasphemers against his holy name'.[3]

Less than a year later, in January 1920, one of the leaders of the monarchist DNVP, Kuno Count Westarp, went a step further. The German Republic, he argued, had been founded against the 'spirit of Bismarck' and thus had no historical right to exist. Westarp was optimistic, however, that the democratic 'system' was only an episode in German history: 'the German Republic of 9 November . . . [and] the knavery of the Treaty of Versailles of 28 June 1919, will

---

[1] Richard Lewinsohn, 'Die Bismarck-Legende', *Die Weltbühne*, XVII (1921), 33–5.
[2] Hermann U. Kantorowicz, *Bismarcks Schatten* (Freiburg im Breisgau, 1921), 11.
[3] 'Bismarck und die Revolution', *Die Tradition*, 5 Apr. 1919.

prove to be a transitory period. . . . On the very foundations of that which was created on 18 January [1871—the day of Bismarck's Imperial Proclamation in Versailles], Prussia and Germany will rise again.'[4]

Divisive and controversial statements such as these were typical of the way in which the deeply fragmented Weimar society interpreted Bismarck's legacy. Conservatives who referred to Bismarck between 1918 and 1933 did so in order to compare the increasingly despised Republic with the mythical figure of the Iron Chancellor and the glorified days of his rule over Germany. For left-leaning liberals and Social Democrats, on the other hand, Bismarck's semi-authoritarian government had interrupted the process of liberalization and democratization which had begun with the Wars of Liberation and culminated in the revolution of 1848. After the military collapse of the *kleindeutsch* Hohenzollern Empire—so ran the Republicans' interpretation of the recent German past—the revolutionaries of 1918 had corrected Bismarck's historical failure and established a more just political system: the Weimar Republic.[5]

The quarrel over Bismarck and his legacy was certainly older than the Republic. Even during the Kaiserreich perceptions of the Iron Chancellor had differed significantly. For those groups which had been stigmatized by Bismarck as 'internal enemies of the Empire'—above all for the Centre Catholics, Left Liberals, and Social Democrats—the experience of the *Kulturkampf* and the anti-socialist legislation of Bismarck's regime continued to dominate the perception of the first Chancellor for decades. Bismarck's critics were, however, confronted with a politically dominant majority of Germans for whom Bismarck was the personification of the German nation, the 'redeemer' who had rescued Germany from its state of disunity and had thereby fulfilled Prussia's 'German mission'. Bismarck himself had contributed significantly to this interpretation. The Imperial Proclamation of 1871 in Versailles' Hall of Mirrors was deliberately held on 18 January, a date of particular symbolic importance: exactly 170 years earlier Frederick I had become the first Prussian king.[6]

In the transition period from Kaiserreich to Republic the Bismarck myth underwent a fundamental change of meaning and purpose. Up until 1918 the narrative had been a constant reminder to the German people that the Empire was the culmination of German history and that every form of criticism against

[4] Kuno Count Westarp, 'Der 18. Januar', *Die Tradition*, 17 Jan. 1920.

[5] On this see Daniel Bussenius, 'Eine ungeliebte Tradition: Die Weimarer Linke und die 48er Revolution 1918–1925', in Heinrich August Winkler (ed.), *Griff nach der Deutungsmacht: Zur Geschichte der Geschichtspolitik in Deutschland* (Göttingen, 2004), 90–114.

[6] See Volker Ullrich, *Die nervöse Großmacht: Aufstieg und Untergang des deutschen Kaiserreiches 1871–1918* (Frankfurt, 1997), 19 ff.

it was a slap in the face of Bismarck, the 'father' of the nation-state. After the end of World War I, however, the myth served as a political *chiffre* of what the German Reich had lost as a result of the 'treason' committed by the 'internal enemies of the Empire'; namely, its role as the leading economic and political power on the European continent. At the same time, the myth was used to remind the German public that their country's former greatness was not owed to parliamentarianism, but to the existence of a towering leader.

In the increasingly unpopular democracy of Weimar, threatened by its internal right- and left-wing opponents, 'the past' in general and the Bismarck myth in particular became a weapon in the struggle of ideologies. Throughout the first German democracy, various conflicting socio-political groups and milieux—monarchists, nationalists, liberals, Centrists, socialists, and Communists—mined the quarry of the past in order to establish credibility and legitimacy for their political goals in the present.

That myths, both old and new, were being created or revived in the transitional period of 1918–19 was no coincidence. According to the philosopher Ernst Cassirer, societies generally invent and reinvent political myths in times of great political unrest and disorientation.[7] And in the Republic of Weimar— probably more than in any other period of modern German history—disorientation and unrest were among the most striking characteristics of the era.

The uncompromising character of the fierce historical-political debate which began with the downfall of the Kaiserreich distinguished the controversy of the years 1918–33 from all previous and subsequent disagreements about Bismarck. The intensity with which the participants in the public debate insisted on the correctness of their particular interpretation of history was the result of one expedient realization: only those who had the past on their side could claim legitimacy for their present-day political views. And legitimacy was desperately needed after the establishment of a political system without precedent in German history. The pseudo-historical debate surrounding Bismarck was therefore only a pretext for a more fundamental question: the historical legitimacy of the Weimar Republic. Was the Republic, as the right-wing opponents of democracy maintained, the result of a 'stab-in-the-back' of the 'victorious' German Army, executed by an unholy and anti-nationally-minded alliance of Social Democrats, Left Liberals, and Centre Catholics? Was it the outcome of a late revenge of the 'internal enemies of the Reich' against

---

[7] Ernst Cassirer, *The Myth of the State* (London, 1946), 364. For similar thoughts see Hans Blumenberg, *Arbeit am Mythos* (Frankfurt, 1996), 41–2 and Carl Schmitt, *Political Romanticism*, reprint of the 1st edn. of 1926 (Cambridge, Mass., 1986), 160.

their former persecutor? Or—as the Republicans argued on the contrary—had the constitution of 1919 brought about the fulfilment of those democratic ideals for which the revolutionaries of 1848 had fought before their suppression by 'reactionaries' under the leadership of Bismarck?

The public debate inflamed by questions such as these mirrored a fundamental problem of Weimar's political culture: the lack of any form of basic consensus about the past, present, and future of the political community.[8] The extreme ideological fragmentation of German society translated into a civil war of memories and historical symbols in which the individual political communities fought over the past in order to give meaning to their policies for the present and future.[9]

The key argument of this book is that the figure of Bismarck played a central role as an anti-democratic myth in the highly ideological battle over the past which raged between 1918 and 1933. It will be suggested that Weimar Germany's political culture, defined as the 'set of subjective orientations to politics in a national population, or a sub-set of the population', can only be explained imperfectly without consideration of the Bismarck myth.[10] Throughout the fourteen years of Weimar's existence, 'Bismarck' remained a constant reminder of past German 'greatness' and achievements that were permanently set against the Republic's perceived weakness. As such, the Bismarck myth served to undermine the establishment of a democratic consensus, which proved to be a vital component in the struggle for survival of Germany's first democracy. At the same time, this study will demonstrate how the Bismarck myth contributed significantly to the rise of Hitler by popularizing and promoting two central elements of right-wing agitation against the Republic of Weimar: anti-parliamentarianism and the belief that only a strong charismatic leader could solve the country's most pressing problems efficiently.

By addressing the Bismarck myth and its impact on Weimar Germany's political culture, this study can be situated within the established school of

---

[8] This has been underlined by Dietmar Schirmer, 'Politisch-kulturelle Deutungsmuster: Vorstellungen von der Welt der Politik in der Weimarer Republik', in Detlef Lehnert and Klaus Megerle (eds.), *Politische Identität und nationale Gedenktage: Zur politischen Kultur in der Weimarer Republik* (Opladen, 1989), 31–60.

[9] Friedrich Stampfer, *Vorwärts*, 18 Jan. 1931, morning edition. The problem of the fragmented political culture in Weimar Germany has been addressed in various recent works, for example in Heinrich August Winkler, *Weimar 1918–1933: Die Geschichte der ersten deutschen Demokratie*, 2nd rev. edn. (Munich, 1994), 285–305. See also Hans Mommsen, *The Rise and Fall of Weimar Democracy 1918–1933*, trans. Elberg Foster and Larry E. Jones (London, 1996). Finally, Detlef Lehnert and Klaus Megerle, 'Problems of Identity and Consensus in a Fragmented Society: The Weimar Republic', in Dirk Berg-Schlosser and Ralf Rytlewski (eds.), *Political Culture in Germany* (London, 1993), 80–95.

[10] Gabriel D. Almond, 'The Study of Political Culture', in Berg-Schlosser and Rytlewski (eds.), *Political Culture*, 13–26, here p. 15.

historiography that investigates what is best described by the German term *Geschichtspolitik*—the politically motivated use of historical narratives within the public discourse.[11] The most basic common assumption of all studies that have emerged from this school in recent years is that each age reconstructs images of the past to suit its present purposes and needs.[12] At least in this respect, the approach owes much to the theoretical groundwork provided by the French inter-war sociologist Maurice Halbwachs.[13] Halbwachs' work is particularly appealing to the historians of political myth-making because of his insistence on the way in which social milieux consciously elaborate a past which corresponds to changing ideological parameters or new political contexts.[14]

Far from being a method pursued only by authoritarian regimes or dictator-ships, the deployment of the past to further a more current political agenda is also a phenomenon of pluralistic societies.[15] Whereas in authoritarian societies the state tends to dictate an official reading of the past, pluralistic societies usu-ally witness a competition between various interpretations of history for universal acceptance. Very few movements (regardless of their ideological origin) have ever failed to attempt a justification of their aims through often contested historical traditions. The closer a political movement or social milieu comes to establishing its own view of the past as universal, the closer it gets to the state of cultural hegemony. In other words, power lies with those who have mastered the past.[16]

---

[11] See Edgar Wolfrum, 'Geschichte als Politikum—Geschichtspolitik: Internationale Forschungen zum 19. und 20. Jahrhundert', *Neue Politische Literatur*, XLI (1996), 376–401. See, too, Petra Bock and Edgar Wolfrum (eds.), *Umkämpfte Vergangenheit: Geschichtsbilder, Erinnerung und Vergangenheitspolitik im inter-nationalen Vergleich* (Göttingen, 1999). Finally, Klaus Schönhoven, *Geschichtspolitik: über den öffentlichen Umgang mit Geschichte und Erinnerung* (Bonn, 2003).

[12] See Bo Strath, 'Introduction: Myth, Memory and History in the Construction of Community', in id. (ed.), *Myth and Memory in the Construction of Community: Historical Patterns in Europe and Beyond* (Brussels, 2000), 33, and Patrick H. Hutton, *History as an Art of Memory* (Hanover and London, 1993), 6. See also the voluminous work on commemorative practices presented by Pierre Nora *et al.* (eds.), *Les Lieux de mémoire*, 3 vols. (Paris, 1984–92). Similar works have recently been published for Italy, Germany, the Netherlands, Denmark, and Austria.

[13] Maurice Halbwachs, *Les Cadres sociaux de la mémoire* (Paris, 1925) and id., *La Mémoire collective* (Paris, 1950). Although the term 'collective memory' has been criticized in recent years because it applies the psychological term 'memory' to larger social entities, it is still widely used. For a critical assessment of the 'collective memory' concept see, for example, Dirk Reinhardt, ' "Kollektive Erinnerung" und "kollektives Gedächtnis": Zur Frage der übertragbarkeit individualpsychologischer Begriffe auf gesellschaftliche Phänomene', in Clemens Wischermann (ed.), *Die Legitimität der Erinnerung und die Geschichtswissenschaft* (Stuttgart, 1996), 87–100.

[14] *Kultur und Gedächtnis* (Frankfurt, 1988); Aleida Assmann, *Erinnerungsräume: Formen und Wandlungen des kulturellen Gedächtnisses* (Munich, 1999); Henry Rousso, *Vichy, un passé qui ne passe pas* (Paris, 1996); Robert Gildea, *The Past in French History* (New Haven and London, 1994).

[15] Edgar Wolfrum, *Geschichte als Waffe: Vom Kaiserreich bis zur Wiedervereinigung* (Göttingen, 2001), 5–7.

[16] Jacques Le Goff, *Histoire et mémoire* (Paris, 1985), 109; Winkler (ed.), *Griff nach der Deutungsmacht*, 7.

In those cases where a certain interpretation of the past transcends historical reality and becomes part of popular culture, it enters the realm of myth. Myths are popular semiotic narratives, usually based on true historical events or persons, which serve the purpose of fostering the self-awareness and integration of a community.[17] Through mythical narratives political abstractions and complex historical realities can be simplified and—for example in the case of the Bismarck myth—personalized. The creation of hero figures in particular has been a dominant feature of myth-making since ancient times, and it became even more important with the emergence of the modern nation-state and the related quest for suitable historical traditions on which a national community's identity could be founded.[18] In the nineteenth century, when nationalism emerged as the secular religion of modernity, the enthusiastic search for mythical hero figures became a universal phenomenon.[19]

As early as 1840, Thomas Carlyle emphasized in his lectures on 'heroes, hero worship and the heroic in history', that hero worship is the strongest and most reliable means for stabilizing a political and social order.[20] The theologian and sociologist Ernest Renan equally maintained the importance of hero worship for the unity of a nation in his famous 1882 address to the Sorbonne University: 'a heroic past, great men, fame . . . that is the social capital on which the idea of a nation is founded.'[21]

While political myths are indispensable for the creation of a national identity, they are equally important for building and sustaining allegiance and successful political mobilization within a community.[22] In this respect, political myths do not necessarily need to have an integrating effect. Particularly in socially and ideologically fragmented societies they can become a mobilizing factor in a politically destabilizing sense. The political culture of Weimar Germany with its lack of consensus is a particularly fruitful example of how rival

---

[17] On this definition see Andreas Dörner, *Politischer Mythos und symbolische Politik: Der Hermannmythos: Zur Entstehung des Nationalbewußtseins der Deutschen* (Reinbek bei Hamburg, 1996), 43.

[18] See, for example, Sebastian P. Garman, 'Foundation Myths and Political Identities: Ancient Rome and Anglo-Saxon England Compared', Ph.D. thesis (London School of Economics, 1994). Also, Alexander Demandt, *Geschichte als Argument: Drei Formen politischen Zukunftsdenkens im Altertum* (Konstanz, 1972). See, too, Eric Hobsbawm, 'Mass-Producing Traditions: Europe 1870–1914', in id. and Terence Ranger (eds.): *The Invention of Tradition*, 2nd edn. (Cambridge, 1996), 263–307; Benedict Anderson, *Imagined Communities: Reflections on the Origin and Spread of Nationalism*, 2nd rev. edn. (London and New York, 1991).

[19] On the blossoming of political myths in nineteenth- and twentieth-century Europe, see Monika Flacke (ed.), *Mythen der Nationen* (Berlin, 1998).

[20] Thomas Carlyle, *On Heroes, Hero-Worship, and the Heroic in History* (London, 1841). The German translation of Carlyle's book was published in three editions between 1846 and 1898.

[21] Ernest Renan, 'Das Plebiszit der Vergeßlichen: über Nationen und den Dämon des Nationalismus—Ein Vortrag aus dem Jahre 1882', reprinted in *Frankfurter Allgemeine Zeitung*, 27 Mar. 1993.

[22] Strath (ed.), *Myth and Memory*, 19–48.

groups constructed myths and challenged each other's interpretations of the past with the aim of either undermining or defending the credibility of the newly founded Republic. Apart from the Bismarck myth four other legends featured prominently in Weimar's civil war of memories: the glorified experience of the trenches as the birth of the *Volksgemeinschaft*, the 'stab-in-the-back' legend of the Weimar right (which, as will be pointed out, was closely intertwined with the Bismarck myth), the democrats' interpretation of the Weimar Republic as an implementation of the ideals of 1848, and the Communist myth of the Majority Social Democrats' 'betrayal' of the proletarian revolution in the winter of 1918–19.

Whereas most of the myths related to the First World War have been the object of scholarly investigations, the same cannot be said about the Bismarck myth after 1918.[23] Most studies on the subject have focused on the years *before* the Weimar Republic came into being.[24] All of these studies have emphasized the Bismarck myth as an essential part of the political culture of Wilhelmine Germany. They have established that by the turn of the century (at the very latest) the politically and personally disputed Bismarck had been replaced in the public debate by a heroic cult figure which embodied the value system and political ambitions of the nationalist-minded German bourgeoisie. Politicians, historians, theologians, teachers, writers, journalists, and artists alike took part in this process, which found its most clearly visible expression

---

[23] On the 'stab-in-the-back' legend, see in particular Friedrich Freiherr von Gärtringen, ' "Dolchstoß"— Diskussion und "Dolchstoßlegende" im Wandel von vier Jahrzehnten', in id. and Waldemar Besson (eds.), *Geschichte und Geschichtsbewußtsein* (Göttingen, 1963), 122–60. See also Anneliese Thimme, *Flucht in den Mythos: Die Deutschnationale Volkspartei und die Niederlage von 1918* (Göttingen, 1969), 68 ff. On the closely related question of war guilt, see Ulrich Heinemann, *Die verdrängte Niederlage: Politische öffentlichkeit und Kriegsschuldfrage in der Weimarer Republik* (Göttingen, 1983). Also Jeffrey Verhey, *The Spirit of 1914: Militarism, Myth, and Mobilization in Germany* (Cambridge, 2000). On the Communist myth of 1918–19 and its protagonists, Rosa Luxemburg and Karl Liebknecht, see Gilbert Badia, 'Rosa Luxemburg', in Etienne François and Hagen Schulze (eds.), *Deutsche Erinnerungsorte*, vol. II (Munich, 2001), 105–21 as well as Manfred Scharrer, *'Freiheit ist immer . . .': Die Legende von Rosa & Karl* (Berlin, 2002).

[24] See, in particular, Lothar Machtan (ed.), *Bismarck und der deutsche National-Mythos* (Bremen, 1994); Thomas Hagemann, *Das Bismarck-Bild in der deutschen öffentlichkeit nach 1890: Mythen-Strukturen, Inhalte, Ausdrucksformen des Bismarck-Kultes und das Beispiel der Verehrerpost aus den Beständen des Archivs der Otto-von-Bismarck-Stiftung in Friedrichsruh*, state exam thesis (University of Paderborn, 1999); Christoph Studt, *Das Bismarckbild in der deutschen öffentlichkeit* (Friedrichsruh, 1999); Leonore Koschnik, 'Mythos zu Lebzeiten—Bismarck als nationale Kultfigur', in *Bismarck—Preussen, Deutschland und Europa: Eine Ausstellung des Deutschen Historischen Museums Berlin, 26. August–25. November 1990*, 3rd edn. (Berlin, 1990), 255–482. See also Hans-Günter Zmarzlik, *Das Bismarckbild der Deutschen—gestern und heute* (Freiburg im Breisgau, 1965), 19; Peter-Arndt Gröppel and Karsten Weber, *Heldenverehrung als politische Gefahr: Der Bismarck-Kult des deutschen Bürgertums im 2. Reich* (Grünwald, 1973). Finally, Hans-Walter Hedinger, 'Der Bismarckkult: Ein Umriß', in Gunter Stephenson (ed.), *Der Religionswandel in unserer Zeit im Spiegel der Religionswissenschaften* (Darmstadt, 1976), 201–15. Most recently, Jakob Hort, *Bismarck in München: Formen und Funktionen der Bismarckrezeption (1885–1934)* (Frankfurt, 2004).

in numerous memorials, postcards, trivial literature, and all sorts of everyday kitsch.[25]

Lothar Machtan, who has edited the most comprehensive collection of essays on the subject to date, has shown that the transformation of Bismarck into the 'German national myth' or *deutscher Nationalmythos* was the concrete response of large parts of the German middle classes to the evident need for national integration.[26] In this respect, the myth defined both what being German was supposed to mean and what was to be condemned as 'un-German'. Consequently, as Machtan and the American historian Michael McGuire have both emphasized, the Bismarck myth was also used as a weapon against those perceived as 'internal enemies of the Empire'.[27] That the Bismarck myth had both an integrating *and* a disintegrating effect was only possible because the narrative was not specifically tied to one concrete interpretation. Bismarck became a mythical projection screen, a label for very different, sometimes even opposite, qualities and attributes.[28] Politically motivated references to the Bismarckian Era (and the way in which it was referred to) were modified constantly to meet changing practical needs.

My own study is deeply indebted to research which has already been undertaken on the Bismarck myth. None the less, there has as yet been no study which takes as its general theme the ideological struggle for a universal interpretation of the Reich's founding father between the parallel political cultures in the years after 1918.[29] The immense importance of this narrative for Weimar Germany's political culture and its presence in almost every key political debate between 1918 and 1933 has never been investigated systematically.

This book thus differs from the many studies which have preceded it in its contextual emphasis. The history of the creation and transformation of the Bismarck narrative into Germany's 'national myth' before 1918 will not constitute its main subject. Instead this study will highlight the myth's function as a

---

[25] Hans-Walter Hedinger, 'Bismarck-Denkmäler und Bismarck-Verehrung', in Ekkehard Mai and Stephan Waetzold (eds.), *Kunstverwaltung, Bau- und Denkmalpolitik im Kaiserreich* (Berlin, 1981), 277–314. See also Hermann Reuter, *Bismarck: Spuren und Wirkungen: die Bismarcks in der Altmark, das Phänomen der Bismarck-Türme und -Denkmäler, Bismarck'sche Kultur- und Wirkungsgeschichte* (Lingen, 1996).

[26] Machtan (ed.), *National-Mythos*, 17.

[27] Michael C. Q. McGuire, 'Bismarck in Walhalla: The Cult of Bismarck and the Politics of National Identity in Imperial Germany 1890–1915', Ph.D. thesis (University of Pennsylvania, 1993).

[28] Rolf Parr, '*Zwei Seelen wohnen, ach! In meiner Brust!' Strukturen und Funktionen der Mythisierung Bismarcks 1860–1918* (Munich, 1992), 118 ff.

[29] The only exception in that respect was a study on Bismarck's perception in the Weimar Republic which was started by Erich Wittenberg in 1969. However, only the first (methodological) volume out of three was ever published. See Erich Wittenberg, *Bismarcks politische Persönlichkeit im Bilde der Weimar-Republik: Eine ideengeschichtliche Beleuchtung einer politischen Tradition* (Lund, 1969).

weapon against the state of Weimar and its destructive influence on the political culture of the first German democracy.

In order to evaluate the impact of the Bismarck myth on Weimar Germany's political culture this study is based on a wide range of sources. The ideologically motivated and competing images of Bismarck in circulation during the Weimar Era were first examined through the eyes of major German daily newspapers and periodicals, which have been selected here according to their political or religious affiliation, their circulation, and the amount of relevant information they contain with respect to the perception and instrumentalization of Bismarck.[30] Newspapers have the capacity simultaneously to mould and reflect public opinion. Hence, newspaper reports can offer clues both on the ways in which opinion-makers portrayed Bismarck, and the manner in which he was perceived by the paper's respective readership.

Of the numerous publications chosen for this analysis, the following were pre-eminent in the period: for the Social Democrats it was the *Vorwärts*, which disseminated the party headquarters' political and historical views. In its influence on the moderately socialist, predominantly working-class and trade unionist milieu *Vorwärts* can be compared with the Communist *Rote Fahne* which served the same purpose for the more radicalized workers.

With respect to the left-liberal press, Theodor Wolff's *Berliner Tageblatt* has been selected because it maintained close contacts with the German Democratic Party, the DDP. Despite their comparatively small circulation, two liberal periodicals, *Weltbühne* and *Hilfe,* deserve consideration for their in-depth analysis of the Bismarck myth between 1918 and 1933. Moderately nationalist views on Bismarck were put forward in Gustav Stresemann's *Deutsche Stimmen* and in *Deutsche Allgemeine Zeitung,* a daily which was acquired by Hugo Stinnes in 1920 and which circulated within the powerful industrial elite.

Official views of the Centre Party's political leadership were often mirrored in *Germania,* a newspaper which was published in Berlin but distributed nationwide. Due to the regional differences within the Catholic milieu, two other Catholic dailies, *Kölnische Volkszeitung* and *Regensburger Anzeiger,* have been considered in this analysis. In addition, the commentaries of two Catholic periodicals, *Hochland* and *Historisch-Politische Blätter für das katholische Deutschland* (from 1923 onwards published as *Gelbe Hefte*), have been analysed.

As the confrontation of the post-war political system with the overwhelming mythical figure of Bismarck was a major preoccupation of Weimar

---

[30] For further details on the newspapers mentioned below, see Kurt Koszyk, *Deutsche Presse im 19. und 20. Jahrhundert: Geschichte der Presse Teil II* (Berlin, 1966), 127–30. With respect to the periodicals, see Heinz-Dietrich Fischer (ed.), *Deutsche Zeitschriften des 17. bis 20. Jahrhunderts* (Pullach, 1973).

Germany's right-wing intellectual and journalistic engagement, the explicitly anti-democratic press was the object of an even more detailed investigation. Among the numerous conservative publications, *Deutsche Tageszeitung* seemed to be particularly important because it was the main information source for the influential agrarian, Protestant milieu of East Elbia. Additionally, *Deutsches Echo,* a publication of the youth organization of the German National People's Party—the Bismarck Youth—has been chosen for its extensive references to Bismarck. For the investigation of Bismarck's role in the election campaigns of 1924–5 it was also necessary to look at the *Korrespondenz der Deutschnationalen Volkspartei.* Taking into consideration the anti-Semitic far-right organizations and parties, time and space has been devoted to *Alldeutsche Blätter* and to the National Socialists' *Völkischer Beobachter.*

The numerous speeches delivered on the occasion of Bismarck's birthday and the day of German unification by prominent historians and right-wing politicians constitute a second group of relevant sources. This reading was supplemented by an investigation of the edited files of the German Chancellory (1918–33) and the bound volumes of the shorthand reports on the Reichstag debates during the Weimar Era. The third important group of sources are the archival party records and the private papers of leading national-liberal or nationalist politicians such as Gustav Stresemann, Alfred Hugenberg, and Kuno Count Westarp.

The Bismarck myth did not, however, manifest itself only in newspaper articles or political speeches. Rather, it was characterized by a great variety of forms. Besides its dissemination by election slogans, journalistic opinion columns, and school textbooks, the myth found expression in memorials, political posters, the two Bismarck films of the mid-1920s, and various kinds of Bismarck memorabilia. These memorabilia, ranging from Bismarck postcards to Bismarck busts, testify to the ubiquity of the myth in the domestic sphere, and can thus serve to explain its endurance and omnipresence in people's everyday lives.

The large variety of sources used for this analysis allows this study to suggest that no one who went to a German school, read the newspapers, or took an interest in Germany's political life between 1918 and 1933 could have avoided confrontation with the Bismarck myth at some stage of his or her life.

2

Prologue: The Bismarck Myth in Wilhelmine Germany (1890–1918)

Bismarck's dismissal and the origins of his mystification

When, on 20 March 1890, Prince Otto von Bismarck was dismissed as Chancellor of the German Reich and Minister President of Prussia, the German public reacted with surprising indifference to the end of his almost fifty-year-long career.[1] To be sure, Bismarck's departure from Berlin on 29 March was accompanied by cheering crowds; but neither the Prussian parliament nor the Reichstag voiced any immediate response to the dismissal of one of the most pre-eminent figures in nineteenth-century European politics.[2] The daily newspapers, which at first uncritically reported the rumour leaked from government circles that Bismarck's request to resign had been accepted on grounds of his ill-health, did not express any grief over the Chancellor's dismissal either. Besides the overall lack of interest there was even a certain degree of jubilation and relief: 'It is good fortune that we finally got rid of him', wrote Theodor Fontane to his friend Georg Friedländer. During his last years in office, Bismarck 'was really only a regent of long habit, who did what he wanted, made everybody wait, and demanded only ever-increasing loyalty'.[3]

Considering these immediate reactions to Bismarck's fall and bearing in mind that he had never enjoyed undisputed personal popularity while in office,

---

[1] John C. G. Röhl, *Wilhelm II: Der Aufbau der Persönlichen Monarchie 1888–1900* (Munich, 2001), 351.

[2] For a detailed account of the part played by Bismarck in German unification as well as for further details on his role in late nineteenth-century German politics see, for example, Wolfgang J. Mommsen, *Das Ringen um den nationalen Staat: Die Gründung und der innere Ausbau des Deutschen Reiches unter Otto von Bismarck 1850–1890* (Berlin, 1993). With respect to the European dimension of the German unification, see Eberhard Kolb (ed.), *Europa und die Reichsgründung: Preußen-Deutschland in der Sicht der großen europäischen Mächte 1860–1880* (Munich, 1980). See also the biographical studies on Bismarck by Otto Pflanze, *Bismarck and the Development of Germany*, 3 vols., 2nd edn. (Princeton, 1990). Finally, Lothar Gall, *Bismarck: The White Revolutionary*, translated from the German by J. A. Underwood, 2 vols. (London, 1986).

[3] Theodor Fontane to Georg Friedländer, 1 May 1890, in Theodor Fontane, *Briefe an Georg Friedländer*, ed. Kurt Schreinert (Heidelberg, 1954), 125. On the context, see Hans-Jürgen Perry, *'Nirgends ist ihm ganz zu trauen': Bismarck im Urteil Theodor Fontanes* (Friedrichsruh, 2002). See also Karl Lange, *Bismarcks Sturz und die öffentliche Meinung in Deutschland und im Auslande* (Berlin and Leipzig, 1927).

it seems surprising, as Otto Pflanze has pointed out, that within only a couple of years of his dismissal Otto von Bismarck was to become the most popular German statesman of all time.[4]

One decisive factor contributing to the positive transformation of Bismarck's public image was the reversal of policy instigated by his successor, Leo von Caprivi. The new Chancellor's conciliatory policy towards the Centre and the Progressive Party was regarded with dismay by Conservatives and National Liberals alike.[5] For the Conservatives, the new Chancellor's attempt to promote the export of industrial goods by dismantling customs barriers in 1893 also aroused their fiercest protest. Controversy over the 'New Course' became all the more heated when Caprivi extended his policy to agrarian countries like Romania and Russia. In reaction, the spring of 1893 saw the foundation of the Agrarian League or *Bund der Landwirte* which rapidly expanded its membership and influence.[6]

In the course of their political campaign against Caprivi, the Agrarian League consciously suppressed the memory of Bismarck as the 'man who in the 1860s and 1870s had helped to lay the foundations for the industrialisation of Central Europe and the rise of the industrial economy and industrial society'.[7] Instead, the League focused on the 'common-sense' trade principles embodied in Bismarck's policies after his protectionist shift of policy in 1878–9. The vociferous protests of the League's members placed Caprivi and Karl Göring, who had been appointed as state secretary of the Imperial Chancellory in 1891, under constant pressure.[8]

---

[4] Otto Pflanze, *Bismarck*, vol. 3: *The Period of Fortification 1880–1898* (Princeton, 1990), 444.

[5] John C. G. Röhl, *Germany without Bismarck: The Crisis of Government in the Second Reich 1890–1900* (London, 1967), 110.

[6] See George Vascik, 'Agrarian Conservatism in Wilhelmine Germany: Diederich Hahn and the Agrarian League', in Larry Eugene Jones and James Retallack (eds.), *Between Reform, Reaction, and Resistance: Studies in the History of German Conservatism from 1789 to 1945* (Providence, RI, and Oxford, 1993), 229–60. See also Hans-Jürgen Puhle, *Agrarische Interessenpolitik und preußischer Konservatismus im wilhelminischen Reich 1893–1914: Ein Beitrag zur Analyse des Nationalismus in Deutschland am Beispiel des Bundes der Landwirte und der Deutsch-Konservativen Partei* (Hanover, 1966). Finally, James N. Retallack, *Notables of the Right: The Conservative Party and Political Mobilization in Germany 1876–1918* (Boston, 1988), 100 ff.

[7] Lothar Gall, 'Die Deutschen und Bismarck', in Ralpf Melville *et al.* (eds.), *Deutschland und Europa in der Neuzeit: Festschrift für Karl Otmar von Arentin zum 65. Geburtstag*, 2 vols. (Stuttgart, 1988), 2. 525–36, here p. 528.

[8] Puhle, *Agrarische Interessenpolitik*, 87–8. The Pan-German League, too, joined in with Bismarck's glorification immediately after its foundation in 1890. See Roger Chickering, *'We men who feel most German': A Cultural Study of the Pan-German League 1886–1914* (Boston, London, and Sydney, 1984), 94–7. See, too, Roland Freisel, 'Das Bismarckbild der Alldeutschen: Bismarck im Bewußtsein und in der Politik des Alldeutschen Verbandes von 1890 bis 1933: Ein Beitrag zum Bismarckverständnis des deutschen Nationalismus', Ph.D. thesis (University of Würzburg, 1964), 69 ff. Finally, Richard Frankel, 'From the Beer Halls to the Halls of Power: The Cult of Bismarck and the Legitimization of a New German Right', *German Studies Review*, XXVI (2003), 543–60.

The allegedly obligatory political tradition represented by the Reich's founder was not only used against Caprivi and his government. In fact criticism articulated with reference to Bismarck was directed mainly against Kaiser Wilhelm II himself.[9] An analysis of the countless letters which Bismarck received in Friedrichsruh after his dismissal revealed an unambiguous link between the hero worship of Bismarck and a critical attitude towards Wilhelm's 'personal regime'.[10] It was for two reasons that Bismarck became the spearhead of conservative opposition to the Kaiser in the years after 1890. First, Bismarck's rhetorical skill allowed him to forcefully articulate the fears for the future held by many of the Kaiser's conservative or national-liberal opponents. Secondly, a demonstrative admiration for Bismarck left no doubt about that person's patriotism. Whoever spoke in Bismarck's name could hardly be suspected of an 'anti-national' political attitude, however fiercely he attacked the Kaiser and the government.[11]

The Kaiser himself gave an unwitting boost to the glorification of Bismarck when, in the summer of 1892, Wilhelm wrote a letter to Emperor Franz Joseph of Austria persuading him not to invite Bismarck to an audience while he was attending his son Herbert's wedding in Vienna. Subsequently, in July, Caprivi published a decree in the *Reichsanzeiger* which barred officials from having any contact with the ex-Chancellor during his journey. The resulting storm of public outrage focused on the injustice which Bismarck had suffered in spite of his pre-eminent role in the foundation of the German Empire.[12]

Various political interests and discontent with Wilhelm's 'personal regime' thus contributed to the retrospective idealization of the first Reich Chancellor by the conservative and national-liberal elites of Wilhelmine Germany. Set against the contemporary political world, and as his retirement from office retreated increasingly into the distance, Bismarck's 'genius seemed to be all the more apparent, his dismissal all the more tragic, the void he left behind even more gaping'.[13]

---

[9] On this see McGuire, *Bismarck in Walhalla*, 32–40.

[10] See Werner Pöls, 'Bismarckverehrung und Bismarcklegende als innenpolitisches Problem der Wilhelminischen Zeit', *Jahrbuch für die Geschichte Mittel- und Ostdeutschlands*, XX (1971), 183–201, here pp. 193 ff., as well as Manfred Hank, *Kanzler ohne Amt: Fürst Bismarck nach seiner Entlassung 1890–1898* (Munich, 1980), 285. See, too, Heinrich Class, *Wider den Strom: Vom Werden und Wachsen der nationalen Opposition im alten Reich* (Leipzig, 1932).

[11] Pöls, 'Bismarckverehrung', 193 ff.

[12] Hank, *Kanzler ohne Amt*, 217–52. On Bismarck's subsequent journey through Germany, which turned into a mass demonstration of sympathy for the old Chancellor, see Otto Gradenwitz (ed.), *Akten über Bismarcks großdeutsche Reise vom Jahre 1892* (Heidelberg, 1921).

[13] Pflanze, *Bismarck*, 3. 445. For similar contemporary statements, see, for example, Max Bewer, *Rembrandt und Bismarck*, 10th edn. (Dresden, 1892), 38.

One of the most significant manifestations of the gradual change in public perception of the Iron Chancellor were the celebrations in honour of Bismarck's eightieth birthday in April 1895.[14] Representatives of countless professional groups and delegations from all parts of Germany gathered in Friedrichsruh to pay their respects to the retired founder of the Reich. Bismarck was granted honorary citizenship by over 450 German cities, and the post office in Friedrichsruh was obliged to take on 23 extra workers to cope with the flood of 9,875 telegrams, and 450,000 letters and postcards which poured in between 25 March and 2 April 1895.[15] There was no mistaking the tenor of these congratulatory messages: addressed to the 'Iron Chancellor', the 'most German of all Germans', or the 'Guardian of the Reich', they all lauded Bismarck's inestimable contribution to the foundation of the Reich in 1871— an achievement that had acquired a quasi-sacred character in the writings of academic historians, as well as in the eyes of the upper echelons of the imperial system.[16] It was evident that large parts of the public now primarily remembered Bismarck as the statesman genius and the founder of the Reich rather than as Bismarck the Prussian Minister President or the East Elbian Junker. As early as 1873, the largely uncritical acceptance of the myth surrounding the unification of the nation on the part of the majority of the German public had prompted the Basel historian Jacob Burckhardt to make the bitter comment that soon 'the whole of world history from the time of Adam will be portrayed as a German victory and centred on the period 1870 to 1871'.[17]

The letters which Bismarck received in Friedrichsruh after his enforced resignation from politics not only confirmed Burckhardt's critical assessment, but were unambiguous proof that the cult of Bismarck's personality from its very beginning reflected the social and political segmentation of German society into socio-political milieux.[18] The letters indicate that admiration for

---

[14] For press comments on Bismarck's 80th birthday see *Schulthess' Europäischer Geschichtskalender*, XXXVI (1895), 78–9. See, too, Hedinger, 'Bismarck-Denkmäler und Bismarck-Verehrung', 277–314.

[15] Koschnik, 'Mythos zu Lebzeiten', 455–8. See, too, Pöls, 'Bismarckverehrung', 187. The letters are collected in the archive of the Otto-von-Bismarck-Stiftung (Friedrichsruh), Sammlung A ('Kanzler'), no. 77–192. For a contemporary assessment, see Ernst Brausewetter, *Fürst Bismarcks 81: Geburtstag-Vollendung des 80. Lebensjahres: Berichte über die Ereignisse vor und an demselben* (Leipzig, 1895).

[16] See Elisabeth Fehrenbach, 'Die Reichsgründung in der deutschen Geschichtsschreibung', in Theodor Schieder and Ernst Deuerlein (eds.), *Reichsgründung 1870/71: Tatsachen, Kontroversen, Interpretationen* (Stuttgart, 1970), 259–90. On the role of the historians in the process of Bismarck's mystification see also Hellmut Seier, 'Bismarck und die Anfänge des Kaiserreiches im Urteil der deutschen Historiographie vor 1914', in Johannes Kunisch (ed.), *Bismarck und seine Zeit* (Berlin, 1992), 359–95.

[17] Jacob Burckhardt, *Briefe*, ed. Max Burckhardt, 6 vols. (Stuttgart, 1960), here 5. 182–3.

[18] See Wolfgang Hardtwig, 'Bürgertum, Staatssymbolik und Staatsbewußtsein im Deutschen Kaiserreich 1871–1914', in id., *Nationalismus und Bürgerkultur in Deutschland 1500–1914: Ausgewählte Aufsätze* (Göttingen, 1994), 191–218. On the milieu-concept see Rainer M. Lepsius, 'Parteiensystem und Sozialstruk-

Bismarck was particularly widespread among the Protestant middle classes. Besides officers, it was artisans, teachers, professors, students, and schoolchildren from Protestant-dominated areas of Germany who formed a disproportionate number of his correspondents.[19] Whereas the social contiguity of the correspondents is hardly a surprise, the geographical base of the correspondence is a somewhat different story: the majority of the telegrams and letters did not stem—as might be expected—from Prussia, but rather from southern Germany (Württemberg-Hohenzollern and the Protestant regions of Bavaria in particular).[20]

Not all contemporaries, however, joined in the retrospective idealization of the man who created the German Reich and assured it a place of respect among the great powers of Europe. Instead, what dominated the minds of certain sectors of the German public was the memory of being stigmatized as 'unpatriotic' by Bismarck in the 1870s and 1880s. A year after the victory of the German army over the French troops at Sedan on 2 September 1870 a solemn celebration of the anniversary of the battle had been instigated on the initiative of the Pietist pastor Friedrich von Bodelschwingh. Despite Bismarck's dismissal and the repeal of the anti-socialist legislation these annual celebrations remained an occasion for virulent attacks from nationalist circles against the 'internal enemies of the Reich', which were taken to include any persons who refused to give their unconditional support to the political and social order of Wilhelmine Germany.[21]

The accusation of 'hostility to the Reich' (*Reichsfeindlichkeit*) was a charge Bismarck himself had found very useful when he was in office, and he had never tired of employing it to discredit persons who attempted to stand in the way of his political goals.[22] The victims of these confrontations, the Centre

---

tur: Zum Problem der Demokratisierung der deutschen Gesellschaft', in Gerhard A. Ritter (ed.), *Deutsche Parteien vor 1918* (Cologne, 1973), 56–80.

[19] Hank, *Kanzler ohne Amt*, 45–6. Hank has equally emphasized that women were overrepresented among Bismarck's correspondents whereas blue-collar workers hardly ever wrote to him (ibid.).

[20] After analysing the correspondence, Werner Pöls has suggested that the ratio was 3:2 (Southern Germany:Prussia). See Pöls, 'Bismarckverehrung', 187 n. 13. Thomas Hagemann, however, without denying the surprisingly high number of letters from southern Germany, maintained that the majority of correspondents were Prussians. See Hagemann, *Bismarck-Bild*, 118.

[21] On Sedan Day and scepticism on the part of the 'internal enemies of the Reich' regarding the annual celebrations on 2 September, see Peter-Christian Witt, 'Die Gründung des Deutschen Reiches von 1871 oder dreimal Kaiserfest', in Uwe Schultz (ed.), *Das Fest: Eine Kulturgeschichte von der Antike bis zur Gegenwart* (Munich, 1988), 306–17. See also Claudia Lepp, 'Protestanten feiern ihre Nation: Die kulturprotestantischen Ursprünge des Sedantages', *Historisches Jahrbuch*, CXVIII (1998), 201–22. Finally, Gerhard Birk, 'Der Tag von Sedan: Intentionen, Resonanz und Widerstand (1871–1895)', *Jahrbuch für Volkskunde und Kulturgeschichte*, XXV (1982), 95–110. From 1896 onwards the day of the Imperial Proclamation (18 January) was celebrated in addition to Sedan Day. See Zmarzlik, *Bismarckbild*, 13.

[22] For the Social Democrats see, in particular, Dieter Groh and Peter Brandt, *'Vaterlandslose Gesellen'*:

Party during the 1870s and the Left Liberals and Social Democrats during the late 1870s and 1880s in particular, would not forget Bismarck's continued attacks against them even after his retirement from politics. On the occasion of Bismarck's eightieth birthday on 1 April 1895, for example, the Social Democratic press expressed its uncompromising criticism of Bismarck, who was accused of being guilty of three wars, and was attacked as a fierce reactionary, as well as an enemy of the working classes.[23] A few weeks earlier *Vorwärts* had already taken the fact that the Berlin butchers' guild wished to elect Bismarck an honorary member as an opportunity for bitter mockery: 'Hopefully the old spokesman of the policy of Blood and Iron will accept this flattering and appropriate honorary membership . . . '.[24]

Another occasion, however, attracted far more public attention than the honorary membership of the butchers' guild. On 14 March 1895 the Berlin city council refused to congratulate Bismarck officially on his eightieth birthday.[25] Little more than a week later, on 23 March 1895, the Reichstag followed Berlin's example.[26] The nationalist press was outraged by this 'alliance of the ungrateful', as the Progressive Party, the Centre, and the Social Democrats were labelled.[27]

The events around Bismarck's birthday in 1895 revealed the fundamental differences in the perception of Bismarck even after his dismissal. They could not, however, conceal the fact that the process of transforming Bismarck into a stylized hero-figure was gaining ground. From the mid-1890s onwards, concrete steps were taken to ensure that Bismarck's controversial internal policies were banished from the collective memory. In this process elementary and secondary schools were to play a central role. Generations of young people were fed an ideologically distorted image of Bismarck, which teachers had little dif-

---

Sozialdemokratie und Nation 1860–1990 (Munich, 1992), 23–5. For Bismarck's constant attacks on Windthorst and the Centre Party see Margaret L. Anderson, *Windthorst: A Political Biography* (Oxford, 1981), 153 ff. See too Bismarck's famous speech of 10 February 1872 as printed in Preußisches Abgeordneten-haus (PAH), Stenographische Berichte, 2. 721–3.

[23] See *Vorwärts*, 24 Mar. 1895. See, too, Paul Singer's Reichstag speech on behalf of the SPD delegation in RT, 23 Mar. 1895, vol. 139, 1673. See, too, Jens Müller-Koppe, 'Die deutsche Sozialdemokratie und der Bismarck-Mythos', in Machtan (ed.), *National-Mythos*, 181–207.

[24] *Vorwärts*, 8 Mar. 1895.

[25] On this see Siegfried A. Kaehler, 'Der 1. April 1895 und sein zeitgeschichtlicher Hintergrund', *Nachrichten von der Akademie der Wissenschaften in Göttingen: Philologisch-Historische Klasse*, III (1948), 30–41.

[26] The proposal to convey official birthday wishes from the Reichstag to Bismarck was rejected by the factions of the Centre Party, the Progressive Party, the SPD, and the minority parties (Poles and Alsatians). See RT, 23 Mar. 1872, vol. 139, 1671–6.

[27] See, for example, *Norddeutsche Allgemeine Zeitung*, 25 Mar. 1895. Equally, *National-Zeitung*, 24 and 26 Mar. 1895.

ficulty imposing on their intellectually unsophisticated charges. In a statement of the Royal Prussian Ministry of Education and Ecclesiastical Affairs, the headmaster of a Berlin grammar school, Konrad Rethwisch, voiced the opinion that Bismarck's role in German history needed to be more strongly emphasized in the school curriculum, since he was the embodiment of 'what we are called to live up to'.[28] Otto Lyon, headmaster of a *Realgymnasium* in Dresden, shared this view. In 1896, in the *Zeitschrift für den deutschen Unterricht*, a periodical held in high regard by schoolteachers, he recommended Bismarck's writings and speeches as compulsory reading material for every school, describing him as 'the German people's most German son' and the 'incarnation of the German character and the German spirit'.[29] These plans to make the cult of Bismarck a regular component of the school curriculum were soon put into practice.[30] While Bismarck personally exerted no direct influence on this particular development, he nevertheless devoted considerable time and effort to cultivating his own historical image in the period following his enforced retirement from politics. Amongst such efforts were his continuous attacks on the policies of his successors and his repeated attempts to defend his own political decisions through a number of periodicals and newspapers, among which Maximilian Harden's *Zukunft*, Hugo Jacobi's *Münchener Allgemeine Zeitung*, and Karl von Hofmann's *Hamburger Nachrichten* were pre-eminent.[31]

Another of Bismarck's attempts to shape his own historical image were his memoirs, *Gedanken und Erinnerungen* or *Thoughts and Reminiscences*, which he commenced in late 1890.[32] What emerged was a self-glorifying portrait of a politician who had managed to unify the nation in the face of enormous obstacles. Yet this statesman had been ungraciously dismissed without explanation, being the victim of conspiracies by men who were not competent enough to lead the Reich in a time of national peril.[33]

[28] Quoted in Wulf Wülfing, Karin Bruns, and Rolf Parr, *Historische Mythologie der Deutschen 1798–1918* (Munich, 1991), 163.

[29] Ibid. 156.

[30] Rudolf Schridde, *Zum Bismarckbild im Geschichtsunterricht: Eine historisch-didaktische Analyse deutscher Geschichtsbücher* (Düsseldorf, 1974), 14–15.

[31] See Rudolf Stöber, 'Bismarcks geheime Presseorganisation', *HZ* CCLXII (1996), 423–51. The articles which Bismarck is said to have inspired or written himself between his dismissal and his death were published in two different collections: Johannes Penzler (ed.), *Fürst Bismarck nach seiner Entlassung*, 7 vols. (Leipzig, 1897–8), and Hermann Hofmann (ed.), *Fürst Bismarck 1890–1898*, 2 vols. (Stuttgart, 1918).

[32] Otto von Bismarck, *Gedanken und Erinnerungen*, 3 vols. (Berlin and Stuttgart, 1898–1919). The first two volumes of *Gedanken und Erinnerungen* were released in 1898. Volume 3, however, which dealt with Bismarck's dismissal and his relationship with Wilhelm II, was only published after the Great War.

[33] For a critical analysis of the memoirs see Otto Pflanze, 'Bismarck's "Gedanken und Erinnerungen"', in George Egerton (ed.), *Political Memoir: Essays on the Politics of Memoir* (London, 1994), 28–61.

Bismarck did not see the publication of the first two volumes of *Thoughts and Reminiscences* in 1898, since he had insisted that they should only be released posthumously. His memoirs were to be his political testament, a calculated move to bind future German decision-makers to his own political ideals. In this respect, *Thoughts and Reminiscences* were astonishingly successful. Bismarck's memoirs were the best-selling German books prior to Hitler's *Mein Kampf*, and they contributed significantly to the process which would start immediately after his death: the transformation of Bismarck into the German 'national myth'.

The German 'national myth'

When Otto von Bismarck died on 30 July 1898, the commemorative articles and obituaries which appeared in German newspapers between the end of July and the middle of August 1898 left no room for doubt that Bismarck's death dissolved all remaining boundaries between the historical figure and the stylized myth.[34] Moreover, the passing of the Iron Chancellor provided the Kaiser with the opportunity to use the myth for his own ends.

The relationship between Otto von Bismarck and Wilhelm II had been far from good ever since the crisis which led to Bismarck's dismissal in 1890. In view of Bismarck's growing popularity, it was feared in governmental circles that Bismarck could 'take millions of hearts with him into his grave' if the Kaiser did not come to terms with Bismarck.[35] Their seemingly amicable meeting in Berlin in January 1894 brought no lasting reconciliation. In March 1895 Bismarck revealed to the press the existence of the 1887 Reinsurance Treaty between Germany and Russia, and its non-renewal after his dismissal.[36] The Kaiser was furious, threatened to imprison the 'evil old man' in the fortress of Spandau, and refused to send Bismarck birthday greetings on 1 April 1897.[37] None the less, when Bismarck eventually died in 1898, Wilhelm did everything in his power to exploit Bismarck's death politically. He immediately gave orders for a state funeral in the Berlin Cathedral, but the offer was declined by the

---

[34] See, for example, the caricature 'Des Helden Heimfahrt', in *Kladderadatsch*, 7 Aug. 1898.

[35] Knesebeck to Eulenburg on 9 December 1893, as quoted in Lothar Machtan, *Bismarcks Tod und Deutschlands Tränen: Reportage einer Tragödie* (Munich, 1998), 89.

[36] In reaction to the non-renewal of the Reinsurance Treaty, *Kladderadatsch* printed a caricature in which Bismarck appeared as Wotan, overshadowing Caprivi who fails to uphold good bilateral relations between Germany and Russia. See *Bismarck-Album des Kladderadatsch, 1849–1898* (Berlin, 1898), 190.

[37] Röhl, *Wilhelm II*, 961. See, too, Christopher M. Clark, *Kaiser Wilhelm II* (Harlow, 2000), 59.

Bismarck family with reference to the last will of the deceased, who wanted to be buried in Friedrichsruh.[38]

It was only after Bismarck's death in July 1898 that the memory of the disagreements between Wilhelm II and Bismarck started to fade. The death of the Iron Chancellor opened the way for the incorporation of the Bismarck myth into the official rhetoric. The *Deutscher Reichs- und Preußischer Staatsanzeiger*, for example, immediately declared that 'the fatherland has lost its greatest son'. Yet only his mortal frame had passed away since the name Bismarck would remain 'a symbol and a prophecy for all time'.[39]

Bismarck's death had a similar effect on some of the 'internal enemies of the Empire'. Only three years after the Centre Party's faction in the Reichstag had voted against a goodwill address on Bismarck's eightieth birthday in 1895, the Centre MP Peter Spahn represented the Reichstag at the memorial service in Friedrichsruh. Three weeks later, a leading Centre politician, Adolf Gröber, explicitly honoured Bismarck as a 'great statesman' at the 1898 *Katholikentag* in the city of Krefeld.[40]

While the Centre increasingly 'normalized' its attitude towards Bismarck, the obituary of the Social Democratic *Hamburger Echo* renewed its criticism of the Iron Chancellor. Under the headline *Mortuum flagellare* (castigation of the dead) the paper refused to acknowledge any positive aspect of Bismarck's work. Bismarck, the *Hamburger Echo* claimed, had always had Prussia's best interests at heart, but never those of Germany. Bismarck's only concern had been 'to secure Prussia's overriding importance and leading position within and over Germany'.[41] The SPD's discontent with the Kaiserreich was revealed in most of the Social Democratic comments on Bismarck's death. And indeed, there was a socialist counter-myth to the nationalists' Bismarck legend: the myth of the coming revolution, the expectation of the great *Kladderadatsch* and the foundation of the *Zukunftsstaat*.[42]

---

[38] The Kaiser's memorial service in the Berlin Cathedral was held in the absence of the Bismarck family. On this and another memorial service, held in the Kroll Opera House, and organized by the non-governmental Berlin Bismarck-Committee, see Machtan, *Bismarcks Tod*, 210–15. Also, Wilhelm Kahl, *Bismarck lebt: Gedächtnisrede bei der allgemeinen Trauerfeier Berlin am 7. August 1898* (Freiburg im Breisgau, 1898).

[39] *Deutscher Reichs- und Preußischer Staatsanzeiger* as quoted in Arthur Rehbein, *Bismarck im Sachsenwald* (Berlin, 1925), 101–2. The poet Ernst von Wildenbruch expressed similar sentiments at the passing of the founder of the Reich ('Keep the Bismarck in you alive!'). See Ernst von Wildenbruch, 'Unser Bismarck', in *Letzte Gedichte* (Berlin, 1908), 43.

[40] See Rudolf Morsey, *Bismarck und die deutschen Katholiken* (Friedrichsruh, 2000), 34–5.

[41] *Hamburger Echo*, 2 Aug. 1898. Cf. too the critical comments in *Vorwärts*, 2 Aug. 1898.

[42] See Reinhart Koselleck, 'Revolution, Rebellion, Aufruhr, Bürgerkrieg', in Otto Brunner *et al.* (eds.), *Geschichtliche Grundbegriffe: Historisches Lexikon der politisch-sozialen Sprache*, vol. 5 (Stuttgart, 1984), 689–788, here pp. 721 ff. Also, Hans-Ulrich Wehler, *Deutsche Gesellschaftsgeschichte*, vol. 3: *Von der 'Deutschen Doppelrevolution' bis zum Beginn des Ersten Weltkrieges 1849–1914* (Munich, 1995), 799.

The progressive-liberal MP Ludwig Bamberger criticized the dead Chancellor from a different perspective. In his review of the first volume of *Thoughts and Reminiscences*, published in 1898, Bamberger supplemented his praise 'for the great things he [Bismarck] had done to raise his nation' with the allegation that the Iron Chancellor was at the same time responsible for the increasing brutalization of political standards. In his memoirs Bismarck had revealed a 'highly dubious' political style: 'If a book like this, which is designed to be devoured by the young and in which the words "humanity" and "civilization" are treated on many pages with nothing but unconditional mockery or as hollow phrases, then the fear does not seem unfounded that the questionable ideal of soldierly *Schneidigkeit* with all its excesses will become dominant in the national character.'[43]

Bamberger's comment was the first of its kind to reveal the truly political nature of the Bismarck myth. Whether he was seen as patron of an imperialist *Weltpolitik*—something Bismarck had in fact repeatedly criticized during the last two years of his life—or the embodiment of supposed 'Teutonic' virtues such as will-power, loyalty, honesty, and perseverance, 'Bismarck' served to foster a national identity and to define what being a 'patriotic German' meant. The fact that it was Bismarck who became the icon of the German bourgeoisie had its basis in his crucial role in the foundation of the Reich in 1871. Nobody else seemed better suited to national self-affirmation, no one was more appropriate to spur the Germans to defend his Empire against imagined and real internal and foreign enemies, than the towering figure of the so-called *Reichsschmied*. In this sense the Bismarck myth can be understood as the response of conservative and national-liberal circles to the manifest popular need for a political hero-figure.[44] Their belief in the almost metaphysical character of the German Reich, and in an authoritarian, non-democratic form of state peculiar to it, was all comprehended and given individual expression in the person of Bismarck.[45] To declare oneself a 'Bismarck-German' became an affirmative political gesture, a profession of faith in the existing state.

A closely related phenomenon was the way in which the myth was used against all those 'internal enemies of the Reich' who might dare to call into question Germany's claims to world power status. Here, the Bismarck myth served as the vehicle of an integral (and at the same time exclusive) nationalism

---

[43] Ludwig Bamberger, *Bismarck posthumus: Sonderabdruck aus der Wochenschrift 'Die Nation'* (Berlin, 1899), 5.

[44] See, for example, Theodor Schieder, *Das Deutsche Kaiserreich von 1871 als Nationalstaat*, 2nd edn. (Göttingen, 1991), 81–96.

[45] Hedinger, 'Bismarck-Denkmäler und Bismarck-Verehrung', 289.

which weighed oppressively upon the political culture of Wilhelmine Germany. Writing retrospectively in 1935, the liberal ex-diplomat Harry Count Kessler noted that at the turn of the century the inclination of the majority of the German middle classes to become 'Bismarckian' and to ostracize socially any critic of 'his' state had created a 'lethal atmosphere' to which 'every independent political character fell victim'.[46]

Among the most forceful contemporary critics of this development was the progressive-liberal Reichstag MP Friedrich Naumann. In August 1899 he protested against the seemingly arbitrary political exploitation of the figure of the *Reichsgründer*: 'There is no connection between the [Bismarck] legend and history: imaginative minds have picked out from his life what suits them, rearranged it, and cloaked the whole thing in dazzling lies. In part this process is natural, but the other half is a conscious effort on the part of certain interested circles. . . . Thus, if the Kaiser attempts to support industrialisation with trade agreements, canal- and shipbuilding, and social reform, in the process of winning over the united left to his cause, then the monster figure of the Junker Bismarck arises from East-Elbia, the peasant founder of the state, the man who was for cavalry and infantry but not for colonies and fleets, the creator of anti-socialist legislation, the father of customs barriers for grain.'[47]

However, Naumann's article did not reflect the convictions of the broader political and social elite. In the years following Bismarck's death, the cult in homage of the *Reichsgründer* found expression in a vast outpouring of post-cards and written ephemera, as well as in the naming of countless Bismarck streets and Bismarck schools all over Germany.[48] Equally important for the political culture of Wilhelmine Germany was a movement which gathered momentum soon after the Chancellor's death and which involved the construction of an ever-growing number of Bismarck memorials.[49] This movement, the most tangible manifestation of the German establishment's cult surrounding the Iron Chancellor, had reached almost obsessive proportions by the beginning of the twentieth century and constituted a classic example of the

[46] Harry, Graf Kessler, *Gesichter und Zeiten: Erinnerungen* (Berlin, 1962), 178 ff.

[47] Friedrich Naumann, 'Die Bismarcklegende', *Die Hilfe*, V (1899), 6 Aug. 1899, 1–2.

[48] See Konrad Breitenborn, *Bismarck: Kult und Kitsch um den Reichsgründer* (Frankfurt, 1990). See also Elisabeth von Hagenow, *Politik und Bild: Die Postkarte als Medium der Propaganda* (Hamburg, 1994), 29 and 45. A 'Bismarck museum' housing an assembly of cult-objects had already been opened in September 1891 in Schönhausen. See Aide Grousilliers, *Das Bismarck-Museum in Wort und Bild: Ein Denkmal deutscher Dankbarkeit* (Berlin, 1899). For a more recent assessment, see Konrad Breitenborn, 'Das Bismarck-Museum in Schönhausen', *Museumskunde*, LVI (1991), 167–74.

[49] On this see Wolfgang Hardtwig, 'Der bezweifelte Patriotismus—nationales Bewußtsein und Denkmal 1786 bis 1933', *Geschichte in Wissenschaft und Unterricht*, XLIV (1993), 773–85.

Bismarck myth's penetration of the public sphere.[50] Between 1898 and 1914 alone, 500 Bismarck memorials and statues were commissioned in Germany, Bohemia, and Austria, of which at least half were completed.[51] Even in the German colonies, tribute was paid to the *Reichsgründer*: monuments were constructed in Darussalam, Tanga, Buea, Muanza, and Samoa; a Bismarck Tower was erected in Cape Nightingale (Cameroon), and Bismarck's name was given to a range of mountains in New Guinea while the nearby islands were named the Bismarck Archipelago.[52] Reproductions of lithographic prints and photographs of these Bismarck monuments were distributed in thousands, thereby penetrating everyday life in Wilhelmine Germany.[53]

Bismarck memorials served as places of political pilgrimage for the ever-growing number of Bismarck-devotees. The most significant of these memorials were the neo-Baroque statue erected in front of the Berlin Reichstag in 1901 and the Rolandesque figure of the Iron Chancellor unveiled in Hamburg in 1906.[54] The enormous Hamburg Bismarck monument in particular was a tribute to the imperial *Zeitgeist*, a 'gigantic symbol of the new German spirit which spreads its pinions over the seas, and which is destined to be a world power and a world culture'.[55]

Besides these and other monuments, so-called Bismarck columns were erected all over Germany. Immediately after Bismarck's death, the *Deutsche Studentenschaft* (German Students' Association) publicly announced its intention to construct memorial columns in the Iron Chancellor's honour: 'As in bygone times the Saxons and Normans erected unpretentious rock pillars over the bodies of their fallen warriors, and placed beacons at the top, so we wish to honour our Bismarck by erecting stately granite beacons on all the high places of our fatherland, where one can view the masterly German countryside. . . . The massive stones will bear no name, but every child will know their meaning.'[56]

---

[50] Wolfgang Hardtwig, 'Erinnerung, Wissenschaft, Mythos: Nationale Geschichtsbilder und politische Symbole in der Reichsgründungszeit und im Kaiserreich', in id., *Geschichtskultur und Wissenschaft* (Munich, 1990), 224–63. For a contemporary analysis, see Arthur Mennell and Bruno Garlepp, *Bismarck—Denkmal für das deutsche Volk* (Chicago, 1895).

[51] See Volker Plagemann, 'Bismarck-Denkmäler', in Hans-Ernst Mittig and Volker Plagemann (eds.), *Denkmäler im 19. Jahrhundert: Deutung und Kritik* (Munich, 1972), 217–52 (text) and 417–42 (pictures).

[52] Ibid.

[53] See Günter Kloss and Sieglinde Seele, *Bismarck-Türme and Bismarck-Säulen: Eine Bestandsaufnahme* (Petersberg, 1997).

[54] On the Hamburg Bismarck memorial see Karen Lang, 'The Hamburg Bismarck Monument as "Lighthouse of National Thought"', in Wessel Reinink and Jeroen Stumpel (eds.), *Memory and Oblivion* (Dordrecht, 1999), 567–79.

[55] Hedinger, 'Bismarck-Denkmäler und Bismarck-Verehrung', 287.

[56] 'Aufruf der Deutschen Studentenschaft vom 3. Dezember 1898', as quoted in Zmarzlik, *Bismarckbild*, 11. On the Bismarck towers and Bismarck columns see Kloss and Seele, *Bismarck-Türme*.

All these Bismarck monuments and columns had one thing in common: they were expressions in stone of 'the elevation of Bismarck to a national symbol as protector and founder of the community'.[57] So that no doubt should remain as to which Bismarck was to be memorialized, only certain quotations were added to the pedestal, the most common of which was the part-sentence: 'We Germans fear God, but nothing else in the world'. The second half of this famous Bismarck quotation, 'and it is fear of God that makes us love and cherish peace', was never to be found on any of the memorials.[58]

The most conspicuous promoters of these monuments were some 300 Bismarck societies spread over the whole of Germany, with a membership totalling around 30,000. Their ranks were recruited first and foremost from the upper-middle and professional classes, the peasantry and the working classes being scarcely represented.[59] The executive board of the largest Bismarck society, the Rhineland-based League for the Erection of a Bismarck National Monument (founded in the spring of 1908), was dominated by prominent politicians from the 'Bülow Bloc'. Apart from Chancellor Prince Bernhard von Bülow as chairman (followed by Theobald von Bethmann Hollweg in 1909), Ernst Bassermann, Johannes Kaempf, and Ernst von Heydebrand und der Lasa were all members of the League.[60]

The social elite equally warmed to the League's project of raising a monumental Bismarck memorial near the city of Bingen (Rhineland). As well as Walther Rathenau, heir to the AEG empire and later Foreign Minister of the Weimar Republic, thirty-seven of the sixty-eight richest industrial families of the Rhineland were represented in the League in 1910. Of the 346 members of the Prussian Upper House sixty-five were members of this organization. The membership lists of 1910 indicate that the idea of a Bismarck National Monument gained most support in the cities: more than two-thirds of the committee members came from communities with more than 20,000 inhabitants; more than 40 per cent from cities with over 100,000 inhabitants. From a political perspective the supporters of the National Liberals and of the conservative parties dominated the executive committee of the League with 146 and 103 members respectively. Although the Progressive Liberals were still quite strong-

---

[57] Thomas Nipperdey, 'Nationalidee und Nationaldenkmal in Deutschland im 19. Jahrhundert', *HZ* CCVI (1968), 529–85, here p. 581.

[58] RT, 6 Feb. 1888, vol. 102, 733.

[59] See Hedinger, 'Bismarck-Kult', 202.

[60] See, in particular, Michael Dorrmann, 'Das Bismarck-Nationaldenkmal am Rhein: Ein Beitrag zur Geschichtskultur des Deutschen Reiches', *Zeitschrift für Geschichtswissenschaft*, XLIV (1996), 1061–87. On the 'Bülow-Bloc' see Katharine A. Lerman, *The Chancellor as Courtier: Bernhard von Bülow and the Governance of Germany 1900–1909* (Cambridge, 1990), 167–247.

ly represented with forty-six members, there were only fourteen Centrists (among them the young Konrad Adenauer), and not a single Social Democrat on the League's executive committee.[61]

Despite the support of some of the most powerful men in Wilhelmine Germany, the Bismarck National Monument at Bingerbrück was never to be built. Before the League's planning phase was concluded, the First World War broke out and the construction works were postponed. However, the Bismarck memorials did not lose their importance when hostilities broke out in 1914. For the first religious service, which followed the Kaiser's order for a general mobilization in Germany, was held at the foot of the Bismarck memorial in Berlin.[62]

Bismarck and the Great War

When Germany went to war, the 'spirit of 1914' was quick to appropriate the Bismarck myth. In the German newspapers of late summer 1914, Bismarck's wars of unification, above all the Franco-Prussian war of 1870–1, were given exemplary character for the approaching conflict with the French *Erbfeind*. Whereas the war against Napoleon III was interpreted as a 'struggle for external unification', the forthcoming conflict would become a war to heal the internal rifts within German society.[63]

Bourgeois intellectuals rejoiced in the idea that the nation was internally united as it entered the 'defensive' struggle, which had been 'forced upon' Germany and celebrated the political truce of 1914 as the beginning of Germany's national regeneration. The distinguished Munich historian Erich Marcks, for example, declared that the prime war aim was to defend 'Bismarck's heritage'. Germany, since 1871 the envy of other European states for its might and strength, had seized the sword which Bismarck had forged.[64]

---

[61] On this as well as on the other statistics quoted in the text see Dorrmann, 'Bismarck-Nationaldenkmal', 1070, and id., ' "Wenn Bismarck wiederkäme": Kunst, Ideologie und Rathenaus Engagement für ein Bismarck-National-Denkmal', in Hans Wilderotter (ed.), *Die Extreme berühren sich: Walther Rathenau, 1867–1922* (Berlin, 1993), 99–108. For Walther Rathenau's work on the Committee, see his diary entries of 21 Jan. 1911, 11 Feb. 1911, 24 June 1911, 20 and 21 Nov. 1911, 4 Dec. 1911, 22 Jan. 1912, and 14 Feb. 1912 in Hartmut Pogge von Strandmann (ed.), *Walther Rathenau: Industrialist, Banker, Intellectual and Politician: Notes and Diaries 1907–1922*, 2nd edn. (Oxford, 1988). See also Alfred Lichtwark and Walther Rathenau, *Der rheinische Bismarck* (Berlin, 1912).

[62] See *Norddeutsche Allgemeine Zeitung*, 4 Aug. 1914.

[63] See Johannes Burkhardt, 'Kriegsgrund Geschichte? 1870, 1813, 1756—historische Argumente und Orientierungen bei Ausbruch des Ersten Weltkrieges', in id. *et al.* (eds.), *Lange und kurze Wege in den ersten Weltkrieg: Vier Augsburger Beiträge zur Kriegsursachenforschung* (Munich, 1996), 9–86.

[64] Erich Marcks, 'Bismarck und unser Krieg', *Süddeutsche Monatshefte*, XI (1914), 780–7. Other leading historians made similar pronouncements at that time. For the role German historians played in 1914 see

The fact that military success failed to materialize did not put an end to the exploitation of Bismarck as a mobilizing force in the Great War. The hundredth anniversary of Bismarck's birth on 1 April 1915 was marked by innumerable popular publications, picture books, and commemorative articles in homage to Bismarck as patron saint of the German troops.[65] The central commemorative celebration in 1915 was held outside the Reichstag in Berlin. It was attended by Chancellor von Bethmann Hollweg and Crown Prince Wilhelm of Prussia as well as by representatives of virtually all important military and civil institutions.[66] Even the SPD, which temporarily lost the stigma as the party of *vaterlandslose Gesellen* or 'unpatriotic fellows' with its approval of the war credits, did not voice any criticism of the event.[67]

Wilhelm II was thus able to speak with some degree of truth of a 'spirit of concord' which had materialized on Bismarck's birthday. The Kaiser hoped that this spirit would 'outlast the war and influence the internal development of the Reich positively after the well-won peace'. If so, he continued, 'we will have won a national existence in which the German people can develop freely and strongly. Then, finally will that proud building be completed for which Bismarck once laid the foundations.'[68]

For many Germans, 'the free development of the German people' referred to by the Kaiser included the annexation of new territories and, in particular, the *Anschluß* of Austria. The concrete experience of the Austro-German arms fraternity led to demands from an increasing number of intellectuals for a revision of the 'limitations' to Germany's borders. The reversal of Bismarck's

Hartmut Pogge von Strandmann, 'The Role of British and German Historians in Mobilizing Public Opinion in 1914', in Benedikt Stuchtey and Peter Wende (eds.), *British and German Historiography 1750–1950* (Oxford, 2000), 335–71. The broader historical context is discussed in detail in Jost Dülffer and Karl Holl (eds.), *Bereit zum Krieg: Kriegsmentalität im wilhelminischen Deutschland 1890–1914* (Göttingen, 1986), 9–19. Also Wolfgang J. Mommsen, 'The Spirit of 1914 and the Ideology of a German "Sonderweg" ', in id., *Imperial Germany 1867–1918: Politics, Culture and Society in an Authoritarian State*, trans. Richard Deveson (London and New York, 1995), 205–16.

[65] See Egmont Zechlin, 'Der Inbegriff des germanischen Menschen: Das Bismarck-Bild 1915: Eine Mischung aus Sage und Mythos', *Die Zeit*, 2 Apr. 1965. The following texts are only a selection of the mass of new publications marking the hundredth anniversary of Bismarck's birth: Arnold Striebitz, *Der Eiserne Kanzler: Ein Lebensbild für das deutsche Volk* (Leipzig, 1915). Noteworthy is Horst Kohl (ed.), *Mit Bismarck daheim und im Felde: Kennworte aus seinen Briefen und Reden* (Berlin, 1915), which went into a record print run of 150,000 copies. Finally, Gottlob Egelhaaf, *Bismarck und der Weltkrieg* (Halle, 1915).

[66] A comprehensive contemporary account of the central commemorative celebration at the Berlin Bismarck memorial can be found in *Berliner Allgemeine Zeitung*, 2 Apr. 1915. For the Bismarck-celebration of the Pan-German League in Friedrichsruh on 1 April 1915, see *Alldeutsche Blätter*, 10 Apr. 1915.

[67] See, for example, *Vorwärts*, 1 Apr. 1915. Whether this was an expression of a changed attitude towards the German nation-state or a result of wartime censorship cannot be said with certainty. On the context see Dieter Groh, *Negative Integration und revolutionärer Attentismus: Die deutsche Sozialdemokratie am Vorabend des ersten Weltkrieges* (Frankfurt, 1973).

[68] Wilhelm II as quoted in *Schulthess*, LVI (1915), 156.

kleindeutsch concept of the nation was already being prophesied at the end of 1914 in an article by the Catholic historian Martin Spahn: 'Through the cannons' smoke', he proclaimed, 'glimmer the borders of a seventy-million-strong Reich—an ideal which inspired the Germans in the eighteenth century and in the Wars of Liberation, and even fifty years ago the *großdeutsch* Party—the borders of a Central European Reich of the German nation. What seemed from 1866 until a few weeks ago an undisputable fact, that the path of historical development of the old Reich had been finally abandoned and a border between Germany and Austria irrevocably fixed, has paled away like an image in a dream. Suddenly the two parts which had been forced apart have grown together again.'[69]

Similar sentiments were voiced by Friedrich Naumann. In his programmatic book *Mitteleuropa*, which first appeared in 1915, Naumann called on his fellow countrymen to adopt a 'new historical consciousness'. In his view Bismarck's *kleindeutsch* solution had been a historical necessity in its time, but was no longer an appropriate national ideal after 1914.[70] Interestingly, the vision of a Central European Empire, which exercised such attraction for Naumann and many others at the time, was seen as a continuity of, rather than a contradiction to, Bismarck's concept of the Reich. In an article in 1915, Naumann expressed his unreserved affirmation of the founder of the *kleindeutsch* Reich: 'Today all of the parties that he overcame agree on a political truce in order to protect his Reich. For his Reich has become everyone's Reich . . . He is no longer a figure of contention for us but a national possession. He is not the representative of a party but the foremost of all Germans.' For Naumann, the real goal of the Great War, to surmount the borders of the current German Empire, was something Bismarck himself had pre-empted with his dual alliance between Germany and Austria in 1879.[71]

This passage is most revealing in light of Naumann's critical stance in 1899 regarding early efforts to exploit Bismarck politically. Naumann was now prepared to invoke the Iron Chancellor in support of his own political and military aims, suggesting the extent to which Bismarck had become a political tool

---

[69] Martin Spahn, 'An den Pforten des Weltkrieges', *Hochland*, XII (1914/15), 14–29, here p. 18. Similarly, Adolf Kapp, 'Der großdeutsche Gedanke einst und jetzt', *Kriegshefte der Süddeutschen Monatshefte* (1914/15), 46–51.

[70] Friedrich Naumann, *Mitteleuropa* (Berlin, 1915), 33. Of all political books published since the 1890s, *Mitteleuropa* was the greatest publishing success after Bismarck's *Gedanken und Erinnerungen*: 100,000 copies were sold within the first year after the first edition came out. Two popular editions followed in July 1916 and October 1917. See Theodor Heuss, *Friedrich Naumann: Der Mann, das Werk, die Zeit*, 3rd rev. edn. (Munich and Hamburg, 1968), 363.

[71] Friedrich Naumann, 'Wer war Bismarck?', *Die Hilfe*, XXI (1915), 185–8, here p. 187.

by this time. Yet the unanimity which Naumann and others thought Bismarck could evoke in the German people was to prove a temporary phenomenon. Bismarck remained beyond criticism only as long as the great majority of Germans were convinced of an ultimate victory. When this belief faded, the latent political and social tensions within the Reich rapidly developed into an acute political crisis. In July 1917 the Majority Social Democrats, the Centre, the Progressive People's Party, and the National Liberals formed the Inter-Party Committee or *Interfraktioneller Ausschuß*, which called for the negotiation of a peace agreement without 'forced cession of territories, and political, economic or financial violations'. It was now, in the July crisis of 1917, that criticism of Bismarck was once again publicly voiced. In an essay on the necessity of a constitutional reform published in October 1917, for example, the sociologist Max Weber heavily criticized Bismarck for not having given the parliament any political power.[72]

In May 1918 Weber articulated his criticism even more clearly: 'The current situation of our parliament is a result of the long rule of Prince Bismarck in Germany and of the attitude which the nation has adopted towards him since the last decade of his Chancellorship.'[73] 'Bismarck's legacy' would be 'a nation without any political will of its own, a nation accustomed to the idea that the great statesmen at its helm would make all the political decisions'.[74] According to Weber, it was the 'Bismarck legend' which was responsible for this develop-ment.[75] With great perspicacity, Weber illuminated the double standards of the German middle classes' attitude towards 'their' Bismarck. At the time of Bis-marck's dismissal the conservatives and national liberals had not commented on the event with a single word: 'Which of the large parties that had followed him up to this point even demanded an account of the grounds for his dis-missal? None of them even stirred themselves, but rather turned their faces to the new leading light. . . . Only when it began to concern their own material interests, above all in tax matters, a few years after Bismarck's dismissal, did they begin to refer to Bismarck as their model, and since then they have played the role of loyal defenders of his traditions.'[76]

Weber's analysis was influenced by recent political developments. In the final phase of the Great War those who held out for a victorious and ann-exationist peace claimed that they were the true defenders of Bismarck's

[72] Max Weber, 'Bismarcks Erbe in der Reichsverfassung' (Oct. 1917), in id., *Gesammelte politische Schriften*, ed. Johannes Winckelmann, 2nd edn. (Tübingen, 1958), 229–32, here p. 230.

[73] Max Weber, 'Die Erbschaft Bismarcks' (May 1918), in id., *Gesammelte politische Schriften*, 299–308, here p. 299.

[74] Ibid. 308.   [75] Ibid. 299.   [76] Ibid. 300–1.

legacy. Opposed to any territorial surrender, these circles founded the German Fatherland Party on Sedan Day 1917, a party which was originally supposed to be launched in Friedrichsruh and named the 'Bismarck Party'.[77] The Fatherland Party, which was financed by contributions from heavy industry, the Agrarian League, and other influential interest groups of the political right, soon became the largest mass organization in Imperial Germany with a membership of around 1.2 million.[78] Its propaganda during the last months of the war fostered the illusion of an ultimate victory, in which a large number of Germans believed up until the last moment. The news of the German armistice offer to President Wilson by the newly appointed Chancellor Prince Max von Baden on 3 October 1918 therefore unleashed a sense of profound shock throughout the German public. The military leadership denied any responsibility for the desperate situation in which Germany found itself. Instead, Hindenburg and Ludendorff claimed that the army threatened to collapse because the Home Front no longer stood behind it. On 1 October 1917, General Ludendorff told his commanders that a new government should be made up of those parties 'whom we have to thank for bringing us to this pass. We shall therefore see these gentlemen come into the Ministry. They must make the peace that has now to be concluded. They must now eat the soup which they have dished up.'[79] The executive committee of the Pan-German League, too, knew whom to blame for the defeat. It was not the Western Allies that had caused the German collapse, but the 'internal enemies of the Reich'. As an immediate reaction to the October reforms and the first refusals in the German Navy to obey orders, the Pan-German League's executive committee called an assembly on 3 November 1918 at the Bismarck memorial in Berlin, so that 'the better Germany' could have the opportunity to give vent to its patriotic feelings 'at the feet of the *Reichsgründer*'.[80] In so doing the Pan-Germans started a tradition of oppositional gatherings at Bismarck memorials all over Germany, suggesting that the fundamental transformation of the Bismarck myth into a

---

[77] See Dirk Stegmann, *Die Erben Bismarcks: Parteien und Verbände in der Spätphase des Wilhelminischen Deutschlands* (Cologne and Berlin, 1970), 499 nn. 333 and 334. The name 'Bismarck Party' had been suggested by Wolfgang Kapp, who had been the chairman of the Königsberg Bismarck Society since 1909. On this see Heinz Hagenlücke, *Deutsche Vaterlandspartei: Die nationale Rechte am Ende des Kaiserreiches* (Düsseldorf, 1997), 118.

[78] Cf. Abraham J. Peck, *Radicals and Reactionaries: The Crisis of Conservatism in Wilhelmine Germany* (Washington, DC, 1978), 203–35.

[79] See *Ursachen und Folgen: Vom deutschen Zusammenbruch 1918 und 1945 bis zur staatlichen Neuordnung Deutschlands in der Gegenwart*, ed. Herbert Michaelis, Ernst Schräpler, and Günter Scheel, vol. 2: *Der militärische Zusammenbruch und das Ende des Kaiserreiches* (Berlin, 1958), 323.

[80] 'Am Berliner Bismarck-Denkmal', *Alldeutsche Blätter*, 9 Nov. 1918.

destabilizing narrative directed against the coming democratic state had emerged even before the founding of the Republic.[81]

In the face of the imminent military defeat of the German Empire, Bismarck, who only a few years earlier had been celebrated as 'the unifier of the nation', became the 'battle standard' of those who were to form the right-wing opposition against the Republic after 1918.[82] This process was hastened by the revolution which began in early November 1918 and which soon led to the collapse of the Kaiserreich, in which the Bismarck myth was rooted. Military defeat and the revolution served to catalyse and reinforce the simmering contrasting ideologies within German society that would determine rivalling Bismarck images in the fourteen years to come.

---

[81] See, for example, the telegram sent to Paul von Hindenburg, in which the local unit of the DNVP in Danzig informs the 'hero of Tannenberg' about a 'Bismarck service' in April 1919 (telegram in Deutsches Historisches Museum, Berlin, Do 99/503). See, too, Otto-von-Bismarck-Stiftung, P 1999/599.

[82] See Studt, *Bismarckbild*, 13.

3

After the Collapse

A farewell to Bismarck's *Kleindeutschland*? Post-war Germany and the struggle for the *großdeutsch* Republic

On 18 January 1919 the Allied Peace Conference convened in Versailles to decide the fate of the defeated German Empire.[1] Both the date of the conference's opening and its location were highly symbolic. Exactly forty-eight years earlier, on 18 January 1871, the German princes had attended the Imperial Proclamation by Otto von Bismarck in Versailles' Hall of Mirrors. It was the same room in which the German delegation led by Hermann Müller (MSPD) and Johannes Bell (Centre) would sign the peace accords in late June 1919.[2]

France had been haunted by the loss of Alsace-Lorraine since its defeat in the Franco-Prussian War of 1870–1.[3] Now, after the German defeat, the time had come to restore France's greatness and to revise the results of 1871. Only three weeks after the German government had concluded an armistice with Marshal Foch on 11 November 1918, a secret memorandum drafted by the French Foreign Ministry proposed massive reductions in the territories of the Reich, possibly even its dissolution, as the precondition for a new international order. France's long-term security interests could only be guaranteed, so the key passage declared, by the 'destruction of Bismarck's work'.[4]

The German public was not aware of such plans being developed in the Quai d'Orsay. Indeed, in the first weeks following the signing of the armistice on 11 November 1918, few Germans concerned themselves with any threat of

---

[1] Manfred F. Boemeke, Gerald D. Feldman, and Elisabeth Glaser (eds.), *The Treaty of Versailles: A Reassessment after 75 Years* (Cambridge, 1998). See, too, Alma Luckau, *The German Delegation at the Paris Peace Conference* (New York, 1971).

[2] See Richard M. Watt, *The Kings Depart: The Tragedy of Germany: Versailles and the German Revolution* (London, 1968), 9–10.

[3] On this see Sally Marks, 'Smoke and Mirrors: In Smoke-Filled Rooms and the Galerie des Glaces', in Boemeke *et al.* (eds.), *Treaty of Versailles*, 337–70, here pp. 347–9. On Versailles' general symbolic importance see Édouard Pommier, 'Versailles: The Image of the Sovereign', in Nora and Kritzman (eds.), *Realms of Memory*, vol. 3: *Symbolism*, 293–324.

[4] Memorandum of the French Foreign Ministry of 25 October 1918 as quoted in Klaus Hildebrand, *Das vergangene Reich: Deutsche Außenpolitik von Bismarck bis Hitler 1871–1945* (Stuttgart, 1995), 390.

2. Crowds at the Berlin Bismarck Memorial outside the Reichstag during the November Revolution, 1918.

the Reich's dissolution or major territorial losses. Instead, they engaged in wishful thinking in the 'dreamland of the armistice period'.[5] Unrealistic as it may seem retrospectively, there was a widely entertained hope in the winter of 1918–19 that the German Reich would be able to compensate for military defeat and the foreseeable loss of Alsace-Lorraine by the incorporation of German-Austria, the rump state left behind by the disintegration of the Habsburg Empire.[6] The *Anschluß* debate in Germany was set in motion with a declaration issued by the provisional National Assembly in Vienna. On 12 November 1918 the Assembly proclaimed that German-Austria was a 'constituent part of the German Republic'.[7]

The German revolutionary government, the Council of People's Representatives, was at first reluctant to react to the Austrian plea for *Anschluß*.

[5] Ernst Troeltsch, *Spectatorbriefe: Aufsätze über die Revolution und die Weltpolitik 1918/22* (Tübingen, 1924), 69.

[6] Stanley Suval, *The Anschluß Question in Germany and Austria in the Weimar Era: A Study of Nationalism in Germany and Austria 1918–1932* (Baltimore and London, 1974).

[7] See 'Gesetz über die Staats- und Regierungsform Deutsch-Österreichs', in Ernst R. Huber, *Deutsche Verfassungsgeschichte seit 1789*, vol. 5: *Weltkrieg, Revolution und Reichserneuerung 1914–1919* (Stuttgart, 1978), 1175. See also Otto Bauer, *Die österreichische Revolution* (Vienna, 1923), 143.

Internally they were sceptical as to whether Germany could 'place a *fait accompli* before the Peace Conference' in 'the light of the overall international situation'.[8] None the less, there can be no doubt that the six members of the revolutionary government—Friedrich Ebert, Philipp Scheidemann, and Otto Landsberg from the MSPD (Majority Social Democratic Party), and Hugo Haase, Emil Barth, and Wilhelm Dittmann from the USPD (Independent Social Democratic Party)—were all equally in favour of *Anschluß*.[9]

German hopes for *Anschluß* predominantly derived from US President Woodrow Wilson's Fourteen Points which envisaged a 'peace of understanding' based on the right of national self-determination and international co-operation.[10] In total misapprehension of political realities, the majority of Germans blithely assumed up until the spring of 1919 that these principles would be the guiding ideas at the Versailles Peace Conference.

Hopes for a 'peace of understanding' accorded with the generally positive, if at times over-optimistic, mood which initially prevailed in post-war Germany. At least until the revolution radicalized in January 1919, the idea of establishing a new political order enjoyed broad social support.[11] For what the chief editor of the liberal *Berliner Tageblatt,* Theodor Wolff, described as 'the greatest of all revolutions' on 10 November 1919 seemed not only to ensure a just peace, but also to guarantee a 'solution to the *großdeutsch* problem which now confronts us'.[12] Particularly during the first few weeks after the armistice, the collapse of Bismarck's state was widely perceived as a precondition for the establishment of the *großdeutsch* Reich. 'We stand here proud and upright, and on the grave of the old Reich we plant our hopes for the Greater Germany', an editorial in *Hilfe* declared in late autumn 1918. 'Unlike our fathers in 1871,' the author of the article, Wilhelm Heile, continued 'we can build our house anew from its very foundations.'[13]

Interestingly enough, the renaissance of the *großdeutsch* idea was also supported enthusiastically by German historians. Ever since the days of Johann

---

[8] On the resolution of the Council of People's Representatives see *Die Regierung der Volksbeauftragten 1918/19,* ed. Erich Matthias and Susanne Miller, 2 vols. (Düsseldorf, 1969), here vol. 1, meeting of 15 November 1918, 45.

[9] See Susanne Miller, 'Das Ringen um "die einzige großdeutsche Republik": Die Sozialdemokratie in Österreich und im Deutschen Reich zur Anschlußfrage 1918/19', *Archiv für Sozialgeschichte,* XI (1971), 1–68.

[10] On Wilson's Fourteen Points, see Thomas J. Knock, *Woodrow Wilson and the Quest for a New World Order* (New York, 1992), 142–7.

[11] See Eberhard Kolb, *The Weimar Republic,* translated from the German by P. S. Falla (London, 1988), 9 ff.

[12] Quotations from *Berliner Tageblatt,* 10 Nov. 1918, morning edition, and from Max Weber, 'Deutschlands künftige Staatsform' (Nov. 1918), in id., *Gesammelte politische Schriften,* 436–71, here p. 441.

[13] Wilhelm Heile, 'Der deutsche Neubau', *Die Hilfe,* XXIV (1918), 559–60.

Gustav Droysen and Heinrich von Sybel, leading German historians had prepared the intellectual ground for Bismarck's *kleindeutsch* solution and had greeted it almost unanimously as the fulfilment of German national history on its implementation in 1871. Prusso-German history was portrayed by them as a 'necessary process of development which led from Luther and the Reformation via the Great Elector and Frederick the Great to the Prussian reform era, and then found its crowning glory in the work of Bismarck'.[14]

After 1918, however, there was a broad consensus within the scholarly community that this image of history was outdated. According to Hermann Oncken, a national-liberal 'Republican by reason', the dissolution of the multi-ethnic Empire of Austria-Hungary had made a unification of the Reich and the German-speaking parts of Austria both possible and necessary. In the current political situation, Oncken maintained, there was one guiding foreign policy goal which the German Republic should strive for: 'the return to the *großdeutsch* idea. For us this is the result of the world crisis . . . Greater Germany has now become possible, because the Austrian monarchy no longer exists, and it has become necessary, because German-Austria cannot survive on its own. Not only has the theoretical justification of the *kleindeutsch* idea of 1848/1866 become redundant. The *kleindeutsch* Reich, too, which has existed from 1871 up to 1918 has lost its legitimacy. The *kleindeutsch* concept . . . therefore has to give way to the *großdeutsch* idea.'[15] To Oncken and others, the Austro-German arms fraternity of 1914–18 had made it abundantly clear that the destinies of the two German-speaking states in the centre of Europe were inevitably intertwined. Thus they deserved to be united in one nation-state. Oncken consequently argued that the lost war and the collapse of the Empire had fulfilled a 'historical purpose'; namely, to bring about the demand for *Anschluß* as the 'richest fruit' of the military defeat of the Kaiserreich.[16]

Oncken's colleague Friedrich Meinecke argued along similar lines. He accused the Kaiserreich's historiography of having idealized Bismarck's solution to the German question: 'It was as though the paths of German history had led inevitably to his [Bismarck's] way, everything that preceded being viewed as a necessary step to the fulfilment which came in 1871.'[17] Leading historians of the early Kaiserreich had played a decisive role in this 'canonization

---

[14] Fehrenbach, 'Reichsgründung', 261.

[15] Hermann Oncken, 'Die Wiedergeburt der großdeutschen Idee', in id., *Nation und Geschichte: Reden und Aufsätze 1919–1935* (Berlin, 1935), 45–70, quotation on p. 61. (The article was first published in *Österreichische Rundschau*, LXIII (1920), 97–114.)   [16] Ibid., 64.

[17] Friedrich Meinecke, 'Der nationale Gedanke im alten und neuen Deutschland', in id., *Nach der Revolution: Geschichtliche Betrachtungen über unsere Lage* (Munich and Berlin, 1919), 47–71, here p. 62.

of the process of national development'.[18] Relentless efforts had been undertaken 'to prove that all previous attempts to solve the German question were somehow faulty or unviable or unworkable or utopian when measured against the matchless solution which Bismarck came up with'.[19]

The propensity to historicize Bismarck's *kleindeutsch* concept of the nation-state was by no means limited to those who—whether from some inner conviction or, as in Oncken's and Meinecke's case, on grounds of 'reason'—took a positive view of the changed political situation in Germany. The Pan-German League, for example, left no doubt as to their negative attitude to the revolutionary overthrow of the state. Nevertheless, the League's leadership felt that the time had arrived to overcome the *kleindeutsch* 'limitations' of the German nation-state and to take a further step in fulfilment of their '*kleindeutsch-großdeutsch-alldeutsch*' programme.[20]

The broad public consensus on the question of a *großdeutsch* extension of the Reich found expression in the emergence of various associations of mixed political complexion such as the Austro-German People's League.[21] The leadership of this League reflected the political diversity of the supporters of *Anschluß* in 1918–19: its first president was the Social Democrat Paul Löbe, supported by a German Nationalist, Otto Hoetzsch, as vice-president. The German-Austrian ambassador to Berlin, Ludo Hartmann, could thus rely on the support of all parties when in early February 1919 he called for a clear statement of commitment to a Greater Germany, thereby emphasizing that he regarded Bismarck's *kleindeutsch* solution as 'insufficient'.[22]

Regardless of the broad consensus on the issue, no other party supported the idea of *Anschluß* more enthusiastically than the MSPD. On the occasion of the opening of the German National Constituent Assembly in February 1919, the leader of the Majority Social Democrats, Friedrich Ebert, called upon the Assembly to 'authorize the forthcoming government to enter into negotiations at the earliest opportunity with the German-Austrian Free State with a view to a permanent union'. The Republic would thereby return to the *großdeutsch* traditions of the first half of the nineteenth century and would reunite 'the bond

---

[18] Friedrich Meinecke, 'Der nationale Gedanke im alten und neuen Deutschland'. [19] Ibid.

[20] Heinrich Claß, 'Der großdeutsche Gedanke', *Alldeutsche Blätter*, 9 Nov. 1918. Claß had argued along similar lines in *Wenn ich der Kaiser wär: Politische Wahrheiten und Notwendigkeiten*, 5th edn. (Leipzig, 1914), 9.

[21] See Suval, *Anschluss Question*, 9 ff. See also 'Österreichisch-deutscher Volksbund', in Dieter Fricke *et al.* (eds.), *Lexikon zur Parteiengeschichte: Die bürgerlichen und kleinbürgerlichen Parteien und Verbände in Deutschland (1789–1945)*, 4 vols. (Leipzig, 1983–6), here 3. 566–8. On the overall public opinion in the Reich see, for example, Duane P. Myers, *Germany and the Question of Austrian Anschluss 1918–1922* (New Haven, 1968). [22] *Berliner Tageblatt*, 4 Feb. 1919, morning edition.

violently sundered in 1866 [the year of the battle of Königgrätz, when the German question was decided in favour of the *kleindeutsch* solution]'. According to Ebert, it was the task of the National Assembly to surmount the 'narrowness' of Bismarck's Reich.[23]

There were several reasons why Ebert and many other representatives of the new political regime were pushing for *Anschluß* in the spring of 1919. First of all, *Anschluß* would 'prove' that the Republic was capable of achieving a more 'comprehensive' solution to the German question than the one which Bismarck himself had been able to offer.[24] Secondly, a commitment to the *Anschluß* movement enabled the parties who had come to power unexpectedly in October 1918 to demonstrate the Republic's attachment to the historical traditions of the German past. Bismarck's *kleindeutsch* solution to the German question and the political system based on the 1871 constitution was represented to the public as a 'false path' to which the Republic could proclaim itself the 'correction'.[25] During the constitutional debates at Weimar, the MSPD and the DDP tried repeatedly to disassociate themselves from Bismarck's Reich. As early as November 1918, Max Weber, who was involved in the drafting of the new constitution, wrote that the essence of this task was 'to find something else to put in the place of what Bismarck had created'.[26] This 'something' needed to be presented as historically legitimate if the Republic was not to be perceived as a form of government which had only come into existence as a by-product of military defeat. In early 1919, the 'father' of the Weimar Constitution, Hugo Preuß, consequently presented his constitutional draft as an 'up-dated form' of the ideals of the 1848–9 Paulskirche parliament.[27] These ideals included both the principles of liberal democracy *and* the quest for a *großdeutsch* fatherland. Hence, his constitutional draft also provided the legal grounds for a *großdeutsch* enlargement—the *Anschluß* of Austria. In Article 2, paragraph 1 of the Weimar Constitution, it was stated that new provinces could be included into the Reich if this was the wish of the population of the province in question.

[23] NV, 6 Feb. 1919, vol. 326, 2.

[24] Stanley Suval, 'Overcoming Kleindeutschland: The Politics of Historical Mythmaking in the Weimar Republic', *Central European History*, II (1969), 312–30, here p. 321.

[25] See the speech by the liberal Foreign Minister Ulrich von Brockdorff-Rantzau in NV, 14 Feb. 1919, vol. 326, 69.

[26] Weber, 'Deutschlands künftige Staatsform', quotations on pp. 437, 444, 446–7, 437. Similar views are presented by Erich Kaufmann, 'Grundfragen der künftigen Reichsverfassung (1919)', in id., *Gesammelte Schriften*, ed. Albert Hilger von Scherpenberg (Göttingen, 1960), i. 253–96. For Weber's influence on the constitutional draft, see Wolfgang J. Mommsen, *Max Weber and German Politics 1890–1920* (Chicago and London, 1984), 332–89.

[27] NV, 24 Feb. 1919, vol. 326, 292. Equally, Ebert, NV, 6 Feb. 1919, vol. 326, 3. Preuß's draft of the constitution is printed in *Deutscher Reichs- und Preußischer Staatsanzeiger*, 20 Jan. 1919.

Additionally, in Article 61, paragraph 2, German-Austria was admitted to the *Reichsrat* with consultative status until it eventually became part of the Reich.[28]

All of these constitutional provisions for *Anschluß* were made obsolete in the beginning of May 1919 when the peace treaty accords were presented to the German delegation at Versailles.[29] In the peace settlement the victorious powers made it very clear that they were not going to countenance any territorial expansion of the Reich. Article 80 of the Versailles Treaty in fact explicitly provided against *Anschluß*, declaring that the independence of Austria 'shall be inalienable, except with the consent of the Council of the League of Nations'.[30]

The German public was generally indignant at the Allied Powers' interdiction of *Anschluß*.[31] For the German Majority Social Democrats, however, this diplomatic defeat was particularly disastrous. Ebert and other leading Social Democrats had repeatedly accused the Kaiserreich of being *kleindeutsch* and thus 'unfinished' or 'incomplete'. As late as 18 March 1919 *Vorwärts* had exclaimed: 'Bismarck's *kleindeutsch* Empire has staggered into the catastrophe of the World War. The *großdeutsch* idea of 1848, however, which aimed at the incorporation of all Germans including the German Austrians . . . will be fulfilled in our days under the black, red, and golden banner, the revolutionary flag of 1848.'[32] The decisive rejection of *Anschluß* by the Allied Powers thus exposed a political flank, which right-wing propaganda knew how to exploit. The conservative weekly *Tradition* had already denounced Social Democratic plans for a peaceful revision of the *kleindeutsch* borders as unrealistic in the beginning of April 1919: 'If Empires could be founded on words and eager German hearts alone, then the idealists of the Frankfurt Paulskirche would have presented us with a greater German fatherland from the Belt to the Adriatic seventy years ago.'[33] After the Allies' ban on *Anschluß*, the editor of *Kreuzzeitung* and later chairman of the German Nationalist Party, Kuno von Westarp, saw this assessment confirmed. He remarked that the 'fathers of the [Weimar] constitution have not succeeded with their plan of achieving a

---

[28] See *Die Verfassung des Deutschen Reiches vom 11. August 1919*, ed. Gerhard Anschütz, 2nd edn. (Berlin, 1921), 30 (art. 2) and 119–20 (art. 61).

[29] See Fritz Klein, 'Between Compiègne and Versailles: The Germans on the Way from a Misunderstood Defeat to an Unwanted Peace', in Boemeke *et al.* (eds.), *Treaty of Versailles*, 203–20.

[30] *Treaty of Peace between the Allied and Associated Powers and Germany* (London, 1925), 51. The words used here are almost identical with those of Article 88 of the Treaty of St Germain. See *Der Staatsvertrag von St Germain* (Vienna, 1919), 58.

[31] For the reactions of the German public see Alfred D. Low, *The Anschluss Movement 1918–19 and the Paris Peace Conference* (Philadelphia, 1974), 375 ff. More generally, Wolfgang J. Mommsen, 'Der Vertrag von Versailles: Eine Bilanz', in Gerd Krumeich (ed.), *Versailles 1919—Ziele—Wirkung—Wahrnehmung* (Essen, 2001), 351–60.

[32] *Vorwärts*, 18 Mar. 1919.   [33] *Die Tradition*, I (1919), 19–20.

großdeutsch Germany, for which they regarded themselves as so superior to Bismarck at the opening of the [constitutional] negotiations'.[34]

The relief which lay behind Westarp's words was only too comprehensible: with the failed attempt to create a *großdeutsch* Republic the democratic left had lost one of its strongest and most popular arguments against Bismarck's Smaller German Reich of 1871. The MSPD was well aware of this dilemma and proved to be particularly reluctant to concede that its *großdeutsch* ambitions had foundered. On 22 June 1919, when the National Assembly, after long and heated debates, finally agreed to the signing of the Versailles Peace Treaty, Paul Löbe assured the plenum that the Republic would continue to fight 'not for Bismarck's Greater Prussia but for *Großdeutschland*, for the unity of all those, no matter where—on the Danube or the Etsch, at the mouth of the Weser, Elbe, Oder, or Vistula—who had learnt the German tongue from the lips of German mothers'.[35]

Following the Allied ban on *Anschluß*, however, the MSPD's promise of a *großdeutsch* Republic lacked something vital: credibility. The notion of transcending the Reich's *kleindeutsch* boundaries—initially a Republican project to stabilize the new political regime—could therefore increasingly be employed by the nationalist right in its struggle to overcome Germany's first democracy. In the following years, right-wing revisionism included the revision of *both* Versailles: the *kleindeutsch* solution of 1871 and the peace settlement of 1919. Blame for the failure to create a Greater German Reich was not attributed to Bismarck. He had solved the German question in the only possible way *at the time*. The Republic, on the other hand, suddenly found itself accused of having failed to seize the opportunity of *Anschluß* when it allegedly had been available.[36] The Republic's diplomatic defeat in Versailles was thus a victory for the right-wing opponents of Weimar democracy. For, paradoxical as it may seem, the Weimar right could now present itself as *großdeutsch* and 'Bismarckian' at the same time.

Bismarck and the foundation of the Weimar Republic

In January 1919, the recently founded conservative DNVP began its campaign for the National Assembly elections with a poster introducing Otto von

---

[34] Count Westarp in *Kreuzzeitung* (7 Sept. 1919), printed in Kuno Graf von Westarp, *Konservative Politik im Übergang vom Kaiserreich zur Weimarer Republik*, ed. Friedrich Freiherr von Gaertringen (Düsseldorf, 2001), 272.
[35] NV, 22 June 1919, vol. 327, 1117.   [36] See, for example, *Die Tradition* II (1920), 897–901.

Bismarck as the figurehead of nationalist opposition against the Republic: 'In order not to lose confidence in Germany's future', ran the caption to the poster, 'we must take heart from our past'.[37]

Bismarck's political instrumentalization after the military collapse of 'his' Reich, the subsequent revolution, and the renaissance of the *großdeutsch* idea would have been difficult to foresee only a few weeks earlier. In the immediate aftermath of the Kaiser's abdication on 9 November 1918, even the most uncompromising right-wing opponents to democracy had made little reference to Bismarck. Partly this was due to the fact that up until 1918 conservatives and nationalists had interpreted the World War as some sort of Darwinian struggle in which two rivalling constitutional forms—the French constitution of 1789 and Bismarck's constitution of 1871—would compete against each other until the superior form emerged victorious.[38] This and the political overthrow of 'their' state put conservative circles very much on the defensive. It was thought amongst right-wing circles that any attempt to demand a return to Bismarck's constitution would lack both credibility and public approval at a time when democracy still enjoyed considerable support among the German population.[39]

Only when this support gradually diminished did the Bismarck myth re-emerge as a political weapon. The radicalization of the revolution in early January 1919 was one aspect which contributed significantly to this development. Its occasion was the dismissal of Emil Eichhorn from his post of Police President in Berlin on 4 January 1919. Eichhorn, a left-wing Independent Social Democrat, refused to resign. His party, the USPD, joined with the recently founded German Communist Party (KPD) in calling for mass demonstrations to protest against Eichhorn's dismissal. The fighting which broke out in the course of these demonstrations was later to become known as the 'Spartacist uprising'. Within only a few days the uprising was crushed violently by volunteer *Freikorps* units formed with the permission of Ebert's Defence Minister, Gustav Noske.[40] It was a Pyrrhic victory. The revolution, first supported or at least tolerated by a vast majority of Germans, lost its innocence. The radical left, whose leaders Rosa Luxemburg and Karl Liebknecht were murdered by *Freikorps* soldiers on 19 January 1919, accused Noske and Ebert of collaboration with reactionary forces.[41] For the German middle classes, on the

---

[37] Machtan (ed.), *National-Mythos*, 35.

[38] See, for example, Erich Kaufmann, *Bismarcks Erbe in der Reichsverfassung* (Berlin, 1917), 145 ff.

[39] Christian F. Trippe, *Konservative Verfassungspolitik 1918–1923: Die DNVP als Opposition in Reich und Ländern* (Düsseldorf, 1995), 45.   [40] See in further detail, Watt, *The Kings Depart*, 254 ff.

[41] Cf. Eric Waldman, *The Spartacist Uprising of 1919 and the Crisis of the German Socialist Movement: A*

other hand, the revolution had shown its true, ugly face. Their traditional aversion to socialism and republicanism asserted itself and contributed to the emergence of Bismarck as a right-wing propaganda device against the Republic. For the bourgeois right, 9 November, the day of the proclamation of the Republic, became synonymous with defeat, 'unspeakable shame', and chaos.[42] Bismarck, in contrast, appeared in public speeches and articles as a warrant of stability and order, the symbol of Germany's former might.[43] At a time 'when all low and mean instincts concealed in the human breast have been let loose among our people', 'nationally'-minded circles felt that only a 'new Bismarck' would be able to put an end to the revolution and restore German 'greatness'.[44]

The signing of the Versailles Treaty on 28 June 1919 also helped to create a political climate in which anti-democratic and anti-western propaganda fell on fruitful ground. The lost war and the establishment of an 'un-German' democratic form of government was portrayed by right-wing organizations as a direct consequence of the November revolutionaries' 'stab-in-the-back' of the otherwise victorious German army. The 'stab-in-the-back' legend of the German High Command went hand in hand with the Bismarck myth. The weekly journal of the Patriotic Leagues, for example, suggested that the 'coup d'état' of 1918 had been planned and carried out by those political groups which Bismarck himself had stigmatized as the 'internal enemies of the Reich'.[45] The Centre Party, the Social Democrats, and the Left Liberals, which formed a coalition government from October 1918 onwards, had committed treason against the spirit of Bismarck by signing the armistice. As 'wreckers of Bismarck's creation' and 'blasphemers against his holy name' they were the ones to blame for Germany's current misery.[46]

The constitutional debates in Weimar confirmed that the Bismarck myth had been quickly adapted to the altered political situation. Right-wing politicians invoked Bismarck's name whenever they expressed their dissatisfaction with the draft constitution which Hugo Preuß had put forward on 20 January 1919. In February 1919, the chairman of the German People's Party (DVP) delegation, Rudolf Heinze, and his DNVP colleague Count

---

Study of the Relation of Political Theory and Party Practice (Milwaukee, 1958), 199–200. See, too, Heinrich August Winkler, 'Die Revolution von 1918/19 und das Problem der Kontinuität in der deutschen Geschichte', *HZ* CCL (1990), 303–19.

[42] Alfred Jacobsen at a meeting of the Pan-German League in Friedrichsruh, as quoted in *Hamburger Nachrichten*, 2 Apr. 1919, morning edition.

[43] See, for example, the Pan-German League's Bamberg Declaration (1919), in Landesarchiv Berlin, Zeitgeschichtliche Sammlung, 243/161.

[44] Dietrich Schäfer, 'Zu Bismarcks 105. Geburtstag', *Neue Preußische Zeitung*, 1 Apr. 1920.

[45] *Die Tradition*, I (1919), 19–20.   [46] Ibid.

Posadowsky-Wehner, insisted that Preuß's draft was unacceptable because it departed too far from Bismarck's constitution. Heinze emphasized that under Bismarck's constitution, the nation had 'reached the finest flowering which the German people have ever achieved since the time of their entry into world history'.[47]

Bismarck also appeared in the National Assembly's highly emotive debate on the future name of the state. Had the new state departed so far from Bismarck's Reich in constitutional terms as to justify changing its name from 'German Reich' to 'German Republic'?[48] The parties' fundamentally different ideologically motivated viewpoints on this issue quickly became apparent when the subject was raised during the second reading of the constitutional draft in July 1919. In presenting his party's position to the plenum, Oskar Cohn of the USPD underlined that Bismarck's Reich was 'past and gone'. Cohn justified his approval of the name change by referring to Bismarck's Reich as a 'historically accidental creation' and 'in world evolutionary terms a transitory phenomenon'. In any case, 'Bismarck's creation' was something which the National Assembly would 'consciously have to turn away from'.[49]

By contrast, Hugo Preuß speaking for the DDP emphasized that his party's aim was first and foremost to fashion for Germany a new constitution based on liberal principles, but that there was no conflict between this and the retention of the name 'Reich' for the state. Indeed, it was important that the old name be retained, to emphasize that the body politic was still Bismarck's nation-state.[50] The DDP, which had emerged from the January elections as the strongest bourgeois party, knew that it owed its success largely to the fact that a substantial number of former national-liberal voters had defected to the DDP in order to counterweight the influence of the workers' parties. For the DDP it thus became important to balance the process of inner renewal and to avoid radical breaks—even on a symbolic level—with the pre-revolutionary past.[51]

The members of the two bourgeois right-wing parties (DVP and DNVP) naturally made even more allusions to Bismarck in the context of the National Assembly's debate about Germany's future constitution. Clemens von

---

[47] NV, 28 Feb. 1919, vol. 326, 396.   [48] See Huber, *Verfassungsgeschichte*, 5. 1192.

[49] NV, 2 July 1919, vol. 327, 1209. The protocol records 'vivid heckling' from the deputies of the DVP and the DNVP during Cohn's speech.

[50] NV, 2 July 1919, vol. 327, 1212. Similar sentiments were voiced by his colleague Bruno Ablaß. See NV, 2 July 1919, vol. 327, 1213.

[51] Jürgen C. Hess, *'Das ganze Deutschland soll es sein': Demokratischer Nationalismus in der Weimarer Republik am Beispiel der Deutschen Demokratischen Partei* (Stuttgart, 1978), 23–75. The DDP received 18.5% of the votes in the general elections of January 1919. See Jürgen Falter *et al.* (eds.), *Wahlen und Abstimmungen in der Weimarer Republik: Materialien zum Wahlverhalten 1919–1933* (Munich, 1986), 46.

Delbrück, a former state secretary in the Imperial Ministry of the Interior and now a member of the DNVP delegation, argued that the name-change proposal would constitute a fundamental 'break with Bismarck's creation'.[52] Referring to Cohn's statement, Delbrück emphasized that Bismarck's foundation of the Reich had been 'neither an aberration nor a product of chance' but an achievement whose significance 'history has fully endorsed and will continue to do so'.[53]

The name-change debate was symptomatic of the clash of different historical traditions in the National Assembly. Between February and July 1919 the German public witnessed the opening battles of the fierce civil war of historical traditions and symbols that would continue to rage in Weimar's politically fragmented society until the collapse of the Republic in 1933. That the debate was conducted with such acrimony was hardly surprising. In its symbolic dimension the name-change debate touched on a central problem facing the new political system: how much of the old to retain, how much to create anew?

Quite similar in this respect was the argument over the colours of the national flag which was also subject to heated disputes both in the National Assembly and among the political public.[54] As opposed to the name-change debate, however, a majority of the delegates of DDP and Centre were here prepared to draw a line of demarcation between Bismarck's Reich and the Republic.[55]

Those principally opposed to adopting black, red, and gold as the new national colours were the DVP and the DNVP. As late as November 1918 prominent representatives of the political right such as the chairman of the Pan-German League, Heinrich Claß, and the editor of *Deutsche Tageszeitung*, Reinhold Wulle, had still supported the adoption of these colours as an 'emblem' of the ideal of *Anschluß*.[56] In the National Assembly, however, there was little detectable enthusiasm left for black, red, and gold amongst the right-wing parties. Instead, the DNVP proposed a motion to keep the colours of 'Bismarck's Reich', a motion which was supported by the DVP and by a minority within the Centre and the DDP.[57]

---

[52] NV, 2 July 1919, vol. 327, 1213. [53] Ibid., 1216.

[54] See Wolfgang Ribbe, 'Flaggenstreit und Heiliger Hain: Bemerkungen zur nationalen Symbolik in der Weimarer Republik', in Dietrich Kurze (ed.), *Aus Theorie und Praxis: Festschrift für Hans Herzfeld zum 80. Geburtstag* (Berlin and New York, 1972), 175–88. For a contemporary view see Egmont Zechlin, *Schwarz Rot Gold und Schwarz Weiß Rot: Geschichte und Gegenwart* (Berlin, 1926). See, too, Elisabeth Fehrenbach, 'Über die Bedeutung der politischen Symbole im Nationalstaat', *HZ* CCXIII (1971), 296–357, here pp. 351–2.

[55] On the position of the Centre Party during the constitutional debates see Rudolf Morsey, *Die deutsche Zentrumspartei 1917–1923* (Düsseldorf, 1966), 196–245.

[56] *Alldeutsche Blätter*, 9 Nov. 1918. Reinhold Wulle's article is printed in *Deutsche Tageszeitung*, 14 Nov. 1918, morning edition.

[57] On this see Anschütz, *Verfassung des Deutschen Reiches*, 31–2.

Speaking on behalf of the DVP, Wilhelm Kahl maintained that keeping the black, white, and red flag was nothing less than a question of 'national honour', a 'matter of patriotic concern'.[58] The DNVP delegate Wilhelm Laverrenz was in full accord on this point when, with a tacit allusion to the results of the revolution and the Versailles Peace Conference, he referred to the old flag as a 'sacred national treasure' that had to be preserved in the light of Germany's recent national decline. He warned that the members of the Assembly should not contemplate abandoning it 'in these days of cruellest humiliation and wretched impotence', unless they wished to abandon 'the last visible symbol which recalls the erstwhile greatness of the Fatherland', a symbol of the 'dawn' of Bismarck's national unification.[59]

Convinced by this argument, the DNVP delegates announced their 'fiercest opposition' to what they denounced as the historical obliviousness of the left: 'You will never erase the memory of this great period', Clemens von Delbrück admonished his political opponents in the plenum, 'and we will do our utmost, to keep the memory of that time alive in this country'.[60]

In the eyes of the Majority Social Democrats, on the other hand, the constitutional break with Bismarck's Reich and the call for a new national flag distinct from that of the old state were self-evidently connected. The Social Democratic Minister of the Interior, Eduard David, noted that the 'new Germany' stood in need of a symbol which would prove to the world that the Reich had experienced an inner renewal. The black, white, and red colours would hardly serve this purpose since they would be associated with Bismarck's Prussian militarism.[61]

In contrast to the debate over the new name for the state, the parliamentary vote on the national flag dispute resulted in the adoption of a compromise solution, which was negotiated by the delegates Max Quarck (MSPD) and Adolf Gröber (Centre Party). According to this compromise the new national colours would be black, red, and gold. The merchant flag, however, would be black, white, and red with a smaller black, red, and golden flag in the upper corner. Although this compromise was adopted by the National Assembly with 211 against 89 votes, the infamous 'Article 3' was to become a permanent subject of dispute.[62] More than any other clause of the Weimar Constitution, 'Article 3'

---

[58] NV, 2 July 1919, vol. 327, 1227–8.   [59] Ibid., 1229–30.   [60] Ibid., 1218.

[61] Ibid., 1125–6. For a similar statement given by Hugo Preuß in the National Assembly, see NV, 24 Feb. 1919, vol. 326, 285. See, too, Alois Friedel, *Deutsche Staatssymbole: Herkunft und Bedeutung der politischen Symbolik in Deutschland* (Frankfurt and Bonn, 1968), 33.

[62] NV, 3 July 1919, vol. 327, 1245–6. Only two years later the controversy over Article 3 burst out anew and eventually brought about the downfall of the Luther government in 1926. Worth comparing is the parliamentary debate on 27 June 1921: RT, 27 June 1921, vol. 350, particularly pp. 4168 ff.

mirrored the Assembly's indecisiveness with respect to the symbolic representation of the newly founded German Republic.

The promulgation of the constitution on 11 August 1919 did not usher in a period of inner consolidation for the Weimar Republic. Quite the opposite was true: those who had failed in their efforts to achieve a more profound transformation of the state and its socio-economic foundations came to regard the Republic as at best a modest improvement on what they considered to be the semi-absolutist nature of Bismarck's Reich. The radical left refused to acknowledge any genuine progressive elements in the Weimar constitution. In their eyes, there was no escaping the fact that Bismarck's authoritarian and privilege-ridden state had survived the war because of the MSPD's renunciation of a more radical social and economic revolution.

The political right—the supporters of the monarchist order and the advocates of a new but equally non-democratic and authoritarian form of government—also held the Weimar Constitution in odium. Whereas the extreme left was convinced of the 'class treason' of the Social Democrats, the radical right accused the SPD of having committed treason against the nation. In this context Bismarck and his constitution of 1871 served as a reference point for right-wing polemics against the Weimar Constitution. When, for example, in 1926 the construction of a national constitutional memorial in Weimar was under discussion, the former national-liberal, then German Nationalist Reichstag MP Gottfried Traub recommended commissioning a sculpture which would portray 'the Jew Preuß' stabbing Bismarck in the back.[63]

Not all of the efforts to convey the superiority of Bismarck's constitution to that of the Weimar Republic took a similarly polemical form. Otto Westphal, for example, based his criticism of the Weimar 'system' on the notion that the 'ideas of 1871' underlying Bismarck's constitution represented a Hegelian concept of the state which had corresponded with the German national character. The Republic, on the other hand, had adopted the 'ideas of 1789' and therefore the 'un-German' constitution of the victors.[64] To Westphal and others, one of the most striking advantages of Bismarck's constitution appeared to be the restricted influence of parties on national politics. Whereas in the Republic ideological and material considerations dominated over the nation's interest, Bismarck's constitution had been based on the belief in a national leader figure, who guided the destiny of the country with a 'strong hand'.[65]

---

[63] *Eiserne Blätter,* IX (1927), 581.

[64] Otto Westphal, *Feinde Bismarcks: Geistige Grundlagen der deutschen Opposition 1848–1918* (Munich and Berlin, 1930), 143–7. A contrasting, rather pro-Republican view is presented in Carl Görler, *Die Weimarer Verfassung im Verhältnis zu ihrem Frankfurter Vorbild und zum Werke Bismarcks* (Annaberg, 1927), 28.

Comments such as these suggest that the National Assembly had failed to convince many Germans that the establishment of a parliamentary democracy was historically legitimate. Moreover, it had failed to create an emotional bond between the Republican state and its citizens. Certainly this was a difficult task to achieve in the context of the lost war and the final outcome of the Versailles negotiations. But Weimar's severe crisis of legitimacy had internal as well as external causes. The inglorious revolution of 1848, which the Republicans chose as their historical reference point to counter the Bismarck myth, was a tradition only held in high regard by a minority of Germans. In the eyes of most Germans, the 1848 revolution had been a disastrous failure, a failure that had proven once and for all that parliaments were incapable of successful political decision-making. Additionally, as Peter Gay has argued, the Republic tried to distinguish itself from the Kaiserreich through sobriety and the absence of pomp which were considered to be democratic virtues. Thus, 'by its very essence, the Republic was a calculated affront to the heroes and clichés that every child knew, many politicians invoked, and, it turned out, most Germans cherished. In the battle of historical symbols the Republicans were at a disadvantage from the start: compared to Bismarck . . . at once superhuman and picturesque, the models available to Weimar were pallid and uninspiring.'[66]

This is not to suggest that the Republicans neglected or even underestimated the power of the Bismarck myth. They never did. Throughout the fourteen years of the first German democracy the Republican parties would fight the Bismarck myth vigorously. However, they failed to create a widely cherished Republican counter-myth, a counter-myth that was desperately needed if the Republicans wanted to emerge victoriously from the battle over Germany's mythical past.

---

[65] See, for example, *Feier der 50. Wiederkehr des Tages der Reichsgründung am 18. Januar 1921 an der Technischen Hochschule Darmstadt* (Darmstadt, 1921), 7.

[66] Peter Gay, *Weimar Culture: The Outsider as Insider*, 4th edn. (London, 1992), 91.

4
Fragmented Society—Divided Memory: Perceptions of Bismarck in Early Weimar Germany

In search of the 'guiding star of patriotic edification': Bismarck in Weimar historiography

The constitutional controversies in Weimar's National Theatre and the accompanying public debates left no room for doubt that the Bismarck myth had survived both the transformation of the political system after 1918 and the renaissance of the *großdeutsch* idea. The immediate post-war controversies also indicated how fundamentally the narrative had changed its character. Whereas the Bismarck myth had served to stabilize the political system between 1898 and 1918, it fulfilled quite the opposite task after the collapse of the Kaiserreich, when it became a weapon to be employed against the Republic of Weimar by its right-wing opponents.

As in 1914, it was historians who, in their capacity as professional interpreters of the past, played a leading role in the adaptation of the Bismarck myth to meet current political requirements. Coming from conservative or at least national-liberal political backgrounds, the majority of Weimar historians provided 'evidence' for the superior character of Bismarck's state while criticizing the Republic for its deficiencies.[1] In a commemorative address before members of the Friedrich-Wilhelm University in Berlin on Reich Foundation Day 1921, the highly respected historian of Eastern Europe, Otto Hoetzsch, for example, denounced contemporary 'fragmentation, party animus, and the destruction and disintegration of all spiritual and material values'. At the same time he invoked the memory of Bismarck as a historical reminder to the living to act 'patriotically' in both the present and future:

---

[1] On general political tendencies within Weimar historiography, see Bernd Faulenbach, 'Nach der Niederlage: Zeitgeschichtliche Fragen und apologetische Tendenzen in der Historiographie der Weimarer Zeit', in Peter Schöttler (ed.), *Geschichte als Legitimationswissenschaft 1918–1945* (Frankfurt, 1997), 31–51.

3. A postcard of 1920 depicting a 'patriotic gathering' at a Bismarck Memorial in Oppeln.

These [memories] demand our faith in people and Fatherland, to toil for Fatherland and State, to creative endeavour, in the hope that the spiritual and moral forces in our nation may give birth to the leaders whose lack we so desperately feel, and whom we, or those who come after us, will be prepared to follow to a new height, the height of a strong and creative German state, in which all members of our people are embraced and in which our obligations to mankind can be fulfilled . . .[2]

In Hoetzsch's view, blame for the 'national decline' since 1918 lay not with those who had held political responsibility in the Kaiserreich but with the par-

---

[2] See Otto Hoetzsch's address in *Reichsgründungsfeier der Friedrich-Wilhelms-Universität zu Berlin* (Berlin, 1921), 6–30, here p. 30.

ties who had pressed for constitutional reform during the Great War and who had come together to form the Weimar Coalition after the November revolution. Hoetzsch's polemic was directed first and foremost against the Centre Party and the Social Democrats, whose 'unpatriotic attitude' or '*vaterlandslose Gesinnung*' he traced back to Bismarck's times. Ever since 1871, the concept of the nation had been rejected by 'the party of political Catholicism . . . and the rising Social Democrats'.[3] The democratic system which both parties supported prevented Germany's inner consolidation, and the Reich's rise to greatness and renewed world importance.[4]

Hoetzsch's statements cannot be dismissed as the isolated comments of an academic outsider. In fact they were typical of the views of the conservative or national-liberal majority of German scholars, who took a critical stance when assessing the republican present while at the same time glorifying the days of Bismarck's rule.[5] Even the Bismarck biographer Max Lenz, who had protested against the politicization of history-writing in the days of the Kaiserreich, now freely vented his aversion to the democratic system when he declared that Bismarck's Reich had been handed over to its internal enemies as a result of the reforms of October 1918.[6] According to Lenz, Bismarck's state had not collapsed because of its army's weakness. Instead, 'cowardice, treachery, and lust for power of fanatic demagogues' had ruined Bismarck's 'glorious Reich'. It was the duty of scholars, he maintained, to remind the people of these 'true reasons' for the loss of the war: 'Always to keep it in mind, and constantly to speak about it—this has to be our motto.'[7]

No one could have agreed more with this 'motto' than Erich Marcks, who described Bismarck's time in office as the 'proud zenith' of Germany's past, in direct contrast to the sombre tones of his portrayal of the post-revolutionary present.[8] Marcks was deeply opposed to the Weimar Republic and its underlying political values. In works like *Die Versklavung des deutschen Volkes* (1921) he

---

[3] Ibid. 15 and 17.

[4] Ibid. See, too, Erich Schaeder, *Reich und Volk: Festrede zur Feier der Reichsgründung, Schlesische Friedrich-Wilhelms-Universität* (Breslau, 1921), 10.

[5] Cf. Bernd Faulenbach, 'Deutsche Geschichtswissenschaft zwischen Kaiserreich und NS-Diktatur', in id. (ed.), *Geschichtswissenschaft in Deutschland: Traditionelle Positionen und gegenwärtige Aufgaben* (Munich, 1974), 66–85.

[6] Max Lenz, 'Partei oder Vaterland?', in id., *Wille, Macht und Schicksal*, 3rd edn. (Munich and Berlin, 1922), 165–6.

[7] Max Lenz, 'Knechtschaft: Rede gehalten in Hamburg am 18. Januar 1921', in id., *Wille, Macht und Schicksal*, 172–83, quotations on pp. 177 and 174. For similar views see Dietrich Schäfer, *Das Reich als Republik: Deutschland und Preußen* (Berlin, 1919), 13, and id., 'Bismarck', *Jung-Bismarck-Berlin*, 1 Apr. 1922.

[8] Erich Marcks, 'Tiefpunkte des deutschen Schicksals in der Neuzeit: Vortrag vor den deutschen Vereinen in Stockholm zur Feier des 18. Januar 1924', in id., *Geschichte und Gegenwart: Fünf historisch-politische Reden* (Stuttgart, Berlin, and Leipzig, 1925), 81–107, here p. 86.

ruthlessly criticized parliamentarianism and the mediocre politicians it created. For Marcks, the memory of Bismarck was a permanent 'source of strength' in an age without moral values.[9] Views such as these made him a popular speaker at right-leaning commemorative celebrations, and may well have been a significant factor in securing his appointment in the mid-1920s as historical adviser for the Bismarck film project, which was heavily criticized by republican circles because of its explicitly anti-democratic tendencies.

No other historian influenced the image of Bismarck in the 1920s and early 1930s more than Marcks, whose hagiographic biography *Otto von Bismarck— ein Lebensbild* was published in twenty-eight editions between 1915 and 1935.[10] Marcks, who had met Bismarck personally in 1893 and who was granted access to the family archives after 1898, was also the driving force behind the 'Friedrichsruh edition' of Bismarck's works.[11]

The 'Friedrichsruh edition', published in nineteen volumes between 1924 and 1935, was designed, according to the editors, to become 'a monument for the Reich's founder erected by Germany at the time of her greatest humiliation'.[12] Such aspirations could hardly fail to influence the selection process of documents that were to be published in the 'Friedrichsruh edition'. Out of the six volumes dedicated to Bismarck's 'political writings', five focused on the eight years between his appointment as Prussian Minister President and the Imperial Proclamation at Versailles. Only one volume was devoted to documents dating from Bismarck's twenty-year-long rule as German Chancellor— including the years of the anti-socialist legislation and the *Kulturkampf*.[13]

Despite (or perhaps because) of the transformation of the political system in 1918–19, historiography in the period continued to portray Bismarck as a leader-figure whose foreign policy achievements largely overshadowed the memory of his repressive and eventually unsuccessful policies against the socialist movement and political Catholicism. Even the minority of those historians who became 'Republicans by reason' made no effort to dispute this

---

[9] Ibid. See, too, Erich Marcks, *Das Deutsche Reich von 1871 bis 1921*, 6th rev. edn. (Leipzig, 1922), 441.

[10] In addition to his publication successes, Marcks received the highest honours for his works. He was a fellow of the Prussian Academy of Arts and Sciences, became President of the Historical Commission of the Bavarian Academy of Arts and Sciences in 1923, and was for some time the editor of *Historische Zeitschrift*. See Jens Nordalm, *Historismus und moderne Welt: Erich Marcks, 1861–1938, in der deutschen Geschichtswissenschaft* (Berlin, 2003).

[11] Otto von Bismarck, *Die gesammelten Werke, Friedrichsruher Ausgabe*, 19 vols. (Berlin, 1924–35).

[12] Introduction to the first volume of the Friedrichsruh edition (1924). The introduction was written by the editors: Erich Marcks, Friedrich Meinecke, and Hermann Oncken.

[13] The 'New Friedrichsruh Edition' (2004–), on the other hand, focuses on documents written between 1871 and 1898. See Otto von Bismarck, *Gesammelte Werke, Neue Friedrichsruher Ausgabe* (Paderborn, Munich, Vienna, and Zurich, 2004–).

glorified view of Bismarck. In Hermann Oncken's writings, too, Bismarck appeared as a national Messiah, for 'he alone knew the path which would lead the whole people out of the desert, and he alone was the man to walk this path, the "*Zwingherr der Deutschheit*", who Fichte had once prophesied'.[14]

The reverential attitude towards Bismarck among leading German historians of the day should not be interpreted purely as a reactionary intellectual stance to the new political system. The military collapse of 1918 was widely perceived as a loss of 'all values in the historical-political sphere'.[15] The attempt 'to use the authority of the past in the face of a threatening present and a gloomy future' became a central motif of national-conservative historians after 1918.[16] The 'shock to German historical consciousness' drove scholars in search of 'the exemplary, a guiding star of patriotic edification' and this they found in Bismarck.[17] In 1922, Johannes Haller, one of the period's leading medievalists, published his book *Epochen der deutschen Geschichte* with which he wished to contribute to the search for 'historical meaning'. His foreword ended with an appraisal of the 'glorious time' of Bismarck's unification of Germany, a period of 'fulfilment and happiness'. In Haller's opinion, the memory of Bismarck, the 'redeemer of the nation', was invaluable for shaping Germany's future.[18] Bismarck nostalgia thus had its origins in a commonly expressed yearning for a government which could both unite the nation, currently divided by the prevailing conflicts of party interests, and restore Germany to the position of power and influence that it had formerly enjoyed when the Iron Chancellor was at the helm.

There was yet another reason why Bismarck occupied such a dominant position in historical writing: the vast majority of historians clung to the paradigm of the primacy of foreign policy.[19] For most historians it was still the Great Powers and their statesmen who were the decisive actors upon which all political action depended.[20] Only academic outsiders such as the *enfant terrible* of

---

[14] Hermann Oncken, *Lassalle: Eine politische Biographie*, 3rd edn. (Stuttgart and Berlin, 1920), 382.

[15] Maximilian von Hagen, *Das Bismarckbild in der Literatur der Gegenwart* (Berlin, 1929), 1.

[16] Hans Herzfeld, 'Staat und Nation in der deutschen Geschichtsschreibung der Weimarer Zeit', in *Veritas-Iustitia-Libertas. Festschrift zur 200-Jahrfeier der Columbia-University New York, überreicht von der Freien Universität Berlin und der Deutschen Hochschule für Politik* (Berlin, 1954), 129–43, here p. 134.

[17] See the introductory remarks in Hans Rothfels (ed.), *Bismarck und der Staat: Ausgewählte Dokumente*, 2nd edn. (Stuttgart, 1953), p. ix.

[18] Johannes Haller, *Epochen der deutschen Geschichte* (Stuttgart, 1922), foreword (not paginated). In the foreword to the 1943 edition of *Epochen der deutschen Geschichte* Haller exclaimed that his 'hopes and beliefs' as articulated in 1922, had 'become reality'.

[19] See Faulenbach, 'Deutsche Geschichtswissenschaft', 66–85.

[20] Evidently, there was a focus on foreign policy in the source publications of the Weimar Republic. See, in particular, *Die große Politik der europäischen Kabinette 1871 bis 1890: Sammlung der diplomatischen Akten des Auswärtigen Amtes*, ed. Johannes Lepsius, Albrecht Mendelssohn Bartholdy, and Friedrich Thimme, 40

Weimar historiography, Eckart Kehr, unsuccessfully questioned the primacy of foreign policy.[21]

Bismarck's foreign policy and the abandonment of his diplomatic strategies after 1890 were among the most frequently investigated topics in Weimar historiography.[22] The period between 1871 and 1914 was divided in historical writings into a Bismarckian Era and a post-Bismarck period, which were generally contrasted with each other. Bismarck's fall from power and the establishment of Wilhelm's 'personal regime' were evaluated as the central reasons for Germany's decline.[23] Bismarck was not held responsible for the outbreak of the Great War and certainly not for the German defeat of 1918.[24] Instead, it was commonly believed that the 'complicated' alliance system which Bismarck had established was never properly understood by his successors. The source publications of the 1920s seemed to confirm 'Bismarck's political genius' for 'all times'.[25] Werner Näf, for example, followed a broad academic consensus when he stated that 'the whole [system of alliances] was based on his [Bismarck's] personality, and could not be held together without those imponderables of geniality and trust, which he incorporated. What he nurtured was alliance politics of the greatest complexity.' Bismarck's foreign policy ideas had been so complex that only he, 'the consummate master of diplomacy, could grasp them'.[26]

Scholars who dared to challenge the dominant image of Bismarck met with hostile criticism from colleagues and professional ostracism. It was well known amongst Weimar historians that any attempt 'to take a critical stance on Bismarck's work' was deemed to indicate a 'lack of national spirit' and could even end an academic career.[27] When, for example, Johannes Ziekursch

---

vols. (Berlin, 1922–7); Lothar von Schweinitz, *Denkwürdigkeiten des Botschafters General von Schweinitz* (Berlin, 1927); Eliza von Moltke (ed.), *Erinnerungen, Briefe, Dokumente: Helmuth von Moltke 1877–1916* (Stuttgart, 1922).

[21] See Eckart Kehr, *Der Primat der Innenpolitik: Economic Interest, Militarism, and Foreign Policy: Essays on German History*, translated from German into English by Grete Heinz (Berkeley, 1977).

[22] For a detailed overview of the extensive literature on Bismarck's foreign policy see Maximilian von Hagen, *Bismarckbild*, 64 ff. and the addenda by the same author in *Zeitschrift für Politik*, XIX (1929), 539 ff.; XXII (1932), 369 ff. and 466 ff.; XXVIII (1938), 197 ff., 241 ff., 404 ff.

[23] See, for example, Wilhelm Schüßler, *Bismarcks Sturz* (Berlin and Leipzig, 1921) and Wilhelm Mommsen, *Bismarcks Sturz und die Parteien* (Berlin, 1924), 44 ff. and 66 ff. Otto Gradenwitz, *Bismarcks letzter Kampf 1888–1898* (Berlin, 1924). On the broader context, see Gisela Brude-Firnau, *Die literarische Deutung Kaiser Wilhelms II zwischen 1889 und 1989* (Heidelberg, 1997).

[24] See, for example, *Deutsche Rundschau*, CLXXXVII (1921), 359 ff.

[25] Hagen, *Bismarckbild*, 2.

[26] Werner Näf, *Bismarcks Außenpolitik 1871–1890* (St Gallen, 1925), 76.

[27] See Walter Goetz, 'Die deutsche Geschichtsschreibung der Gegenwart', in id., *Historiker in meiner Zeit: Gesammelte Aufsätze* (Cologne and Graz, 1957), 415–24, quotation on p. 420.

suggested that Bismarck had founded the Reich 'against the spirit of the time' (an argument first put forward by Friedrich Nietzsche) and that it therefore had 'contained within it the seeds of its own destruction', critics competed to write the most negative reviews of his book.[28] Nevertheless, Ziekursch refused to abandon his view that there were clear structural faults inherent to Bismarck's constitution from the start. They were responsible at least in part, he suggested, for the Reich's collapse in 1918.[29]

Ziekursch differed from the majority of German historians in his belief that the constitution of 1871 had been a rejection of the democratic principles of the Paulskirche parliament of 1848–9. In his view, the 'false development' of domestic policy after 1871 was rooted in the Prussian constitutional conflict, in which the competing ideas of 'a monarchical form of government with an overlay of pseudo-constitutionalism administered by the Junkers with the help of the army and the civil service' on the one hand, and a 'parliamentary government in the hands of the higher bureaucracy' on the other, had fatally been decided in favour of the former.[30]

It was not without significance that such arguments were largely marginalized in Weimar's scholarly discourse and that historians generally failed to assess Bismarck's historical role critically. Throughout the Weimar era institutions of higher education instead proved to be strongholds of the Bismarck cult.[31] This had ramifications in the wider community. Through their lectures and writings some of the most respected German scholars ensured that the Bismarck myth acquired the halo of intellectual credibility, which in turn conferred respectability on the pseudo-historical arguments employed by right-wing circles in their attacks upon the Republic.

Bismarck and the Weimar right

Despite the many ideological and programmatic differences between the highly heterogeneous right-wing movements in Germany's first democracy, the Weimar right found its common battle standard against the Republic

---

[28] See Karl-Georg Faber, 'Johannes Ziekursch', in Hans-Ulrich Wehler (ed.), *Deutsche Historiker*, vol. 3 (Göttingen, 1972), 109–23.

[29] Johannes Ziekursch, 'Bismarcks Innenpolitik', *Der Eiserne Steg*, III (1926), 47–57.

[30] Johannes Ziekursch, *Politische Geschichte des neuen deutschen Kaiserreiches*, vol. 1: *Die Reichsgründung* (Frankfurt, 1925), 69.

[31] See Konrad H. Jarausch, *Deutsche Studenten 1800–1970* (Frankfurt, 1984), 124. Also Hans P. Bleuel and Ernst Klinnert, *Deutsche Studenten auf dem Weg ins Dritte Reich: Ideologien-Programme-Aktionen 1918–1933* (Gütersloh, 1967), 8–9.

within a couple of months after the collapse of the Kaiserreich: Bismarck.[32] No other historical reference point was used more often in public debate to criticize the 1919 Constitution, the Versailles Treaty, and the Republic's supposed lack of historical legitimacy. The Weimar right may have been deeply divided, but adoration for the 'glorious days' of the Iron Chancellor and the exemplary character of Bismarck's charismatic leadership was shared by *all* right-wing parties and movements.

It was commonly asserted in right-wing circles that in the Republic party politics had triumphed over 'national interest'. Under a charismatic, 'Bismarckian' type of leader, on the other hand, the pettiness of political disunity would come to an end.[33] In nationalist circles the hope for a 'new Bismarck' who would overcome the 'squabbling of the parties' remained common currency throughout the fourteen years of the Weimar Republic.[34]

Contemporary popular literature reinforced such views. In 1921, the writer Otto Autenrieth achieved a commercial success with his novel *Bismarck der Zweite: Der Roman der deutschen Zukunft* (*The Second Bismarck: A Novel about Germany's Future*), in which the protagonist, Otto von Fels, discovers that 'he is destined by providence to become the saviour of Germany and the world, Bismarck the Second'.[35] By suggesting that the prospects for Germany's future were dependent upon the emergence of a new Bismarck, Autenrieth's novel was very much in line with the dominant narratives in Weimar historiography, which contrasted the Bismarckian era with the 'leaderless' Republic.

Against the background of such interpretations of Bismarck by leading German historians, it was not surprising that the conservative daily *Deutsche Tageszeitung* referred to results of 'scholarly research' when on 18 January 1921 it sharply contrasted the Republic with the 'sublime period' of Bismarck's reign.[36] Under Bismarck, 'the dreams of every generation and every party for the last century had been brought to fulfilment'. The revolution of 1918–19 had effected a rupture with this 'glorious' past. As opposed to Bismarck's unification of the German nation, which had been the result of a 'social movement and

---

[32] On the highly heterogeneous Weimar right see in particular Kurt Sontheimer, *Antidemokratisches Denken in der Weimarer Republik: Die politischen Ideen des deutschen Nationalismus zwischen 1918 und 1933*, 4th edn. (Munich, 1994), 26. On the nationalist-conservative DNVP as the largest party of the anti-Republican right before the rise of National Socialism see Werner Liebe, *Die Deutschnationale Volkspartei 1918–1924* (Düsseldorf, 1966), 51–9.   [33] Sontheimer, *Antidemokratisches Denken*, 180–233.

[34] On this see Klaus Schreiner, ' "Wann kommt der Retter Deutschlands?" Formen und Funktionen von politischem Messianismus in der Weimarer Republik', *Saeculum*, XLIX (1998), 107–60. See, for example, Count Westarp's speech at a DNVP convention to celebrate Bismarck's birthday in 1927, quoted in *Der Tag*, 1 Apr. 1927.

[35] Otto Autenrieth, *Bismarck der Zweite: Der Roman der deutschen Zukunft* (Munich, 1921), 190.

[36] So, for example, *Deutschen Tageszeitung*, 18 Jan. 1921, morning edition.

transformation that proceeded from deep within the German people', the November revolution had been a 'politically coloured and cleverly constructed mutiny'.[37]

Deutsche Tageszeitung and other nationalist or *völkisch* papers also adopted the historiographical view that it had been the moment of Bismarck's dismissal which marked the beginning of the Reich's downfall. Here, 'the tragic blame' lay with both Wilhelm II and the German people themselves: 'A ruler, a people, a country on whom such guilt weighs' are doomed to misfortune, 'unless they recognize their fault and return to the basic principles and examples of state-craft set by that statesmanlike hero who was dismissed and driven into the wilderness against all the laws of decency and morality'.[38]

In the eyes of the vast majority of Germans, Wilhelm II's rule had been a dis-astrous failure.[39] Even the monarchists within the DNVP and the 'Stahlhelm' hardly ever referred to Wilhelm II in their demands for a restoration of the Hohenzollern dynasty.[40] Instead it was Bismarck who was employed by German monarchists to illustrate the past glory of the Kaiserreich.[41] The pub-lication of the third volume of Bismarck's *Thoughts and Reminiscences* in 1919 constituted a temporary blow to these attempts, but only a year later, during the Kapp-Lüttwitz putsch, Bismarck reappeared as a figurehead of the monarchists' anti-republican propaganda.[42] At least for the DNVP, the

---

[37] Quotations from *Deutsche Tageszeitung*, 17 Jan. 1921, evening edition; *Deutsche Tageszeitung*, 9 Nov. 1921, morning edition. Similarly, though with stronger critical emphasis on Bismarck's successors, 'Bismarck', *Die Tradition*, 1 Apr. 1922.

[38] Heinrich Claß, 'Bismarcks Schatten', *Alldeutsche Blätter*, 27 Mar. 1920. This view was not limited to the far right. In the national-liberal press, too, Wilhelm II and Bismarck's successors were blamed for the decline of the German Reich. See the anonymous article 'Wenn Bismarck wiederkäme . . .', *Deutsche Stimmen*, XXXI (1919), 27–9. See also Max Lohan, 'Bismarcks Sturz im Lichte der Gegenwart', *Deutsche Stimmen*, XXXII (1920), 231–9.

[39] The critical literature on Wilhelm II published after 1918 is too numerous to be listed here in detail. See, for example, Erich Le Mang, *Die persönliche Schuld Wilhelms II: ein zeitgemäßer Rückblick* (Dresden, 1919); Emil Neyen, *Wilhem II: Sein Werk: 450 Milliarden neuer Schulden und 21 fliehende Könige* (Berlin, 1919); Walther Rathenau, *Der Kaiser* (Berlin, 1919); Edgar von Schmidt-Pauli, *Der Kaiser: das wahre Gesicht Wilhelms II.* (Berlin, 1928). For a detailed analysis of critical attitudes towards Wilhelm II within the German aristocracy, see Stephan Malinowski, *Vom König zum Führer: Sozialer Niedergang und politische Radikalisierung im deutschen Adel zwischen Kaiserreich und NS-Staat* (Berlin, 2003), 249–53.

[40] On monarchism in Weimar, particularly between 1920 and 1923, see Walter H. Kaufmann, *Monarchism in the Weimar Republic* (New York, 1953).

[41] The best example of the monarchists' employment of Bismarck is the fact that the DNVP's youth organization was named 'Bismarck Youth'.

[42] The DNVP deeply regretted the publication of the last volume of *Thoughts and Reminiscences*. In their view, Bismarck's criticism of Wilhelm II would strengthen anti-monarchism. See Westarp papers, political correspondence, in BA (Berlin), N2329. During the monarchist Kapp-Lüttwitz putsch of 1920 a leaflet was distributed which juxtaposed Wilhelm I, Bismarck, and Hindenburg against Ebert, Bauer, and Noske. See Johannes Erger, *Der Kapp-Lüttwitz-Putsch: Ein Beitrag zur deutschen Innenpolitik 1919/20* (Düsseldorf, 1967), 90.

popular catchphrase 'Back to Bismarck' meant nothing less than a return to the political system of the Kaiserreich.

For the *völkisch* right, on the other hand, the slogan 'Back to Bismarck' implied more than merely a call for the restoration of the pre-war political status quo. According to Heinrich Claß, for example, the period of Bismarck's government represented only the highest point of national development *to date*, 'the starting-point of Germany's great future'. The task facing the present generation was to 'build on' Bismarck's *Kleindeutschland*, for 'once a people stops struggling for more, it is already beginning to give itself up'.[43]

Neo-conservative intellectuals such as Arthur Moeller van den Bruck, Oswald Spengler, and Hans Freyer equally rejected a return to the morally 'decadent' bourgeois culture of Wilhelmine Germany. Yet they were full of praise for Bismarck, whose Wars of Unification were interpreted as a period of moral purification.[44]

Similar, although not identical, emphasis was given to representations of Bismarck by leading politicians of the National Socialist German Workers' Party (NSDAP). The Nazi Party had arisen out of the German Workers' Party in 1920, and while at first only one among many *völkisch* and anti-Semitic splinter groups, it soon surpassed its right-wing competitors with a unique radicalism. Upon the 'ruins of that proud Reich which Bismarck's genius had created', *Völkischer Beobachter* declared in early 1921, a new state embracing all members of the German people would have to be created. With frightening clarity the author—none other than Adolf Hitler himself—explained how this inwardly renewed and outwardly expanded Reich would be governed. While under Bismarck 'risible means' had been used to combat 'parties which were hostile to the state', Hitler promised that in future times 'parasites, exploiters, and agitators' would be 'rounded up to the last man'.[45]

Although he was critical of Bismarck's 'moderate' domestic policies, Hitler emphasized the importance of this 'great man' for the nationalist movement in the Weimar Republic. The name of Bismarck, Hitler suggested, had to remind the German people in a time of national distress that there were good reasons 'to be proud to call oneself a German'.[46] Hitler's references to the founder of the

[43] Heinrich Claß, 'Zum achtzehnten Januar', *Alldeutsche Blätter*, 22 Jan. 1921.

[44] Arthur Moeller van den Bruck, *Das Dritte Reich*, ed. Hans Schwarz, 3rd edn. (Hamburg, 1931), 231; Oswald Spengler, *Preußentum und Sozialismus* (Munich, 1920), 6; Hans Freyer, *Das politische Semester: Ein Vorschlag zur Universitätsreform* (Jena, 1933). See, too, Wolfgang Hardtwig, 'Der Bismarck-Mythos: Gestalt und Funktionen zwischen politischer Öffentlichkeit und Wissenschaft', in id., *Hochkultur des bürgerlichen Zeitalters: Ausgewählte Aufsätze* (Göttingen, forthcoming).

[45] *Völkischer Beobachter*, 20 Jan. 1921.   [46] Ibid.

Reich had much the same purpose as the idealizing tendencies in conservative circles: Bismarck's rule was to act as a positive template—a period of national dignity and greatness—against which the unpalatable features of Weimar Germany could be set. In comparison to the Bismarckian Era, the Republic was no more than a transitional period, a momentary nadir in history, which it was the self-appointed duty of the Weimar right to surmount.

Catholic and liberal perceptions of Bismarck

On 18 January 1921, *Regensburger Anzeiger* recommended that Catholic Germany should recall with profound 'gratitude' Bismarck's unification of Germany as 'the moment of birth of an unhoped-for and unparalleled cultural and economic rise for the German nation'.[47]

This view, propagated by a paper affiliated with the Centre's Bavarian sister party, the BVP, was echoed elsewhere in the Catholic press. *Germania*, for example, proclaimed that the Kaiserreich—'the crowning achievement of Bismarck's statesmanlike policies'—had been 'the fulfilment of a thousand years of German history'.[48] At the same time, *Germania* described the current Centre Party as 'a party with genuine German sentiments', for it was—in its own revealing words—'in heart and mind fully and completely aware of the significance of 18 January 1871'.[49]

Both articles were evidence of a high degree of continuity in Catholic Germany's attitude towards Bismarck, despite the revolution of 1918–19. Ever since Bismarck's death in 1898, political Catholicism in Germany had adopted an increasingly positive stance towards its former arch-enemy, the Chancellor of the *Kulturkampf* legislation. To a certain extent, the Centre Party's worship of Bismarck as an unrivalled German statesman was and had always been an attempt to take the wind out of the sails of those who sought to condemn political Catholicism as 'unpatriotic and untrustworthy'.

The Centre Party's attempts to prove its 'national trustworthiness' by praising Bismarck's work were not always approved by German Catholics. In 1922, the Catholic historian Franz Xaver Hoermann, for example, warned that the tendency to emphasize the success of Bismarck's foreign policy at the cost of underplaying his failures in domestic policies presented a severe danger to

---

[47] *Regensburger Anzeiger*, 17 Jan. 1921, evening edition.
[48] *Germania*, 18 Jan. 1921.
[49] Ibid. Likewise, *Kölnische Volkszeitung*, 17 Jan. 1921, evening edition.

democracy. A selective assessment of the Reich's founder encouraged those call-ing for a 'new Bismarck', a man who would 'once again raise Germany to the height of 1870–71'.[50]

Hoermann was correct in identifying hopes for a restoration of 'former greatness' as one of the dominant motifs in the middle classes' attitude towards Bismarck. This was also true for national-liberal circles. Almost all of the news-papers which supported the DVP stressed the role of the National Liberal Party in bringing about the Reich's unification.[51] They also credited the National Liberals with responsibility for the economic upturn in the years immediately after the Empire's foundation, an economic boom which national-liberal papers contrasted sharply with the continuing inflation of the post-war years.[52]

Newspapers associated with the DVP identified two major reasons for Germany's current political misery: first, the Allies' peace conditions imposed on the defeated Reich, and, secondly, the widespread inclination of the Germans to neglect the historical models of their 'great' past, a past in which Bismarck's role had been pre-eminent. This historical neglect, Paul Oswald suggested in *Deutsche Stimmen*, was a result of the left's cunning strategy to ban Bismarck from public consciousness and to attempt instead to establish tradi-tions more 'suitable' for their own political goals: 'The memory of him [Bismarck] poses an obstacle to the full victory of the democratic idea . . .'.[53] All Germans had to understand, however, that historical oblivion with respect to Bismarck was 'an indication of the low level of our national feelings and thoughts' and that 'to fight the memory of Bismarck means nothing less than to erode the basis of our national unity and to deprive us of the last thing we have left nowadays'.[54]

However strong the critique of the contemporary state of German society and the economy may have been, the national-liberal elites were none the less notably restrained in their criticism of the government. The fact that the DVP was represented in the government coalition since the general elections of 1920 certainly contributed to this stance. The DNVP, which had attacked the DVP for entering the government coalition, was reminded that a revision of the 'sec-

[50] Franz X. Hoermann, 'Die Etappen und das Schlussresultat der Bismarckschen Politik', *Historisch-Politische Blätter für das katholische Deutschland*, CLXX (1922), 655–66, here p. 656; id., *Großdeutschlands vierhundertjähriger Niedergang zum Kleindeutschland: Die erste Ursache des heutigen politischen Zusammen-bruchs* (Regensburg, 1924).

[51] *Deutsche Allgemeine Zeitung*, 18 Jan. 1921, morning edition.

[52] See, for example, *Deutsche Allgemeine Zeitung*, 17 Jan. 1921, morning edition.

[53] Paul Ostwald, 'Bismarck oder Stein?', *Deutsche Stimmen*, XXXIV (1922), 222–4, here p. 222.

[54] Quotations from Paul Ostwald, 'Ist Bismarcks Werk ein Irrtum?', *Deutsche Stimmen*, XXXII (1920), 483–6, here p. 486, and id., 'Bismarck oder Stein?', 224.

ond Versailles' of 1919 was only to be achieved if the Germans stood together as they had done in the days of Bismarck.[55]

It was this very unity which the German Vice-Chancellor Rudolf Heinze emphasized in a public address in Munich on 17 January 1921. Heinze reminded his audience that the nation had to return to 'internal unity' in order to surmount the oppressive conditions of the peace accords imposed by the Western Allies. Heinze heavily criticized the Peace Settlement by pointing out the difference between the 'first and the second Versailles'. Bismarck's conditions in the Frankfurt Peace Treaty of 1871 were 'harmless' in comparison to the Versailles Treaty and France's attempts to ruin the German Reich politically and economically.[56]

What was missing in the Vice-Chancellor's speech (and, in fact, in any of the DVP's commemorative articles around 18 January 1921) was a clear and unequivocal commitment to the Republic. Commentary emanating from the left-liberal milieu, on the other hand, discussed the memory of Bismarck in an unmistakable spirit of support for parliamentary democracy and of opposition to the constitutional monarchy that Bismarck had established. In an editorial for the *Berliner Tageblatt*, Theodor Wolff made it clear that he interpreted the countless articles on Bismarck in the conservative press from 1918 onwards as a 'call to action' on the part of the right against the Republic. With respect to the forthcoming Reich Foundation Day of 1921, Wolff expressed the fear that this day would provide right-wing teachers with the opportunity to impose their reactionary ideas in schools and universities, the very places where future decision makers were moulded intellectually.[57] This insight should not, however, lead the right to conclude that the democratic forces were about to capitulate in the struggle over the past. Rather, the government and the democratic parties had to stress their commitment to Republican ideals 'at every opportunity, in clearly stated words and with clearly visible actions' until the 'German youth recognizes in them the seeds of a new greatness, and the chorus of doubters and critics no longer attracts support or enjoys credibility'.[58]

Wolff was not the only left-liberal intellectual who called for a depoliticization of the public debate revolving around Bismarck. The liberal-democratic jurisprudence professor Hermann Ulrich Kantorowicz also argued that a rational reconsideration of the nationalist interpretation of the past was a matter of fundamental importance for the Republic. In an article, which soon

---

[55] *Deutsche Allgemeine Zeitung*, 17 Jan. 1921, morning edition.

[56] Rudolf Heinze's speech is printed in part in *Berliner Tageblatt*, 17 Jan. 1921, evening edition.

[57] *Berliner Tageblatt*, 17 Jan. 1921, evening edition. See also *Frankfurter Zeitung*, 18 Jan. 1921, evening edition.   [58] *Berliner Tageblatt*, 17 Jan. 1921, evening edition.

afterwards was published as a pamphlet entitled *Bismarcks Schatten*, Kantorowicz warned his readers not to underestimate the effects of the right's constant employment of the founder of the Reich as a political weapon against the Republic. Bismarck, who according to Kantorowicz had changed the political and ethical value system of the bourgeoisie in an entirely negative sense, was *the* embodiment of the authoritarian state. 'As long as Bismarck's shadow falls over it,' Kantorowicz concluded, 'the young tree of German democracy can never thrive.'[59]

Kantorowicz's statements caused a huge scandal in his home town of Freiburg. Only three days after his article had appeared on 16 November 1921, an anonymous response was published in the German Nationalists' *Breisgauer Zeitung*. It was revealed a couple of weeks later that the author was a colleague of Kantorowicz, the famous Freiburg historian Georg von Below. In his article, Below accused Kantorowicz of attempting 'to erase all memory of Bismarck within Germany'.[60]

Despite Below's attacks, Kantorowicz remained a sharp critic of the Bismarck myth. In 1927 he wrote in an English journal: 'It is a very general mistake, common among my fellow countrymen, and shared by many foreigners, to consider Bismarck the founder of German unity. He did the contrary: by stigmatising Catholics, socialists and democrats as enemies of the Fatherland, unworthy of having any share in power, he split up the people into a mass of parties, each distrusting and hating the other, and made political life the dismal thing it is still in my country.'[61]

The liberal labour expert Heinz Potthoff arrived at similar conclusions. In an attempt to counteract the mythologization of Bismarck's image, he claimed that the Iron Chancellor was largely responsible for contemporary social conflicts. By branding certain social and political groups 'enemies of the Reich', Bismarck had created an atmosphere of enmity and mistrust in Germany.[62] Potthoff abhorred the fact that the 'poisonous accusation' of being 'anti-national' had reappeared in the political debate after 1918. Bearing in mind the precarious stability of the political, economic, and social order, the term 'national', he suggested, should not be applied to those pursuing party political

---

[59] Kantorowicz, *Bismarcks Schatten*, 5. The book was based on the article 'Bismarcks Schatten, Anmerkungen zu Robert Riemanns "Schwarzrotgold"' which was published on 13 November 1921 in the Sunday edition of the Social Democratic *Basler Anzeiger*.

[60] See Karlheinz Muscheler, *Hermann Ulrich Kantorowicz: Eine Biographie* (Berlin, 1984), particularly 59 ff. Also Donald L. Niewyk, *The Jews in Weimar Germany* (Manchester, 1980), 64.

[61] Hermann U. Kantorowicz: 'The German Constitution in Theory and Practice', *Economia*, VII (1927), 37 ff., here p. 40.   [62] Heinz Potthoff, 'National!', *Die Hilfe*, XXVI (1920), 23–4.

interests but to those willing to accept political responsibility in the democratic state of Weimar.[63]

In their attempts to deconstruct the Bismarck myth, Potthoff and
Kontorowicz could count on the support of some popular novelists such as
Emil Ludwig, who in 1924 staged a critical theatre play on Bismarck in
Potsdam. This was followed in 1926 by the publication of his popular biography on the Iron Chancellor.[64] While nationalist papers started a witch-hunt
against Ludwig, democrats such as Rudolf Olden praised the biography as a
book 'with a politically educational effect . . . a highly useful contribution to
the stabilization of the German Republic.'[65]

Left liberals were, however, not merely concerned to deconstruct the
Bismarck myth but, together with the Social Democrats, also strove to establish
their own democratic tradition, in which the Wars of Liberation, the Prussian
reform era, and the March revolution of 1848 had a central significance.[66] A
concrete manifestation of the democratic left's attempt to create and institu-
tionalize a Republican tradition of its own were the annual commemoration
ceremonies on Constitution Day to celebrate the signing of the Weimar
Constitution on 11 August 1919. The organization of these celebrations, which
had begun in 1921 during Joseph Wirth's Centre-Left coalition government,
was one of the central tasks of Edwin Redslob, who had been appointed as
Reichskunstwart in 1920.[67] The *Reichskunstwart*, subordinate to the Ministry of
the Interior, was responsible for every form of state representation including the
organization of the national commemoration festivals on 9 November.[68] However, these events were only of emotional relevance to a small minority of Social
Democrats and Left Liberals. It was widely perceived that 9 November was
anything but a glorious, identity-forging foundational event which inspired
romantic notions. 'Though November 1918 meant the end of the war,' Sebastian
Haffner wrote in his memoirs, 'it recalls no sense of joy, only a bad mood, defeat,

---

[63] Ibid. See, too, Emil Ludwig, 'Bismarck—nach dem Zusammenbruch', *Die Weltbühne*, XVII (1921),
697–700. Finally, Eugen Ehrlich, *Bismarck und der Weltkrieg* (Zurich, 1920), 31.

[64] Emil Ludwig, *Bismarck: Triologie eines Kämpfers* (Potsdam, 1924). Kaiser Wilhelm II subsequently filed
a lawsuit against Ludwig which Wilhelm lost. See Christoph Gradmann, *Historische Belletristik: Populäre historische Biographien in der Weimarer Republik* (Frankfurt and New York, 1993), 96 n. 61. Ludwig's Bismarck
biography was published as *Bismarck: Geschichte eines Kämpfers* (Berlin, 1926).

[65] Rudolf Olden, 'Emil Ludwigs Bismarck', *Berliner Tageblatt*, 5 Dec. 1926.

[66] See, for example, *Berliner Tageblatt*, 18 Jan. 1921, morning edition.

[67] See the autobiography by Edwin Redslob, *Von Weimar nach Europa: Erlebtes und Durchdachtes* (Berlin,
1972).

[68] Annegret Heffen, *Der Reichskunstwart—Kunstpolitik in den Jahren 1920–1933: Zu den Bemühungen um
eine offizielle Reichskunstpolitik in der Weimarer Republik* (Essen, 1986).

anxiety, senseless gunfights, confusion and bad weather.'[69] A comment printed in *Kölnische Volkszeitung* was even more pointed in this respect: 'There will be no paintings of the likes of Werner's Imperial Proclamation to announce the birth of the new Germany; it will simply be good when the memory of those dark, grey, ugly November days is erased once and for all . . . !'[70]

Most democrats were well aware of the political disadvantage deriving from the Republic's association with military defeat and revolution. For this reason they were concerned to defuse the divisive quarrel about the past which was having an obviously destabilizing effect on contemporary politics. Wilhelm Heile, for example, writing in the magazine *Hilfe*, warned his readers on Reich Foundation Day in 1921 not to focus their attention on disputed historical and political symbols but to work first and foremost for a consensus which transcended party interests.[71]

Yet it soon enough became evident that Heile's appeal had fallen on deaf ears. This fact did not escape the notice of the editor of *Hilfe*, the liberal Reichstag MP Gertrud Bäumer. She admitted that her magazine's conciliatory efforts during the celebrations of the fiftieth anniversary of the Reich's foundation had ultimately failed. The way in which the political leaders of the right had used the celebrations to stir up enmity against their political opponents and the Republican state was, according to Bäumer, 'the strongest and perhaps most notable symptom that we have lost the heritage of 1871, namely unity'.[72]

Bismarck and the divided left

In focusing on the right's instrumentalization of Bismarck against the Republic, Gertrud Bäumer had overlooked a crucial element of Weimar's battle over the past: the ideological divisions within German society did not follow a simple left–right scheme. Instead, the left was itself caught up in a fierce intellectual battle over the legacy of the past.

Certainly, the spokesmen of the politically divided working-class movement were united in adopting a critical tone in their allusions to Bismarck.[73] Never-

---

[69] Sebastian Haffner, *Defying Hitler: A Memoir*, translated from German into English by Oliver Pretzel (London, 2000), 19. [70] *Kölnische Volkszeitung*, 19 Jan. 1924, 1st morning edition.
[71] Wilhelm Heile, 'Zum 18. Januar', *Die Hilfe*, XXVII (1921), 18–19.
[72] Gertrud Bäumer, 'Rückblick auf die Feiern der Reichsgründung', *Die Hilfe*, XXVII (1921), 33.
[73] On the divided labour movement of the early Weimar Republic see Heinrich August Winkler, *Von der Revolution zur Stabilisierung: Arbeiter und Arbeiterbewegung in der Weimarer Republik 1918–1924*, 2nd rev. edn. (Berlin and Bonn, 1990), particularly 243–82. For critical contemporary assessments of Bismarck by the socialist and Communist press see, for example, *Vorwärts*, 19 Jan. 1921, morning edition, and *Rote Fahne*, 19 Jan. 1921, morning edition.

theless, it would be rash to assume that this resulted in some form of a 'united proletarian front' against the exploitation of Bismarck by right-wing circles. In contrast to the Communists' propaganda, the moderate socialist press always linked their attacks on Bismarck with a clear support of the Republic and its constitutional values. The revolution of 1918 and the achievements of the National Constituent Assembly were represented by the SPD as a return to the liberal-democratic tradition which had been suppressed by Bismarck.[74]

The distinguished Social Democratic journalist Richard Lewinsohn in an article for *Weltbühne* sought to explain to his readers why he regarded the foundation of Bismarck's Reich as nothing but a 'princes' business'. He noted that the 'German tribes were united long before Bismarck began his campaign for unity. Already after the Wars of Liberation and particularly since 1848 they had wanted the unification.' Bismarck's Reich was not the one for which the March revolutionaries had struggled. Rather it was an 'accumulation of violence directed within and without'. The aim of the Republic, in contrast, was to be an 'institution of peace and law'.[75]

The Social Democratic argument that the November revolution represented a break (in a positive sense) with Bismarck's legacy was sharply contested by the spokesmen of the radicalized socialist subculture. In clear opposition to the Social Democrats, leading Communists were keen to stress that the recent revolution had done little to alter the political and economic circumstances of the workers.[76] The central message disseminated by the Communist leadership was that the Majority Social Democrats bore full responsibility for this, having 'betrayed' the interests of the workers by their 'treason' during the revolutionary winter of 1918–19. On the occasion of the fiftieth anniversary of the Reich's foundation, the KPD party newspaper, *Rote Fahne*, concerned itself only briefly with the right's celebrations or their content. The paper was much more interested in a brief (and politically uncompromising) public address issued by President Ebert and Chancellor Konstantin Fehrenbach on the occasion of Reich Foundation Day 1921.[77] From the Communist paper's point of view, it was 'unbelievable' that a self-proclaimed working-class party leader such as Ebert could publish a 'proof' of his devotion to the old Reich, thereby

---

[74] See, for example, *Vorwärts*, 18 Jan. 1921, morning edition.

[75] Richard Lewinsohn, 'Die Bismarck-Legende', *Die Weltbühne*, XVII (1921), 33–5, here p. 35. The SPD's ambition to deconstruct the Bismarck cult manifested itself in numerous acts of highly symbolic importance. In Munich, for example, the SPD-led local government removed the Bismarck bust from the town hall in June 1919 and ordered that there would be no further state-sponsored celebrations at the Bismarck memorial at Lake Starnberg. See Hort, *Bismarck in München*, 113–14.

[76] *Rote Fahne*, 18 Jan. 1921, morning edition.

[77] The address is printed in *Schulthess*, LXII (1921), 10.

idealizing the Imperial Proclamation of Versailles.[78] 'The proletariat', *Rote Fahne* maintained, had by contrast no reason 'to shed a single tear' for Bismarck's Reich: 'It was not *its* Reich, it was its prison.'[79]

Given that these polemics took place only a few weeks before the elections for the Prussian Lower House on 20 February 1921, it is likely that the Communists' strident tone was part of their campaign tactics. However, there can be no doubt that this reading of the recent past was one of the most important identity-forging legends nurtured in the Communist milieu. It manifested itself in the creation of the KPD's own *lieux de mémoire* in which the graveyard in the Berlin district of Friedrichsfelde featured prominently. Among the most famous Communists buried here were Rosa Luxemburg and Karl Liebknecht, Leo Jogiches, who was shot dead in March 1919 in the Berlin-Moabit prison, and the socialist historian Franz Mehring, who had died in the same year. The KPD provided the financial resources for a monument on the Friedrichsfelde cemetery to commemorate those who had been killed in the revolution of 1918–19. On 13 June 1926, after more than two years of construction works, the monument designed by the Bauhaus architect Mies van der Rohe was eventually completed.[80] Even before the erection of the monument, in fact ever since 1920, left-wing radicals organized annual commemoration marches which ended on the Friedrichsfelde graveyard. The idea that Ebert, Scheidemann, and Noske had prevented a 'genuine revolution' in 1918–19 by forging an alliance with the 'bourgeois reaction' played a key role in the speeches held on these occasions. It was repeated constantly because this legend fulfilled exactly the same purpose for the KPD as the Bismarck myth did for the right: it served to unite the party's followers and to define them against the 'system'.[81]

This myth of victimhood, which played an essential role in the political self-affirmation of the German Communists, was repeatedly linked to the memory of Bismarck. When, for example, Reichstag President Paul Löbe (SPD) stated in a short address to the plenum on 19 January 1921 that Bismarck's unification of Germany had been the fulfilment of 'the decades-long desire of progressively-minded spirits in our country', the leader of the KPD, Paul Levi, immediately asked permission to address the house.[82] Levi

---

[78] *Rote Fahne*, 18 Jan. 1921, evening edition.
[79] *Rote Fahne*, 18 Jan. 1921, morning edition.
[80] *Rote Fahne*, 14 June 1926, morning edition.
[81] *Rote Fahne*, 17 Jan. 1921, evening edition. On the Communist heroes of this legend, Rosa Luxemburg and Karl Liebknecht, see Scharrer *Legende von Rosa & Karl*.
[82] RT, 19 Jan. 1921, vol. 346, 1887–8.

scarcely waited to reach the podium before bursting into 'vehement protest against the exploitation of a historical event as a demonstration of support for imperialist rationalization and the present bourgeois class system embodied in Ebert's Republic, namely that fifty years earlier the king of Prussia received the imperial crown from the hands of the German princelings'. The KPD and the workers it spoke for, he insisted, remained convinced that 'the window-dressing the Reich underwent after the November revolution . . . has in no way altered its basic character'.[83]

In spite of its common historical roots and shared experience of persecution under the Iron Chancellor, the ideologically divided German working class was unable to overcome its internal political differences even on the subject of Bismarck, the 'father' of the anti-socialist legislation. The Social Democrats were the political party most willing to support the Republic, employing arguments to counteract the Bismarck myth in ways which drew them close to the intellectuals of the liberal left. Leading representatives of the radicalized workers' movement, on the other hand, accused the SPD of having betrayed the revolution. Instead of establishing a proletarian dictatorship in 1918–19, the KPD suggested, the MSPD had avoided a radical break with Bismarck's Reich.

To say that the working class lacked consensus about the past, present, and future of the political community is to underline a conclusion which can be applied generally to the whole of Weimar society. This lack of consensus and the 'inner rejection of the peace' by sectors of the German population prevented the easing of political tensions after the revolution.[84] It created a political climate in which the most determined enemies of the Republic would stop at nothing, not even at assassinating political opponents. Between 1918 and 1922 alone, 22 politically motivated assassinations were committed by left-wing radicals and 354 by right-wing extremists.[85] The most prominent victim of this violent development was murdered in 1922: Foreign Minister Walther Rathenau.

[83] Ibid. 1888.
[84] Quotation from Mommsen, *Weimar Democracy*, 89.
[85] See Gay, *Weimar Culture*, 21.

5

Fighting the 'Enemies of the Reich': Bismarck and the State Crisis of 1922–1923

Bismarck and the Law for the Protection of the Republic

On the morning of 24 June 1922, the German Foreign Minister Walther Rathenau was shot dead on his way to the Wilhelmstraße by members of the militant nationalist 'Organisation Consul'.[1] The German public was up in arms about yet another terrorist act by this radical right-wing organization, from whose ranks had already come the assassins of the former Reich Finance Minister Matthias Erzberger.[2] Spontaneous strikes in numerous large industrial workplaces all over Germany were as much an expression of the public outrage as the various large-scale demonstrations, at which hundreds of thousands of people (in Berlin more than a million) gave voice to their consternation.[3]

The pressure of public opinion and the severity of the crime caused President Ebert to promulgate, at the cabinet's request, an emergency decree for the protection of the Republic two days after the attack. As a result of this emergency decree it became possible to ban anti-republican organizations as long as there was reasonable suspicion of anti-constitutional intent.[4] The cabinet, led by the Centre politician Joseph Wirth, soon agreed that the Reich President's emergency decree must be converted into a long-term 'Law for the Protection of the Republic'.[5] In early July 1922, a suitable draft was presented to the Reichstag.

Apart from the problem of achieving consensus on the proposed constitutional amendments, the central question during the bill's first reading was how a political climate could have emerged in which leading Republicans had to

---

[1] See Martin Sabrow, *Der Rathenaumord: Rekonstruktion einer Verschwörung gegen die Republik von Weimar* (Frankfurt, 1999).

[2] See, for example, *Rote Fahne*, 24 June 1922, evening edition; *Vorwärts*, 24 June 1922, evening edition; *Germania*, 25 June 1922; *Deutsche Allgemeine Zeitung*, 24 June 1922, evening edition.

[3] See *Schulthess*, LXIII (1922), 80–1.   [4] Ibid. 79–80.

[5] *Akten der Reichskanzlei, Das Kabinett Wirth II, 26. Oktober bis 22. November 1922*, ed. Ingrid Schulze-Bidlingmaier (Boppard, 1973), cabinet meetings of 25 June 1922 (pp. 896–901) and 26 June 1922 (pp. 901–6).

4. 'Exceptional legislation'—a front-page caricature in *Simplicissimus* draws an analogy between Bismarck's anti-socialist legislation (1878) and the Law for the Protection of the Republic (1922).

fear for their lives. Gustav Stresemann, whose DVP was crucial for the attainment of the necessary two-thirds majority for passing the bill, protested against the 'injustice of wanting to make those, who are today leading figures in the Republic, responsible for the dire situation and poverty in which the German people find themselves'. In the same speech, Stresemann clearly ascribed the rapid deterioration of the political climate to the 'struggle over the past', which had also, he suggested, contributed to the murder of

Rathenau.[6] The 'tumultuous agreement' with which his audience greeted Stresemann's speech confirmed that the threat to the state's internal stability from the battle over the past was acknowledged by the majority of political decision makers.[7]

By rejecting the USPD's demand to incorporate in the law a 'proscription of the monarchist assassins' flag [black, white, and red]', Stresemann at the same time lent force to his conviction that a republican mind-set could not be dictated 'from above'.[8] The DVP leader emphasized instead the importance of arriving at a basic socio-political consensus that was impossible to achieve by legislation alone. He suggested that the various historical traditions used by representatives of all parties to legitimize their positions were not as opposed as was commonly imagined. Stresemann exemplified his view by referring to the ongoing controversy over the national flag. He claimed to honour, now as before, the old black, white, and red flag of the Reich as the 'symbol of a nation which achieved unity and greatness after a long struggle'. He also insisted, however, that the same was true for the 'historical traditions associated with black, red, and gold'. After all, German patriots had already fought for the idea of national unity in the Wars of Liberation and in the years 1848–9 before Bismarck succeeded with his 'policy of Blood and Iron'.[9]

Wilhelm Kahl, another member of the DVP Reichstag delegation, supported Stresemann's views and expressed his desire for an end to the historical-political trench warfare. Unlike Stresemann, however, he resolutely protested against the tendency of left-wing publicists and politicians 'to class whole parties as murderous and to hold them responsible for a certain assassination'. Kahl insisted that such accusations had resulted in the 'poisoning' of peaceful political coexistence, as manifested in the left's 'merciless' attacks upon the right's annual celebrations of 18 January, in which the Weimar left had deeply wounded 'our feelings of piety, remembrance, and thankfulness'.[10]

None the less, the DVP was prepared in principle to support the Law for the Protection of the Republic.[11] The German Nationalists consequently found

---

[6] RT, 5 July 1922, vol. 356, 8307. The attempt to mediate between rivalling historical traditions promoted by the right and the democratic left is a recurrent pattern in Stresemann's writings and speeches. See Gustav Stresemann, *Bismarck und wir* (Berlin, 1916), 4–6 as well as his article 'Das alte und das neue Deutschland', published in March 1925 in the French magazine *L'Europe nouvelle*. The article is reprinted in Gustav Stresemann, *Vermächtnis: Der Nachlaß in drei Bänden*, ed. Henry Bernard, here vol. 2: *Locarno und Genf* (Berlin, 1932), 327–32.   [7] RT, 5 July 1922, vol. 356, 8310–11.

[8] For Rosenfeld's speech see RT, 5 July 1922, vol. 356, 8307. For Stresemann's speech see RT, 5 July 1922, vol. 356, 8309.

[9] Ibid.   [10] RT, 11 July 1922, vol. 356, 8426–7.

[11] See, too, the speech of Rudolf Heinze, leader of the DVP's Reichstag delegation, in RT, 25 June 1922, vol. 356, 8059. Also Ernst R. Huber, *Deutsche Verfassungsgeschichte seit 1789*, vol. 7: *Ausbau, Schutz und Untergang der Weimarer Republik* (Stuttgart, 1984), 255 ff.

themselves in an isolated position. The DNVP leadership was aware of the extent to which their situation had deteriorated since 24 June. As the public protests demonstrated, the assassination of Rathenau had stabilized rather than weakened the Republic. The DNVP suddenly found itself politically ostracized and stigmatized as the new 'internal enemy of the Reich'.[12]

In these circumstances the party leadership reacted with a defensive strategy. Members of the DNVP publicly claimed that the Law for the Protection of the Republic was a form of enslavement of opinion unambiguously directed against the right, by which freedom of speech would be stifled. A restriction of the freedom of speech, the nationalist MP Walther Graef pointed out, was totally unacceptable, especially as the German people were in the middle of a 'vicious conflict of ideologies' in which public controversy over the past, present, and future of the Reich had to be conducted with all possible clarity. Graef then attacked the Centre on the basis that in the 1870s political Catholicism had objected to similarly unjust treatment under Bismarck. *Germania* in particular, he claimed, had criticized Bismarck's government on many occasions. Hence, the (Catholic) Chancellor should not react so 'sensitively' if the German Nationalists' press decided to enforce the same right in a similar situation.[13]

The strategic approach of anti-democratic right-wing opposition to the Law for the Protection of the Republic was thus made clear: the DNVP, forced by Rathenau's murder into uncomfortable proximity with fanatical terrorists, tried to represent itself as the victim of legal exclusion by those parties which Bismarck had 'identified' as 'patriotically unreliable'. Accused of preparing the intellectual ground for Rathenau's murder, the DNVP rejected the Law for the Protection of the Republic as a means to stifle legitimate parliamentary opposition. Some commentators even suggested that if the law (which, in analogy to the anti-socialist legislation of the 1870s, was referred to as the 'Nationalist Law' in right-wing circles) came into effect, then a similar strengthening of the 'victims' would result as had occurred during Bismarck's struggle against political Catholicism and Social Democracy.[14]

Graef's speech, and the all too transparent intention behind his words, caused the Social Democratic Minister of Justice, Gustav Radbruch, to pillory the devious behaviour of the German Nationalists. After making defamatory speeches against democratic politicians, the DNVP deputies dared to declare themselves victims of a policy of exclusion.[15] Radbruch strongly opposed any

[12] See Chancellor Wirth's famous speech in RT, 25 June 1922, vol. 355, 8058. For the violent attacks against DNVP offices in different German cities see *Schulthess*, LXIII (1922), 78.

[13] RT, 11 July 1922, vol. 356, 8414.

[14] See Hans Weberstedt, 'Am Grabe Bismarcks', *Die Tradition*, 29 July 1922. See, too, the caricature 'Exceptional Legislation' printed in *Simplicissimus*, XXVII (1922), 241.

[15] RT, 11 July 1922, vol. 356, 8416–17.

comparison between the Law for the Protection of the Republic and Bismarck's exceptional legislation of the 1870s and 1880s; while Bismarck's legislation had been explicitly directed against specific political views, the planned legislation merely aimed to protect the current constitutional system.[16]

Johannes Bell supported these statements and rejected the DNVP's criticism on behalf of the Centre Party. In contrast to the *Kulturkampf* legislation, which had targeted a religious minority, the Law for the Protection of the Republic would 'equally apply to all citizens'. According to Bell, had it been otherwise, the Centre would never have stood in support of the Law's acceptance. After all, political Catholicism had for too long 'suffered from the pressure of unbearable exceptional legislation'. Bell insisted that the experience of the *Kulturkampf* had been so traumatic for the Centre Party that it would never support any unjust legislation.[17]

It is hardly surprising that the DNVP's attempts to draw a parallel between the current measures for the protection of the Republic and Bismarck's anti-socialist and *Kulturkampf* legislation aroused such strong reactions among representatives of both the SPD and the Centre Party. Whenever Centrist or Social Democratic spokesmen referred to Bismarck's domestic policy it was made clear that no future legislation which put political convictions on trial would ever gain their approval.[18] More than half a century after Bismarck's creation of the German Empire, the memory of the 'internal foundation of the Reich' touched a raw nerve in the collective memory of the socialist and Catholic population. It was precisely on this 'weakness' that the anti-democratic political right preyed. None the less, the DNVP failed to prevent the passing of the bill. The DDP Reichstag delegate Walther Schücking acknowledged the nationalist opposition's right to well-founded criticism of the government and warned parliament against a return to those 'old-fashioned Prussian methods' through which Bismarck had finally brought about the 'largest bankruptcy' which 'any state has ever suffered in world history'. But Schücking made it clear that the draft legislation under consideration was fully reconcilable with the democratic principles of the Weimar constitution. As opposed to Bismarck's illiberal and ideologically motivated legislation, the Republic had created a thoroughly justifiable piece of legislation to counteract the enemies of democracy.[19]

---

[16] Ibid. See also the speech of the Social Democratic Reich Minister of the Interior Adolf Köster, who declared that the Law for the Protection of the Republic was 'no second Socialist Law'. RT, 5 July 1922, vol. 356, 8289.   [17] RT, 5 July 1922, vol. 356, 8293. For similar comments, see *Germania*, 12 July 1922.

[18] See, for example, the 1921 review of the 3rd volume of Bismarck's *Gedanken und Erinnerungen* in *Historisch-Politische Blätter für das katholische Deutschland*, CLXX (1922), 62–4. See, too, Paul Kampffmeyer, 'Bismarck und die Sozialistengesetze', *Sozialistische Monatshefte*, LXVII (1928), 747–52.

[19] RT, 11 July 1922, vol. 356, 8430–1.

Schücking considered it vital to impart these 'insights' about Bismarck to the younger generation in view of the lack of democratic convictions in broad spheres of society. The 'task of the future' was to provide the young with a history written 'from the viewpoint of the German people' and not to hold on to the nationalist myths 'which we have learnt in the Prussian primary schools and in the Royal Prussian grammar schools'.[20]

On 18 July 1922, the Law for the Protection of the Republic was passed in the Reichstag with a comfortable two-thirds majority, although the deputies of DNVP, KPD, and BVP voted solidly against it.[21] The law provided against further insults to the Republican flag and physical attacks on representatives of the Republic by establishing more severe punishment for crimes against the constitution and by creating a central Court of Justice for the Protection of the Republic in Leipzig. Both in its theory and in its practice, the Law for the Protection of the Republic did not justify a comparison with Bismarck's exceptional legislation of the 1870s and 1880s. Whereas the former aimed at the reduction of radical agitation through legally justifiable means supported by two-thirds of the Reichstag deputies, the latter had sacrificed constitutional principles in favour of political calculation.[22]

Despite the DNVP's defeat in the parliamentary vote of 18 July 1922, the Law for the Protection of the Republic gave the Weimar right no real cause for concern. First, the law was restricted to a five-year period. Moreover, the independent justice apparatus which had remained largely unchanged since the days of the Kaiserreich, made sure that the Law for the Protection of the Republic was predominantly used against left-wing offenders. Criminal acts against the Republic committed by the right, however, were all too often treated with indulgence.[23]

Bismarck and the Battle of the Ruhr

The threat to Weimar's domestic political peace represented by the assassination of Walther Rathenau was followed just a few months later by a new challenge. This time it was not posed by internal enemies of democracy, but rather

---

[20] Ibid. 8434.   [21] RT, 18 July 1922, vol. 356, 8737–9.

[22] On Bismarck's exceptional legislation see Wolfgang Sauer, 'Das Problem des deutschen National-staates', in Hans-Ulrich Wehler (ed.), *Moderne deutsche Sozialgeschichte* (Cologne, 1966), 407–36. See, too, Anderson, *Windthorst*, 165 ff.

[23] See Gotthard Jasper, *Der Schutz der Republik: Studien zur staatlichen Sicherung der Demokratie in der Weimarer Republik 1922–1930* (Tübingen, 1963), 196 ff. See, too, Christoph Gusy, *Weimar—die wehrlose Republik? Verfassungsschutzrecht und Verfassungsschutz in der Weimarer Republik* (Tübingen, 1991), 134 ff.

by the French government led by Prime Minister Raymond Poincaré. On 9 January 1923 the Allied reparations commission declared (against the will of the British representative) that Germany had deliberately defaulted on its required coal deliveries for 1922. This was the pretext for the occupation of the Ruhr region by French and Belgian troops two days later. Massive protests, often combined with strong verbal attacks on the French 'arch-enemy', immediately broke out in Germany.[24]

Wilhelm Cuno, formerly director of HAPAG and Chancellor of a bourgeois minority cabinet since November 1922, had predicted such a response immediately after the publication of the reparations commission's report: 'If it comes to sanctions and the use of force', he prophesied, 'then the next consequence will be a strong wave of nationalist feeling'. In this event, he argued, every effort should be made 'to make this wave of feeling useful for the state, not to let it run uncontrolled, or ally itself with the swastika or the red, white, and black banners, but to ensure that it serves the purposes of unity and reconciliation within the German people'.[25]

The call for internal unity was also raised in the Reichstag, which met in Berlin for an extraordinary sitting on the day after the occupation of the Ruhr. Here, too, it seemed as if the French military actions would reconcile internal tensions, at least superficially.[26] Since the occupation of the Ruhr was seen as an act of French aggression threatening the very existence of the Reich, a broad consensus emerged in the German public.[27]

The emergence of a 'political truce' was hailed by many contemporaries. At Berlin's Friedrich-Wilhelm University, for example, the representative of the student body declared that the Germans had found their own way 'back to the national thought and thus to a national strength of mind'. Just as in Bismarck's time, the nation was now 'united and strong' in resistance against the external threat.[28] The Tübingen historian Wilhelm Weber also considered it apposite to

---

[24] See Mommsen, *Weimar Democracy*, 128–46. For contemporary reactions see, too, Paul Wentzke, *Ruhrkampf: Einbruch und Abwehr im rheinisch-westfälischen Industriegebiet*, 2 vols. (Berlin, 1930–2). Also, Heinrich Claß, 'Um die deutsche Freiheit', *Alldeutsche Blätter*, 20 Mar. 1923.

[25] AdR, *Das Kabinett Cuno, 22. November 1922 bis 12. August 1923*, ed. Karl-Heinz Harbeck (Boppard, 1968), cabinet meeting of 9 January 1923, 122–9, quotation on pp. 122–3, n. 3. See, too, the shortened version of the public address issued by President Ebert and the Cuno government on 11 January in *Schulthess*, LXIV (1923), 8–9.   [26] For more on the Reichstag debate, see RT, 13 Jan. 1923, vol. 357, 9423 ff.

[27] Quotations from *Deutsche Tageszeitung*, 19 Jan. 1923, evening edition; *Berliner Tageblatt*, 28 Jan. 1923, morning edition. Objections to the 'National Front of Unity' or *nationale Einheitsfront* were raised, for example, in *Vorwärts*, 13 Jan. 1923, evening edition.

[28] Gerhard Hoef's speech in *Reichsgründerfeier der Friedrich-Wilhelms Universität zu Berlin, gehalten in der neuen Aula am 18. Januar 1923* (Berlin, 1923), 13–14. See also the address of Emil W. Mayer in *Feier der Reichsgründung, veranstaltet am 18. Januar von der Universität Giessen* (Giessen, 1923), 3–5.

call upon the 'spirit of 1870–71'. Weber suggested that France had won a Pyrrhic victory in the Treaty of Versailles. Her military action in the Ruhr would facilitate Germany's rebirth as an internally united nation. In accordance with its 'divine purpose' the German Reich would once again take its place among the great powers. Then, the Germans would follow Bismarck's dictum, and 'fear God but nothing else in the world!'[29]

Although the actions of Poincaré's government were unanimously condemned by the German public, the means of carrying out the struggle against French aggression remained controversial. The majority of German politicians considered passive resistance to be the best reaction to Poincaré's policy of 'productive mortgages', but conservative circles in particular regretted the government's lack of 'resolution to defend the territorial unity of those regions of the Reich which were handed down to us by the *Reichsgründer*, cost what it may'.[30] *Deutsche Tageszeitung* suggested that Germany had accepted the loss of Alsace-Lorraine, spoils of the war of 1870–1, far too readily. 'Encouraged' by this lack of 'active, stubborn resistance', the 'arch-enemy in the West has not given up its hope to further destroy the unity of the Reich. The setback in the Ruhr represents a concerted effort to carry out this plan belatedly. . . . Only if we pass this ordeal by fire can we once again be worthy of our fathers.'[31] As nationalist circles attempted to revive the memory of the German victory of 1871 and the 'spirit of 1914', Bismarck was represented in armour, sword in hand, on the front cover of a right-wing magazine.[32]

By contrast, Rudolf Pannwitz, a journalist committed to the republican cause, called for calm and moderation. In an article for *Weltbühne*, published in early February 1923, Pannwitz asked what Bismarck would do if he saw his 'well built, badly defended house in ruins'. As 'a realist', Pannwitz suggested, 'he would not respond . . . according to the principles which others than him have made into Bismarck's tradition and Bismarck's system . . .'. According to Pannwitz, Bismarck would have accepted the lost war and paid the due reparations.[33]

That Bismarck could be invoked to justify two thoroughly different solutions to the current crisis may seem surprising in light of the political trench

---

[29] Wihelm Weber, *Vom vergangenen und vom zukünftigen Deutschen: Eine Gedächtnisrede zur Reichsgründung für die Stuttgarter und Hohenheimer Studenten* (Tübingen, 1923), quotations on pp. 1, 10, and 12.

[30] Commentaries approving the policy of passive resistance can be found, for example, in *Berliner Tageblatt*, 23 Jan. 1923, morning edition. In contrast see *Deutsche Tageszeitung*, 18 Jan. 1923, evening edition.

[31] Ibid. See also *Deutsche Tageszeitung*, 5 Mar. 1923, evening edition.

[32] See the illustration 'Bismarck, hilf!' ('Help, Bismarck!'), *Jung-Bismarck-Berlin*, Apr. 1923.

[33] Rudolf Pannwitz, 'Was würde Bismarck tun?', *Die Weltbühne*, XIX (1923), 208.

warfare of the previous years. It was the perceived threat to German territorial integrity that stimulated a search for suitable historical comparisons and lessons to be learnt from the past. As early as autumn 1922, Walter Goetz had indicated that Franco-German relations in Bismarck's days were of 'highly significant current interest' not just for right-wing anti-democrats, but also for those forces loyal to the Republic. Especially after 2 September 1870, the date of the German victory over the main French army at Sedan, 'the same questions, difficulties and sufferings' were 'present in different forms'. Then German troops had stood on French soil, now the opposite was true. Unlike Poincaré, however, Bismarck had not been full of the 'desire for destruction'. While the Reich's founder had never interfered with French sovereignty, France had used its position of power 'methodically for unjust ends' since the end of the Great War.[34]

Vorwärts came to a similar assessment in January 1923 when comparing Bismarck's actions during the Franco-Prussian War of 1870–1 with Poincaré's present policy. The most important conclusion drawn by *Vorwärts* was that Bismarck had not immediately resorted to military sanctions when the French had fallen behind on their reparations payments. Poincaré, on the other hand, was not prepared to make comparable concessions because his aim was the destruction of the German Reich. The Social Democratic paper nevertheless estimated France's chances of success as low. It predicted that Poincaré would achieve through his policy of violence precisely what Bismarck had tried to avoid, namely the internal unity of his opponent. If Bismarck had encouraged French ideas of revenge by his annexation of Alsace-Lorraine, then Poincaré would make the same mistake in the current situation. He would 'create a mood among the German people for which the German government can take no responsibility'.[35] Bismarck's French campaign thus also offered a historical point of comparison for the forces loyal to the Republic. This reference point was deliberately employed in order to demonstrate the injustice of Poincaré's actions and to 'prove' the lack of historical precedent for France's actions against Germany. Liberals as well as Social Democrats thereby positively represented an era in German history which they had previously criticized. The temporary about-face in their attitude to Bismarck appeared to them to be justified by the changed political context.

---

[34] Walter Goetz, 'Die deutsche Außenpolitik von 1871–1890', *Die Hilfe*, XXVIII (1922), 317–19, quotation on p. 318. For a similar assessment see the book published by Goetz's colleague, Hans Herzfeld, *Deutschland und das geschlagene Frankreich 1871–1873: Friedensschluß, Kriegsentschädigung, Besatzungszeit* (Berlin, 1924).

[35] *Vorwärts*, 16 Jan. 1923, morning edition. Similarly, *Germania*, 18 Jan. 1923.

However, a political climate in which even the left drew on Bismarck in justifying its political ambitions did not last long. The 'National Front of Unity' increasingly tottered under the effects of the hyperinflation resulting from passive resistance, and right-wing criticism of Cuno's policies was again formulated with reference to Bismarck. Heinrich Claß, for example, felt obliged to remind Chancellor Cuno in mid-July 1923 that Bismarck, in contrast to the current leadership, would never have tolerated French occupation of German soil. Instead, Claß asserted, Bismarck would have opposed the French with a policy of 'Blood and Iron' and taken up the 'struggle with all possible strength' to 'make Germany free'.[36] In July 1923, *Völkischer Beobachter*, too, regretted the 'lack of political instinct' and 'national will' on the part of the Cuno government. What Germany desperately needed, what 'the sad present avidly hopes for', was a leader of Bismarckian proportions who would take 'firm hold of the rudder'.[37]

Gustav Stresemann, who took over the Chancellorship on 13 August 1923 as head of a Grand Coalition government, was certainly not the leader *Völkischer Beobachter* had hoped for. In the eyes of the German right, Stresemann had abandoned his nationalist beliefs by entering into a coalition government with the SPD, thereby stabilizing 'the hated system of defeat and weakness epitomized by the term Weimar'.[38] Stresemann's policies during his hundred days in office reinforced their criticism. When the policy of passive resistance against the French became financially unbearable and the long-cherished hope for Great Britain's diplomatic intervention finally proved to be unfounded, Stresemann put an end to the Battle of the Ruhr on 26 September 1923.[39] This decision—inevitable as it was in practical terms—met with considerable opposition from nationalist circles.[40] Stresemann countered the nationalists' criticism by emphasizing that his decision was in line with Bismarck's flexible foreign policy. After he had criticized the DNVP's putative loyalty to principle as inappropriate to Germany's current international position, he stressed that

the man who puts his principles foremost should lay his wreath at the foot, not of Bismarck's statue, but of that of Eugen Richter [leader of the Progressive Liberal Party and one of Bismarck's most determined opponents in the Reichstag]. It is only political philistines who perpetually hold fast to principles. . . . Bismarck had the capacity of looking facts in the face and of taking account of circumstances. We were maintaining

---

[36] Heinrich Claß, 'Nach fünfundzwanzig Jahren', *Alldeutsche Blätter*, 20 July 1923.
[37] *Völkischer Beobachter*, 31 July 1923. [38] Mommsen, *Weimar Democracy*, 154.
[39] *Schulthess*, LXIV (1923), 177–8.
[40] See, for example, the Reichstag speech by the *völkisch* politician Albrecht von Graefe, RT, 28 Sept. 1923, vol. 361, 11929. See, too, the response in *Berliner Tageblatt*, 28 Sept. 1923, morning edition.

at that time a comparatively steady rate of progress, whereas now we are living in a revolutionary period. . . . We are finding out how hard it is for a defenceless nation to carry out foreign policy. We can have nothing to do with the pacifists who are proud of this state of affairs. Unlike them, we feel bitterly the disgrace of having disarmament imposed upon us. However, just as we believe in Bismarck's theory of practical politics, we must ask those who claim to be followers of Bismarck to deal in practical politics and not drift into a policy of illusions. We had to abandon our struggle in the Ruhr, and have proved our willingness to make reparations to the limit of our capacity.[41]

Statements of this sort were highly characteristic of Stresemann, who propagated an image of Bismarck which deviated significantly from that of the nationalist right. Stresemann, who had studied history and economics in Berlin, often drew on the knowledge he had acquired as an undergraduate in the course of his political career.[42] Despite his annexationist convictions during the First World War, Stresemann had advocated a strengthening of parliamentary power within the Imperial Constitution, a position he had justified by referring to Bismarck. In a Reichstag debate of October 1916 he admitted that 'Bismarck's personality had been a great impediment to German parliamentary development'. The restriction of parliamentary power had not mattered as long as Bismarck, the genius politician, was at the helm. After Bismarck's dismissal in 1890, however, the powerless parliament had been unable to mitigate the policies of Bismarck's less talented successors. Stresemann insisted that in 1892 Bismarck himself had advocated a strengthening of parliament's rights: 'Without a Reichstag which can maintain a constant majority, which is capable of fulfilling the duties of a people's assembly, of criticizing the government, controlling, warning, moderating, which is capable of realizing the equilibrium that our constitution wished to create between government and the people's representatives—without such a Reichstag I fear for the endurance and solidity of our national institutions.'[43]

After the German defeat and the revolution of 1918, Stresemann founded the German People's Party, whose deputies in Weimar's National Assembly voted against the new constitution. Stresemann himself was decidedly against revolution and revolt, and made no secret in the early years of the Weimar Repub-

[41] 'Through Toil and Sacrifice to Freedom', speech delivered at the convention of the German People's Party in Hanover, 30 March 1924, in Gustav Stresemann, *Essays and Speeches on Various Subjects*, with an introduction by Rochus von Rheinbaben (London, 1930), 209–10.

[42] In 1897 Stresemann had attended a series of forty-two lectures on nineteenth-century German history by the Bismarck expert Max Lenz. Stresemann's shorthand notes can be found in Politisches Archiv des Auswärtigen Amtes, Stresemann papers, vol. 362.

[43] Bismarck as quoted by Stresemann in RT, vol. 308, 26 Oct. 1916. See, too, Gustav Stresemann, 'Zu Bismarcks Gedächtnis', in id., *Vermächtnis*, vol. 3: *Von Thoiry bis zum Ausklang*, 282–9.

lic of his enduring monarchist convictions and his attachment to the former glory of Imperial Germany. Even during and immediately after the Kapp-Lüttwitz putsch of 1920, Stresemann took an ambiguous position. At a meeting of the DVP's executive committee on 28 March 1920 Stresemann proclaimed that 'the ideal of our lives lies in ruins' as a consequence of the military defeat and the revolution of 1918–19. He reminded his audience that in September 1866 the National Liberal Party had granted Bismarck indemnity after the Prussian constitutional conflict (1862–6), even though he had violated the legislation for approving budgets as laid down in the Prussian Constitution. The purpose (in this case Bismarck's creation of the German Reich) had justified the unlawful means. Stresemann continued: 'I am of the opinion we must be clear about one thing: there is no parallel with the events of 13 March [1920; the day the Kapp putsch began], but if our lord God and fate send us another man who will once again, without observing all of Weimar's laws, create a great Germany, then our party will give him that same indemnity that the statesmen of the National Liberal Party once granted Bismarck.'[44]

Nevertheless, as Jonathan Wright has argued, the Kapp putsch made it clear to Stresemann that any attempt to restore the monarchy was bound to end in civil war.[45] It was Stresemann's pragmatic approach to the Republic which brought the former implacable enemy of socialism to the conclusion that it was necessary to bridge the gulf between his own party and the SPD, the two parties representing the conflicting social and economic interests of industry and the working class. At the DVP's Stuttgart party conference in 1921, Stresemann suggested the DVP should return to the government coalition. In reply to the reproach that in order to do so the DVP would have to make concessions to the Centre and the SPD, Stresemann again referred to Bismarck: 'I ask you to go back in German history, to consider the greatest statesman the world had in the nineteenth century, Bismarck. Were his politics anything other than the politics of compromise? . . . Was this policy of the achievable not a hundred times more national-minded and forward-looking than the policies of those who felt the necessity to attack it?'[46]

Stresemann's willingness to co-operate with the Weimar coalition parties after 1920 was never forgiven by the nationalist opposition. His 1923 decision

[44] Stresemann at the DVP's executive committee meeting of 28 March 1920, as quoted in Eberhard Kolb and Ludwig Richter (eds.), *Nationalliberalismus in der Weimarer Republik: Die Führungsgremien der Deutschen Volkspartei*, 2 vols. (Düsseldorf, 1999), here I. 285. The records testify to 'long, rapturous praise and applause'.

[45] See Jonathan Wright, *Gustav Stresemann: Weimar's Greatest Statesman* (Oxford, 2002), 150 ff.

[46] Gustav Stresemann's speech at the DVP's party conference in Stuttgart on 1 December 1921, in id., *Schriften*, ed. Arnold Harttung (Berlin, 1976), 222 ff., here p. 228.

to abandon the policy of passive resistance in the Ruhr was hardly designed to improve relations between the Chancellor and his right-wing critics. Rhetorical attacks were not the only problems Stresemann's government had to deal with in the late autumn of 1923. Immediately after the abandonment of passive resistance the Bavarian state government declared a state of emergency and transferred all power to Gustav von Kahr, previously the Minister President of Bavaria. This clear breach of the constitution by the Bavarian state government was only the most recent climax in the long smouldering conflict between the Reich and the southern German state which had become, since the Kapp putsch of 1920, an 'Eldorado' for right-wing political extremism.[47]

Bavaria's provocative actions, matched just hours later by Friedrich Ebert's declaration of a state of emergency in the Reich, spawned a tumult of angry protest in the democratic press. The liberal historian Walter Goetz described the Bavarian government's action as 'pure madness' and as an attempt 'to destroy Bismarck's work by criminal negligence'. The fathers of those who were responsible for this policy would in all certainty 'never have dreamt that the nation's deep longing for unity would be reversed just fifty years later in a conflict over the competence of the federal state, and that in this way Bavaria would thus work for the German arch-enemy [France] against Germany'.[48]

Even if Goetz's accusation that Kahr would 'once again drive Germany into the misery of the old system of loosely linked small states' was slightly farfetched, he was correct about one thing: the political situation for the Republic was more serious than it had ever been before. Germany stood on the brink of a civil war, and attacks against the democratic 'system' were perpetrated not just from the political right, but also from the left. However, neither the 'German October' nor Hitler's attempted coup of 9 November 1923 were to bring about the end of the Weimar Republic.[49] Even the fall of Stresemann's government on 23 November 1923 could not alter the fact that Germany's future seemed far less grim in the second half of November 1923 than it had only a few weeks earlier. The attempted putsches of the right and the left had failed, their organizers were discredited in the medium term, and hyperinflation had been eliminated.

Weimar had therefore survived the post-war crisis which began in 1919 and culminated in 1923. The Republic proved capable of withstanding the threats to democracy from the left and the right. The Kapp putsch of 1920 was impres-

---

[47] Kolb, *Weimar Republic*, 38. For details of the constitutional problems involved in this step see Huber, *Verfassungsgeschichte*, 7, 364–5.

[48] Walter Goetz, 'Bayern und die Reichsgründung', *Die Hilfe*, XXIX (1923), 368–9.

[49] On the 'German October' and the Hitler putsch see Winkler, *Weimar*, 223–43.

sively fended off by a general strike and rapidly collapsed.[50] Three years later, following the French occupation of the Ruhr and hyperinflation, the ability of the Republic to weather these storms seemed to augur well for the future. The endurance of this stability would, however, largely depend on the Republic's ability to instil a belief in democratic principles in the people's minds. In this respect, as Hermann Ulrich Kantorowitz put it in 1921, the path which the supporters of the Republic would have to tread to consolidate democracy could only lead 'over the rubble of the Bismarck cult'.[51]

[50] On the Kapp-Lüttwitz putsch and the subsequent general strike see Erwin Könnemann (ed.), *Der Kapp-Lüttwitz-Ludendorff-Putsch* (Berlin, 1996).
[51] Kantorowicz, *Bismarcks Schatten*, 11.

6

Bismarck as an Election Campaigner

'You must vote thus, or you are voting for the wrong party!' Bismarck and the Reichstag elections of 1924

The Reichstag elections of 4 May 1924 ended ignominiously for the 'Weimar coalition' parties. The Republican powers suffered their worst result prior to the disastrous elections of 1932; together they received merely 36.9 per cent of the valid vote. Only the Centre Party was able to consolidate its result of June 1920. The DDP, on the other hand, fell from 8.3 per cent to 5.3 per cent. The worst blow was struck against the Social Democrats, reunited with the USPD's 'right' wing since 1922, whose share of the Reichstag mandates went down from 171 to 100 seats.[1]

The prime beneficiary of this huge loss of support for the moderate socialist left was the KPD, who could attribute the increase in their mandate from 17 to 62 seats largely to the fact that they had been able to attract the support of the majority of former USPD voters. Apart from the KPD, the radical right, too, could regard itself as an election victor: with a share of 19.5 per cent of the vote, the DNVP became the second strongest party in the Reich. Its right-wing splinter party, the *völkisch* Freedom Party or *Freiheitspartei*, which had allied itself with the National Socialists, registered 6.5 per cent—barely 3 per cent less than the moderate nationalist DVP, whose result was 4.7 per cent worse than in the June elections of 1920.[2]

The central object of contention during the spring election campaign of 1924 following the dissolution of the Reichstag on 13 March 1924 had been the

[1] On the election results see Falter, *Wahlen*, 69. See, too, Elfi Bendikat and Detlef Lehnert, '"Schwarzweißrot gegen Schwarzrotgold": Identifikation und Abgrenzung parteipolitischer Teilkulturen im Reichstagswahlkampf des Frühjahres 1924', in Detlef Lehnert and Klaus Megerle (eds.), *Politische Teilkulturen zwischen Integration und Polarisierung: Zur politischen Kultur in der Weimarer Republik* (Opladen, 1990), 102–42.

[2] After having formed an alliance with the ten MPs of the Farmers' League, the DNVP, being the largest parliamentary group, had the right to appoint the president of the Reichstag. For a detailed analysis of the election results, including the shift in voting patterns, see Heinrich August Winkler, *Der Schein der Normalität: Arbeiter und Arbeiterbewegung in der Weimarer Republik 1924–1930*, 2nd rev. edn. (Berlin and Bonn, 1988), 177–88.

(Exzellenz Scheidemann bei der Kaßler Vappenparade)

Ein Mundwerk des
schwarz-rot-gelben Deutschland

Der Staatsmann des
schwarz-weiß-roten Deutschland

Deutscher Wähler vergleiche!
Wähle schwarz-weiß-rot!
Wähle Deutschnational!

Thiele & Schwarz, Wörthstr. 8

5. 'Compare them, German voter! Vote for black, white, and red! Vote for the German Nationalists!' Philipp Scheidemann, 'a mouthpiece of the black, red, and yellow Germany', is juxtaposed to Bismarck, the 'statesman of the black, white, and red Germany'. DNVP election poster, 1924.

Dawes Plan. After Stresemann's government had called for a review of German solvency on the basis of Article 234 of the Treaty of Versailles in October 1923, the allied commission of experts, led by the American banker Charles Dawes, came to the alarming conclusion that the German annuities could not be reconciled with the country's industrial productivity. The report, presented on 9 April, provided for a temporary settlement of the reparations question. After a four-year recovery phase, the annuities were to be gradually raised to the sum of 2.5 billion marks in gold as set down in the London payment plan.[3]

---

[3] See Kolb, *Weimar Republic*, 58–61.

6. 'Bismarck on 11.8.1867: "Politics is the art of the possible!" Vote for the German People's Party!' DVP election poster, 1924.

The Dawes Plan, which included the promise of an international loan of 800 million marks to revive Germany's economy, was a considerable success for German diplomacy and its aim to achieve a gradual revision of the Versailles peace treaty. It certainly compared favourably with the results of the London conference of 1921. Nevertheless, the nationalist opposition was up in arms about the Dawes commission's suggestions. First, the DNVP protested against the fact that the duration of payments had not been fixed. Secondly, they objected to the proposal to establish allied control of two central German institutions, the Reichsbank and the Reichsbahn. Karl Helfferich, the DNVP's expert for financial issues, had as early as 6 March evoked 'the danger of a new and even worse Versailles' in the Reichstag and thereby established his party's position in the forthcoming campaign.[4]

---

[4] RT, 6 Mar. 1924, vol. 361, 12620. See, too, Liebe, *Deutschnationale Volkspartei*, 76–7.

The DNVP's criticism of the Dawes Plan was strengthened by repeated references to Bismarck, just as their criticism of the Versailles Treaty had been a few years earlier.[5] Bismarck, or so Oskar Hergt claimed at the German Nationalists' party conference in Hamburg before the Dawes Plan's publication, would never have agreed to a new 'enslavement' as embodied in the Dawes commission's proposals.[6]

The DNVP's party conference in Hamburg, which was held on Bismarck's birthday, left no doubt that the nationalist right was determined to instrumentalize the Iron Chancellor in their forthcoming election campaign. Besides the larger-than-life bust of Bismarck behind the lectern, this intent was reflected in the conference's motto: 'spirit of our Bismarck—show us the way'.[7] The aim of the DNVP, as the Reichstag MP Max Wallraf proclaimed to the thunderous applause of the party delegates, was to re-establish the political system created by Bismarck in 1871.[8]

The speech of the conservative MP Wilhelm Laverrenz struck exactly the same chord. Above all, he raised the phrase 'Back to Bismarck' to the status of a leitmotif for the German Nationalists.[9] It was only logical that the DNVP offered Bismarck's grandson, who was also called Otto, the opportunity to stand for the party in the forthcoming general elections in the Weser-Ems constituency. Otto von Bismarck Jr. accepted the candidature for a Reichstag mandate without hesitation.[10]

The tone and substance of the DNVP's conference speeches were reflected pictorially in the campaign posters portraying the Reich's founding father, which adorned the streets of German towns and cities from the beginning of April 1924 onwards. One of these posters communicated to the observer the basic contents of the Bismarck myth in a very tangible way: a black, red, and gold railway track and a black, white, and red track were depicted with Bismarck as signalman at their junction to ensure that the rapidly approaching train, symbolizing Germany, would choose the 'right' way in both senses of the word. The intended message was unambiguous: to protect what they had inherited from Bismarck, the German electorate would have to vote for the

---

[5] See, for example, *Regensburger Anzeiger*, 9 Nov. 1920, morning edition.

[6] Hergt's speech is printed in *Deutsche Tageszeitung*, 1 Apr. 1924, morning edition.

[7] *Korrespondenz der Deutschnationalen Volkspartei*, 31 Mar. 1924. The liberal press ridiculed the German Nationalists' cult of the past. See, for example, the article 'Die Primadonnen im völkischen Flitterröckchen', *Berliner Tageblatt*, 2 Apr. 1924, evening edition.

[8] *Korrespondenz der Deutschnationalen Volkspartei*, 2 Apr. 1924.

[9] Laverrenz's speech, as quoted in *Neue Preußische Zeitung*, 31 Mar. 1924.

[10] See Rehbein: *Bismarck*, 116. See, too, Otto-von-Bismarck-Stiftung, Friedrichsruh, J 24. In both Reichstag elections of 1924, Otto von Bismarck Jr. won this constituency for the DNVP.

DNVP. A vote for the 'Weimar coalition' parties, on the other hand, was nothing less than treachery against the German nation embodied by Bismarck.[11]

In order to distinguish Bismarck (and implicitly the German Nationalists) from the 'incapability' of republican politicians, another pictorial motif was introduced: against Bismarck, 'the statesman of the black, white, and red Germany', Philipp Scheidemann was disparaged as 'a mouthpiece of the black, red, and yellow Germany'. The juxtaposed portraits of the German bourgeoisie's most highly respected politician, and one of the chief hate figures for the political right since the end of the Great War, were completed by the exhortation: 'Compare them, German voter!'[12] This poster was regarded as such a success by leading DNVP officials that it was used in the subsequent general election campaigns as well.

The strategic use of Bismarck as patron saint of the DNVP's election campaign found unanimous support within the party. Kuno Count Westarp effectively stated in an article for the *Neue Preußische Zeitung* (of which he was the editor), that no other historical figure was as well suited as Bismarck to promote the aims of the DNVP. He demanded that it should become part of the public consciousness that future governments could 'in no way ignore Prusso-German history and Bismarck's life's work' without being penalized for so doing by the electorate.[13] Westarp received intellectual support from the historian Dietrich Schäfer, who in the same newspaper promoted a new 'Bismarckian mentality'. This he defined as a power of will and creativity which 'was able to found the German Reich and which will raise it again from its contemporary humiliation'.[14]

A vote for the DNVP on 4 May 1924 was thus presented to the electorate as an opportunity to return to the path which Bismarck had paved. In the German Nationalists' election manifesto, which was released in late March, the party promised a 'return to the basis of the German constitution as created by Bismarck'.[15] In order to win over Catholic voters, the DNVP's party newspaper also emphasized that the party leadership was striving for a return to the 'moral foundations' of Bismarck's Reich, but that a 'renewal of the *Kulturkampf*' would be regarded as a 'great misfortune'.[16]

---

[11] See the following posters: 'Wählt Liste 5: Deutschnational', BA (Koblenz), Plak. 2/29/84, and 'Wählt Deutschnational', BA (Koblenz), Plak. 2/29/11. On the general importance of political posters in Weimar's election campaigns see Rainer Schoch, 'Das politische Plakat der Weimarer Republik: Voraussetzungen und Entwicklungstendenzen', in id. (ed.), *Politische Plakate der Weimarer Republik 1918–1933* (Darmstadt, 1980), 6–13.   [12] 'Deutscher Wähler vergleiche!', BA (Koblenz), Plak. 2/29/6.
[13] *Neue Preußische Zeitung*, 31 Mar. 1924, 'Bismarck-Beilage'.   [14] Ibid.
[15] The DNVP's election manifesto, *Deutsche Tageszeitung*, 23 Mar. 1924, Sunday edition.
[16] *Korrespondenz der Deutschnationalen Volkspartei*, 28 Apr. 1924. The DNVP had its own committee for

The scale of the mobilizing references to the Iron Chancellor as a symbol of German Nationalists' policies during the election campaign of spring 1924 was without precedent, although the enlistment of Bismarck as a campaign weapon by the party was not previously unknown. As early as 1919, during the election campaign for the National Assembly, the DNVP had lobbied for votes using the likeness of the Reich's founder.[17]

When the DNVP used images of Bismarck in 1924, it could therefore rely on certain symbolic associations, the dissemination of which had been developed in many ways over the years. In January 1924, for example, the *Deutsche Tageszeitung* had praised Bismarck's Germany, a return to which, it was suggested, was imperative if the country wished to rise to continental dominance. The memory of Bismarck should serve to make every patriotically minded political force duty-bound to emulate him. The experiences of the crisis year 1923 had 'proven' once again that Germany could not survive 'without the restoration of its freedom and honour, without a renewal of the old Prussian spirit, discipline and without duties or a constitution which is true to its national identity'. This 'profession of faith' was to be 'transmitted to our German people in their flesh and blood. That is only possible by turning away from all internationalist thoughts and non-German ways . . . If this renewal of our national spirit succeeds, then the German nation will one day break the chains which today keep it fettered, outside and in. Then it will rise again to new freedom and strength.'[18]

This message was repeatedly conveyed to the electorate by the German Nationalists and it met with various reactions from other political parties. The democratic left objected to the right's continuous attempts to use the past as a weapon against Weimar by emphasizing that the Republic was deeply rooted in the liberal-democratic tradition of 1848. The DDP, for example, campaigned with posters depicting the Paulskirche parliamentarian Ludwig Uhland.[19] The German People's Party, however, attempted to establish itself as the actual 'Bismarck Party' against its false conservative competitors.[20] In this struggle for Bismarck's heritage, the DVP politicians' references to Bismarck differed

---

German Nationalist Catholics, the 'Reichsausschuß deutschnationaler Katholiken'. The Committee repeatedly emphasized that Bismarck had only fought against the 'ultramontane' tendencies within political Catholicism, not against Catholicism itself. See the file 'Reichsausschuß der Katholiken', in Archiv für Christlich-Demokratische Politik, Centre Party papers, VI-051/A668 (press clippings). See, too, BA (Berlin), R 8005/467-480.

[17] Machtan (ed.), *National-Mythos*, 35.
[18] *Deutsche Tageszeitung*, 18 Jan. 1924, morning edition.
[19] See Lothar Gall (ed.), *Aufbruch zur Freiheit* (Frankfurt, 1998), 270.
[20] *Deutsche Allgemeine Zeitung*, 29 Apr. 1924, morning edition.

significantly from those of the DNVP. Although the DVP's election manifesto stressed the necessity of preserving 'Bismarck's inheritance', its rhetorical flourishes remained free of anti-republican phraseology.[21]

The DVP's attempts to enlist support through capitalizing on Bismarck did not, however, meet with great success. Despite the successful stabilization of the currency after the crisis year of 1923, the electorate was yet still more receptive to the kind of radical slogans formulated by the DNVP with reference to Bismarck. Stresemann's political aims found less support as many DVP voters transferred their allegiance to the German Nationalists.[22]

The coalition negotiations after the general elections of 4 May were tortuous. The German Nationalists' press never tired of reminding the DVP (which had presented itself so 'enthusiastically' as a Bismarckian party) that Bismarck would have regarded it as imperative 'to fight Social Democracy with united forces'.[23] None of the moderate parties, however, was willing to participate in a government under the DNVP candidate for Chancellor, and former Admiral of the Fleet, Alfred von Tirpitz, as long as the conservative right stuck to the central tenet of their election manifesto: the rejection of the Dawes Plan.

The only practicable solution to this dilemma was the reconstitution of the bourgeois minority cabinet under Wilhelm Marx. At the beginning of June, Ebert finally gave him the authority to form a government. The lack of a parliamentary majority was, however, an unresolved problem, and, once the Dawes legislation had been passed with the support of part of the DNVP's delegation, the path appeared clear for a *Bürgerblock* cabinet. Stresemann in particular wanted to draw the DNVP into a share of governmental responsibility to prevent it from reaping further electoral rewards by nationalist agitation.[24] The DDP and parts of the Centre Party, however, refused to form a coalition with the DNVP. Consequently, Ebert had to dissolve the Reichstag and call for new general elections on 7 December.[25]

In the following weeks, Stresemann appealed to all constitutional parties to unite behind a foreign policy of *Realpolitik*—a term he adopted from Bismarck. This he defined, contrary to the political ideas linked with the name of Bismarck on the Weimar right, as a policy free of the illusions of both the right

[21] Bendikat and Lehnert, 'Schwarzweißrot gegen Schwarzrotgold', 112.

[22] Hagen Schulze, *Weimar: Deutschland 1917–1933*, 4th rev. edn. (Berlin, 1994), 288.

[23] *Korrespondenz der Deutschnationalen Volkspartei*, 16 May 1924.

[24] The hope for a stabilization of the Republic through an integration of the DNVP in the government was central for Stresemann between 1923 and 1929. See Larry E. Jones, 'Stabilisierung von Rechts: Gustav Stresemann und das Streben nach politischer Stabilität 1923–1929', in Karl H. Pohl (ed.), *Politiker und Bürger: Gustav Stresemann und seine Zeit* (Göttingen, 2002), 162–93.

[25] Further details in Winkler, *Weimar*, 267–8.

and left, a policy 'which is conscious of the limitations of our power and which seeks understanding and peace'.[26] The foreign policy goals of the DVP were presented as a continuation of Bismarck's political ideas under changed conditions. Bismarck, just like Stresemann, it was suggested, would have pursued a policy leading to European stability and lasting peace.[27]

The German Nationalists' party leadership, on the other hand, continued to follow their successful strategies developed during the previous general elections. The DNVP's poster campaign, which had many similarities with their enlistment of Bismarck in the spring, was as much a part of this continuity as their consistently aggressive criticism of Stresemann's foreign policy.[28] The president of the dissolved Reichstag, Max Wallraf, for example, reminded a gathering in Munich of Bismarck's statement about the German people, who feared God but nothing else in the world. The motto of Stresemann's foreign policy, however, seemed to be: 'We Germans do not fear God, but we do fear everything else in the world!'[29] Despite the resignation of Oskar Hergt as party leader, the DNVP, now under the temporary leadership of the prominent Protestant layman Friedrich Winckler, renewed its claim to the 'glorious colours' black, white, and red and emphasized the importance of the elections as the 'day of the great struggle against black, red, and gold'.[30]

The idea that a German Nationalist election victory would equate to a 'breakthrough of patriotic consciousness', as the DNVP maintained in their campaign, was a point of view not shared outside the conservative camp. Franz Mischler, a member of the paramilitary republican *Reichsbanner Schwarz-Rot-Gold*, for example, underlined the contrast between the allegedly *kleindeutsch* German nationalism of the DNVP and the *großdeutsch* patriotism of the democratic parties.[31] The SPD's success in the second general election of 1924 and

[26] Speech to the DVP party conference, 14 Nov. 1924, BA (Berlin), R 45, II/29, published as Gustav Stresemann, *Nationale Realpolitik: Rede des Reichsaußenministers Dr. Stresemann auf dem 6. Parteitag der Deutschen Volkspartei in Dortmund am 14. November 1924* (Berlin, 1924). Already in 1916, Stresemann had emphasized similar ideas. See Stresemann: *Bismarck und wir*, 10–11.

[27] See Roland Thimme, *Stresemann und die Deutsche Volkspartei 1923–1925* (Lübeck and Hamburg, 1961), 55–7; 'Bismarck am 11.8.1867: Politik ist die Kunst des Möglichen! Wählt Deutsche Volkspartei!', BA (Koblenz), Plak. 2/25/13.

[28] On one of the DNVP's posters for the second Reichstag elections of 1924, Bismarck points to the DNVP's list on the ballot-paper and says: 'Put your cross in this circle. You must vote thus, or you are voting for the wrong party!' See BA (Koblenz), Plak. 2/29/56.

[29] Wallraf, as quoted in *Korrespondenz der Deutschnationalen Volkspartei*, 26 Nov. 1924.

[30] Quotations from *Deutsche Tageszeitung*, 21 Oct. 1924, evening edition, and the DNVP election manifesto as printed in *Deutsche Tageszeitung*, 29 Oct. 1924, morning edition.

[31] See Karl Rohe, *Das Reichsbanner Schwarz Rot Gold: Ein Beitrag zur Geschichte und Struktur der politischen Kampfverbände zur Zeit der Weimarer Republik* (Düsseldorf, 1966), 233. See also Hubertus von Löwenstein, *The Tragedy of a Nation: Germany 1918–1934* (London, 1934), particularly 210–25.

the equally remarkable loss of votes for the radical parties was not, however, primarily a result of the *Reichsbanner*'s campaign. The de-radicalization of the German electorate had been brought about by the evident upswing of the German economy as a result of an influx of foreign credits.[32]

Although the advance of the DNVP had been 'stopped in its tracks', as the *Vorwärts* declared with relief a few days later, the election results of 7 December made *two* forms of government possible: either a Grand Coalition of parties from the SPD to the DVP or a right-wing *Bürgerblock*.[33] After the negotiations initiated by Wilhelm Marx to include the SPD had failed due to the DVP's resistance, Ebert gave the task of forming a government to the independent former Finance Minister, Hans Luther. On 19 January Luther was able to present his centre-right *Bürgerblock* cabinet to the Reichstag. It was the first government of the Weimar Republic to include *both* allegedly 'Bismarckian' parties—the DVP and the German Nationalists.

The making of a 'new Bismarck': The Hindenburg elections of 1925

With the involvement of the DNVP in Luther's cabinet, criticism of the government by the conservative nationalist press was temporarily silenced and directed instead even more strongly against the Social Democratic head of state, President Friedrich Ebert. During the so-called 'Barmat scandal' and the trial for libel of Erwin Rothardt, a nationalist journalist who had publicly accused the President of high treason during the November revolution, Ebert was exposed to great hostility from the right.[34]

Ebert's early death on 28 February 1925, which resulted from the delay of surgery during the Rothardt trial, necessitated early elections for the country's highest political office. As none of the candidates achieved the necessary majority in the first round of voting on 29 March, the representatives of the SPD, DDP, and the Centre appointed Wilhelm Marx as their common candidate for the second round.[35] Given that the 'Weimar Coalition' parties enjoyed the sup-

---

[32] Falter, *Wahlen*, 70.   [33] *Vorwärts*, 9 Dec. 1924, morning edition.

[34] See Wolfgang Birkenfeld, 'Der Rufmord am Reichspräsidenten: Zu Grenzformen des politischen Kampfes gegen die frühe Weimarer Republik 1919–1925', *Archiv für Sozialgeschichte*, V (1965), 453–500.

[35] Although with 38% of the overall vote the common candidate of the DNVP and the DVP, Karl Jarres, far exceeded his Republican rivals' share of the vote (Braun 29%, Marx 14.5%, and Hellpach 5.8%), his chances of defeating a common candidate of the 'Weimar Coalition' parties were more than doubtful. On the election result, see Falter, *Wahlen*, 76.

port of the majority of the electorate, a victory of the so-called *Volksblock* seemed almost certain. It took several days for the right-wing parties to respond to the *Volksblock*'s challenge and to agree that only one candidate would be able to defeat Marx: the former Field Marshal Paul von Hindenburg.[36]

Hindenburg, in retirement since the end of the Great War, only allowed his candidacy to go forward after being urged to do so by his old friend von Tirpitz. Although he made no secret of his continued commitment to monarchism, Hindenburg enjoyed considerable respect even outside conservative circles.[37] His reputation as the 'victor of Tannenberg' outshone the catastrophic scale of the defeat in the Great War, for which he in fact shared a good deal of responsibility, and guaranteed him the sympathy of many of those who had not voted for Jarres in the first round of the presidential elections. That Hindenburg had attended Bismarck's Imperial Proclamation in Versailles as a young officer was also useful because it served to confirm the status conferred on him by the nationalist right as a 'symbol of faith in the history of Prussia and Germany'.[38]

The representatives of the democratic left could not deny that the nomination of Hindenburg would make it more difficult for their own candidate Marx to win the forthcoming elections. Ernst Feder, a highly analytical observer of contemporary events, reminded his political companions that in Hindenburg the so-called *Reichsblock* had found a candidate to be taken even more seriously than Jarres because the majority of the population would see in him a 'new Bismarck'. The task of all democrats would therefore be to clarify the blurred distinction between myth and reality in relation to Hindenburg. To this end Feder emphasized that Bismarck had been three years younger when he retired in 1890 than Hindenburg would be were he to reach office.[39]

The fact that Feder referred to Bismarck in his article was far from coincidental. Feder's analysis was largely based on his experiences during the first round of the presidential elections. When Jarres had agreed to stand for the presidency, conservative papers had promoted him as a 'Bismarckian type of leader'[40] who, if elected, would 'make use of the lessons of history for the present and future of our people'.[41] Indeed, in the first public speech of his

---

[36] Stresemann at first objected to Hindenburg's candidacy, but feared correctly that to withdraw from the *Reichsblock* would also endanger the stability of Luther's coalition government. See Thimme, *Stresemann*, 133–8. See, too, Noel D. Cary, 'The Making of the Reich President 1925: German Conservatism and the Nomination of Paul von Hindenburg', *Central European History*, XXIII (1990), 179–204.

[37] Andreas Dorpalen, *Hindenburg and the Weimar Republic* (Princeton, 1964), 44 ff.

[38] Kuno Graf Westarp in *Neue Preußischen Zeitung*, 15 Apr. 1925.

[39] *Berliner Tageblatt*, 8 Apr. 1925, evening edition.   [40] *Deutsche Tageszeitung*, 29 Mar. 1925.

[41] *Hamburger Nachrichten*, 22 Mar. 1925, morning edition. On the nomination of Jarres as the *Reichsblock*'s candidate for presidency, see Manfred Dörr, 'Die deutsch-nationale Volkspartei 1925 bis 1928', Ph.D. thesis (Marburg, 1964), 120–1. See also *Korrespondenz der Deutschnationalen Volkspartei*, 13–17 Mar. 1925.

campaign on 22 March 1925, Jarres pointed out his credibility as a 'Bismarck-ian' politician by reminding his audience of his visit to Hamburg and Friedrichsruh on the occasion of Bismarck's eightieth birthday on 1 April 1895.[42] Further, the presidential candidate suggested that Bismarck's dismissal was the 'origin of our national misery' and had led the Germans directly to the 'second Versailles' of 1919. Jarres' speech, given at the foot of the gigantic Bismarck memorial in Hamburg, culminated in the words: 'If we want to lead our people towards a new future' then 'we need to go back to Bismarck'. His audience greeted these words with endless applause.[43]

If Jarres had been only the promoter of 'Bismarckian ideals', Hindenburg was to become their embodiment in the second round of voting. Indeed, the *Reichsblock's* campaign was dominated by an attempt to convert the hope for a 'saviour' into votes and to project, on an ever-increasing scale, 'Bismarckian qualities' onto Hindenburg.[44] This process had begun during the Great War when postcards portrayed the 'two icons of Germanness', Hindenburg and Bismarck, side-by-side.[45] The mythological connection between Bismarck and his 'successor' Hindenburg was thus already established and the election campaigners of 1925 were well aware of its political appeal.

Once more Field Marshal von Hindenburg appeared on the *Reichsblock's* non-programmatic posters as a leader who had proved his ability to convert dangerous developments into positive outcomes at the Battle of Tannenberg. Hindenburg was represented as the epitome of the Reich's dutiful servant. The parallels to the Bismarck posters of the previous year—equally based on nostalgia, and the cult of loyalty and leadership—were difficult to ignore. Hindenburg's campaign manager, Gerhard Schulze-Pfaelzer, did not, in retrospect, attempt to conceal that he had created a stylized hero figure with Bismarckian character traits for the race against Marx. His strategy was based on the conviction that the 'German national character' demanded 'patriarchal models' and would associate more readily with a personality to whom 'mystical powers of salvation were ascribed'.[46]

---

[42] Jarres as quoted in *Hamburger Nachrichten*, 23 Mar. 1925, evening edition.

[43] Ibid. See, too, the photograph of Jarres' campaign rally at the Hamburg Bismarck memorial, printed in Rehbein, *Bismarck*, 119.

[44] See, for example, the campaign poster with the caption 'The Saviour'. The poster is printed in Schoch, *Politische Plakate*, 111. For evidence that Hindenburg was attributed with Bismarckian qualities since the Battle of Tannenberg, see Wülfing *et al.*, *Historische Mythologie*, particularly 197–209. See also the poem 'Zwei Pfeiler der Deutschheit' as printed in Paul Lindenberg (ed.), *Hindenburg-Denkmal für das deutsche Volk* (Berlin, 1923), 400.

[45] See Hagenow, *Politik und Bild*, 28–9.

[46] Gerhard Schulze-Pfälzer, *Von Spa nach Weimar: Die Geschichte der deutschen Zeitenwende* (Leipzig and Zurich, 1929), quotations on pp. 32 and 34.

Under the pressure of the campaign the *Weltbühne* felt obliged to take a position on Hindenburg's 'Bismarckian traits'. In an anonymous article published in early April it stated that Hindenburg was in no way 'as inspired and ardent a genius as Bismarck'. To honour him as a 'representative of the good old times', when 'Bismarck had still directed the fate of the Reich', was conceivable. To promote the two completely different characters as equal, however, was the result of a 'horrifying lack of political instinct, simple human decorousness and logical consistency'.[47]

The *Volksblock*'s campaign strategists attempted to distinguish themselves from the *Reichsblock*'s Bismarck cult by highlighting the liberal tradition of the 1848 revolution upon which the Republic had been founded. One of the *Volksblock*'s posters therefore suggested: 'What our ancestors thought in '48, their grandchildren have realized! Who wants to betray the banner [an allusion to the black, red, and golden flag in the poster] which Grimm and Uhland unfurled?'[48]

Nevertheless, individual publicists attempted to instrumentalize Bismarck for the republican cause. *Germania*, for example, protested against the *Reichsblock*'s attempts to hijack Bismarck for their candidate's own ends. The paper represented the Iron Chancellor as a level-headed statesman who, in the third volume of his *Thoughts and Reminiscences*, had emphatically warned against a national political leadership comprising of generals on the basis that the world of politics was not 'a battlefield'. The Centrist newspaper deemed this alone sufficient ground to militate against the candidacy of the political novice Hindenburg. If Bismarck had been alive, the article concluded, he would have voted for Marx.[49]

When Hindenburg prevailed on 26 April 1925 by only 900,000 votes over his opponent Marx, the degree of disappointment in the republican camp was only matched by the triumph displayed by the right.[50] While prominent liberals like the ex-diplomat Harry Count Kessler saw in Hindenburg's victory the approach of 'one of the darkest chapters in German history', spontaneous gatherings of Hindenburg's supporters took place at Bismarck memorials all over Germany to celebrate the *Reichsblock*'s triumph.[51] Right-wing papers such as

---

[47] 'Hindenburg', *Die Weltbühne*, XXI (1925), 535–9, quotations on pp. 535 and 539.

[48] Gall, *Aufbruch zur Freiheit*, 270.

[49] 'Bismarck rät: Wählt Marx!', *Germania*, 25 Apr. 1925. See, too, the similar comment by Carl Sonnenschein, 'Vor der Entscheidung', in Archiv für Christlich-Demokratische Politik, VI-051 (Centre Party, press clippings), no. A 166.   [50] Falter, *Wahlen*, 77.

[51] Harry Count Kessler's diary entry of 26 Apr. 1925, in Harry Graf Kessler, *Tagebücher 1918 bis 1937*, ed. Wolfgang Pfeiffer-Belli (Frankfurt and Leipzig, 1996), 461. See, too, Peter Fritzsche, 'Presidential Victory and Popular Festivity in Weimar Germany: Hindenburg's 1925 Election', *Central European History*, XXIII (1990), 205–24.

Alldeutsche Blätter expressed the expectation that Hindenburg would lead the German people to the same 'glorious heights of moral purity' it had experienced under Bismarck's rule.[52]

There were several reasons for Hindenburg's election victory. The KPD's decision to keep Ernst Thälmann in the race although he was bound to lose carries as much weight as the BVP's recommendation to vote against the Centre politician Marx and for the North German Protestant Hindenburg. What was central to Hindenburg's victory, however, was the desire amongst the German public for a strong Bismarck-like leadership which could put an end to the divergent party interests and bring Germany to new prosperity and world standing.[53] Considerations of this nature led many who had refrained from voting in the first round to vote for the *Reichsblock*'s candidate in the second round.[54] This was precisely what the liberal *Frankfurter Zeitung* assumed in its analysis of 27 April 1925: 'The feverish fantasies of the impoverished, lower classes, their national consciousness deeply wounded, have woven a romantic wreath around the general's head without being aware that they owe their personal and national impoverishment to that very system whose representative they honour in the general. Romantic yearning for lost honour and influence: that is what led these un-political classes to the ballot box and Hindenburg to victory.'[55]

However unsatisfactory Wilhelm Marx's narrow defeat may have been for the democrats, Hindenburg's victory at the same time provided a respite from right-wing-hostility. In the mood of 'national triumph' even the executive committee of the Pan-German League, barely unsurpassed in its anti-democratic radicalism until this point, declared itself willing to follow Hindenburg under the black, red, and golden banner: in association with him the colours would once again recall 'the deep yearning for German unity and freedom, which . . . the true German democrats of '48, in contrast to today's, carried in their hearts, and who finally, under Bismarck's strong creative genius, saw their deepest desires realised under the black, white, and red banner'.[56]

Comments of this type were generally linked to the hope for a tangible change of policy.[57] As Noel D. Cary has argued, it was the *Reichsblock*'s ultimate

---

[52] 'Heil Hindenburg', *Alldeutsche Blätter*, 2 May 1925. See, too, Jürgen Falter, 'The Two Hindenburg Elections of 1925 and 1932: A Total Reversal of Voter Coalitions', *Central European History*, XXIII (1990), 225–41.

[53] See the caricature of *Kladderadatsch*, 'The pilot is coming on board (1925)', as printed in Wolfgang Hofmann (ed.), *Hindenburg-Album des Kladderadatsch* (Berlin, 1927), 52. It draws an analogy with the famous Bismarck caricature of *Punch* ('Dropping the Pilot') of 29 Mar. 1890.

[54] For an analysis of the election see Winkler, *Schein der Normalität*, 229–45.

[55] *Frankfurter Zeitung*, 27 Apr. 1925, morning edition.

[56] 'Heil Hindenburg', *Alldeutsche Blätter*, 2 May 1925.

[57] See, for example, General Graf von der Goltz, 'Was nun?', *Die Tradition*, VII (1925), 145–9.

Der Lotse besteigt das Schiff

7. 'The pilot is coming on board': a caricature in *Kladderadatsch* (1925) shows the newly elected President Paul von Hindenburg entering the *Deutschland*, a reference to the *Punch* caricature 'Dropping the pilot', published in 1890 after Bismarck's dismissal.

objective to install a Reich President 'with the political shrewdness of a Bismarck, who, like the Iron Chancellor, would use his office to confound the parliament and refashion the Weimar state from above'.[58] However, even if the radical change which Hindenburg's supporters hoped for did not occur, the

[58] Noel D. Cary, 'Making of the Reich President', 180.

Reichsblock's election victory marked a caesura in the history of the first German democracy. With Hindenburg's triumph in the 1925 presidential elections began a 'quiet constitutional change'—Weimar's transformation into a 'conservative Republic'.[59] This also meant that the conservative and nationalist supporters of the Bismarck cult could now rely on a like-minded figure at the very heart of the republican system.

In Weimar's battle over the past, Ebert had been a frequent promoter of the 'tradition of 1848'. In 1923, on the occasion of a commemoration celebration in the Frankfurt Paulskirche to honour the revolutionaries of 1848, Ebert had praised the 'spirit of unity, freedom, and justice' which had prevailed during the 1848 revolution and which would be the guiding principle of the constitution of 1919. This spirit, so Ebert concluded, 'shall lead us into a brighter future'.[60] With Ebert's death and Hindenburg's election victory, future commemoration celebrations of the 1848 revolution could no longer count on the support of the head of state. Instead, Hindenburg was only too prepared to enhance with his personal patronage the status of projects such as the Bismarck films of 1925 and 1927, and the intended construction of a Bismarck National Monument.

The political framework created in 1918–19 continued to exist after 1925, but with Hindenburg's election victory the advantage in Weimar's battle over the past had shifted in favour of those who hoped to destabilize the Republic by active recourse to the Bismarck myth.

[59] Winkler, *Schein der Normalität*, 244.
[60] Ebert's speech in the Frankfurt Paulskirche as quoted in *Schulthess*, LXIV (1923), 103–4. See, too, Dieter Rebentisch, *Friedrich Ebert und die Paulskirche: Die Weimarer Demokratie und die 75-Jahrfeier der 1848er Revolution* (Heidelberg, 1998). Finally, Bussenius: '48er Revolution', 90–114.

7

In the Shadow of Stabilization

'Let us take him as our guide today': Bismarck and Stresemann

The year 1925 did not only enter history books on account of the Hindenburg elections. A second event in this year equally warrants historical consideration: the signing of the Locarno Treaties on 26 October 1925.[1]

From the beginning, the atmosphere of the negotiations at Locarno differed significantly from the spirit of post-war hostility at Versailles. In the main treaty (the so-called security pact), Germany, France, and Belgium agreed to refrain from using force to alter the existing western German border. Britain and Italy guaranteed this agreement and pledged to come to the aid of the attacked country, be it France or Germany. With respect to the eastern German border, however, the Luther government was not prepared to go beyond the conclusion of arbitration treaties with Poland and Czechoslovakia, which were not internationally guaranteed and thus only of symbolic significance.[2]

As far as Germany's accession to the League of Nations was concerned (which was a condition of the treaties' ratification), the German delegation at Locarno was also able to chalk up a major success. The Allies guaranteed an interpretation of the 'intervention article' 16 of the League of Nations' constitution that went a long way towards meeting German interests. According to this interpretation, the Reich was only duty bound to co-operate with League sanctions in proportion to its military and geographical situation. Germany did not therefore have to fear that it would be forced to support economic sanctions against the Soviet Union, or even, in case of a new Russo-Polish war, permit French troops to cross German territory against its will.

---

[1] For a detailed account of the Locarno negotiations see Jon Jacobson, *Locarno Diplomacy: Germany and the West 1925–1929* (Princeton, 1972). See, too, Edward D. Keeton, *Briand's Locarno Policy: French Economics, Politics and Diplomacy 1925–1929* (New York and London, 1987). Finally, Peter Urbanitsch, 'Großbritannien und die Verträge von Locarno', Ph.D. thesis (Vienna, 1968).

[2] See the cabinet meeting of 2 October 1925, in *Akten der Reichskanzlei: Die Kabinette Luther I und II, 15. Januar 1925 bis 17. Mai 1926*, ed. Karl-Heinz Minuth, 2 vols. (Boppard, 1977) here I. 665 n. 24.

All in all the diplomatic achievements of October 1925 signified the fulfilment of one of Germany's short-term post-war aims. Its influence on the world political stage had been increased to the extent that, despite continuing limitations on its sovereignty, it could once again deal with the European great powers on an equal footing. At the same time, Germany did not rule out the possibility of a peaceful revision of its eastern border.

Gustav Stresemann, Foreign Minister and therefore responsible for the success of the negotiations, had good grounds to assume that the Locarno Treaties would find approval from the parties across the political spectrum.[3] Instead, however, the centre-right coalition under Chancellor Luther foundered as a direct consequence of the question of Locarno's ratification. Stresemann must indeed have been surprised when on 22 October the *Korrespondenz der Deutschnationalen Volkspartei* published an article denying all of the treaties' advantages, which it had acknowledged only three days before.[4]

The conservatives' abrupt change of policy, which finally led to the DNVP's withdrawal from the centre-right coalition government on 25 October, was the result of a power struggle within the party, in the course of which the DNVP's radical or *völkisch* wing had put increasing pressure on the moderate leadership.[5] One figure who had worked particularly hard to bring about this situation was the spokesman of the party's radical right wing, Alfred Hugenberg.[6] With the help of his newspaper empire, Hugenberg succeeded in mobilizing the party's regional committees, the DNVP's central committee, and the majority of the Reichstag delegation against the more moderate party leadership.[7]

The DNVP's criticism of the Locarno settlement crystallized around three major issues: the arbitration pact, which Germany concluded with Poland, Germany's membership of the League of Nations, and the consequences of both for German relations with the Soviet Union. To abandon the 'Eastern option' by joining the League was seen by many contemporaries as a limitation

---

[3] On 19 October, even the *Korrespondenz der Deutschnationalen Volkspartei* praised the accomplishments of the negotiators, as did the DNVP's ministers in the cabinet on the day of Luther's and Stresemann's return from Locarno. See *Korrespondenz der Deutschnationalen Volkspartei*, 19 Oct. 1925. See also the cabinet meeting of 19 October, in *Kabinette Luther I und II*, 2. 786–9. On Stresemann's Locarno policy see, in particular, Jonathan D. Wright, 'Stresemann and Locarno', *Contemporary European History*, IV (1995), 109–31.

[4] *Korrespondenz der Deutschnationalen Volkspartei*, 22 Oct. 1925.

[5] See the detailed account of Grathwol, *Stresemann and the DNVP*, 135 ff. as well as *Schulthess*, LXVI (1925), 154. See also Dörr, *Deutschnationale Volkspartei*, 178. Finally, see the resolution of the party leadership of 29 October 1925 as published in *Korrespondenz der Deutschnationalen Volkspartei*, 30 Oct. 1925.

[6] On Hugenberg see John A. Leopold, *Alfred Hugenberg: The Radical Nationalist Campaign against the Weimar Republic* (New Haven and London, 1977).

[7] See Heidrun Holzbach, *Das 'System Hugenberg': Die Organisation bürgerlicher Sammlungspolitik vor dem Aufstieg der NSDAP* (Stuttgart, 1981), 180 ff.

to Germany's freedom of action in foreign policy. Moreover it was portrayed as the repetition of a mistake already made after Bismarck's fall in 1890: the non-renewal of the Reinsurance Treaty.[8]

Behind the demands for a return to Bismarck's 'pro-Russian foreign policy' were a number of different motives. For the electro-technical industry, namely for AEG and Siemens, the wish to strengthen economic links with Russia was predominant.[9] Others, like the influential chief of the Army's High Command, General Hans von Seeckt, were primarily interested in military co-operation. As early as June 1920, during the interventionist war in the Soviet Union, Seeckt had taken a strongly pro-Russian position in a policy paper on relations between the Weimar Republic and the Soviet Union prepared for President Ebert. Despite his well-known anti-Communist convictions, Seeckt advised that political, economic, and military links between the two countries should be strengthened.[10] Seeckt suggested that the government should once again 'be guided by the principles of Bismarck's policies'.[11]

Against this background, it is not surprising that Gustav Stresemann felt the need to refer to Bismarck in his broadcast address to the German people in November 1925, in which he justified his policy of reconciliation. He emphasized that the Locarno agreement was a fundamental breakthrough in the process of the revision of the post-war international system since it provided for British protection of the German Western border against a French invasion:

The very fact that England, who has hitherto been the ally of France, should solemnly undertake to protect Germany with all her land and sea forces against an attack on the

---

[8] See, for example, Otto Hoetzsch, 'Die deutsch-russischen Beziehungen von 1871–1914', in *Politisches Archiv des Auswärtigen Amtes, Berlin: Akten des Parlamentarischen Untersuchungsausschusses für die Schuldfragen des Weltkrieges*, vol. 12. On Hoetzsch and his work see Gerd Voigt, *Otto Hoetzsch 1876–1946: Wissenschaft und Politik im Leben eines deutschen Historikers* (East Berlin, 1978), 199–200. Others who argued similarly to Hoetzsch were Gerhard Ritter, *Die Legende von der verschmähten englisch-deutschen Freundschaft 1898–1901* (Freiburg, 1921); Hans Rothfels, 'Zur Geschichte des Rückversicherungsvertrages', *Preußische Jahrbücher*, CLXXXVII (1922), 265–92; Gustav Roloff, *Die Bilanz des Krieges: Ursprung, Kampf, Ergebnis* (Königstein im Taunus, 1921).

[9] On the AEG's and Siemens' position see Hartmut Pogge von Strandmann, 'Rapallo—Strategy in Preventive Diplomacy: New Sources and New Interpretations', in Volker R. Berghahn and Martin Kitchen (eds.), *Germany in the Age of Total War: Essays in Honour of Francis Carsten* (London and Totowa, NJ, 1981), 123–46. [10] Otto Geßler, *Reichswehrpolitik in der Weimarer Zeit* (Stuttgart, 1958), 186.

[11] In accordance with this, Seeckt welcomed the conclusion of the German–Soviet Trade Agreement of May 1921 as well as the Treaty of Rapallo and the Berlin Treaty of 1926 as first steps to a return to a 'Bismarckian foreign policy'. See Hans von Seeckt, *Aus seinem Leben 1918–1936* (Leipzig, 1941), 305. See also Graf Westarp's Reichstag speech during the Locarno debate, in RT, 23 Nov. 1925, vol. 388, 4496. Similar viewpoints were articulated in *Neue Preußische Zeitung*, 5 Nov. 1925. A more detailed assessment (albeit from a Communist viewpoint) is to be found in Sigrid Wegner-Korfes, *Otto von Bismarck und Rußland: Des Reichskanzlers Rußlandpolitik und sein realpolitisches Erbe in der Interpretation bürgerlicher Politiker 1918–1945* (Berlin, 1990), 193–203.

part of the French, is a matter of the very greatest political importance. This was admitted by no less a person than Prince Bismarck. One passage, indeed, in the instructions given by him to Prince Hatzfeldt [Prince Paul von Hatzfeldt, German ambassador to the Court of St James, 1895–1901] in January 1888 sounds almost prophetic: 'It is not a question of preponderance of strength in the event of war, but of preventing war. Neither France nor Russia will disturb the peace if they have official information that they will inevitably and immediately be opposed by England. I consider that if it becomes known that England is protected from a French invasion by her alliance with Germany and Germany against a French invasion by her alliance with England, peace in Europe will be assured so long as the alliance exists. I believe that such an alliance would be greeted all over Europe with feelings of relief and reassurance.'[12]

Stresemann's attempt to portray the politics of Locarno as a continuation of Bismarck's policy reached its height in the following words: 'Let me remind anyone who is sceptical as to the moral value of such an agreement [Locarno] that the phrase about "imponderable factors in politics which no statesman can afford to disregard" was uttered by the most matter-of-fact politician the world has ever seen; I mean Otto von Bismarck. Let us therefore take him as our guide today.'[13]

Stresemann's speech demonstrated the Foreign Minister's political acumen. He countered the right's attempt to use the Reich's founder in their protests against Locarno by invoking Bismarck as the spiritual inspiration for his own foreign policy. Reaction from the right was quick to emerge. As early as 4 November, one day after Stresemann's broadcast, *Neue Preußische Zeitung* protested 'against what happened yesterday, namely the introduction of Bismarck as justification for a policy which is based on a completely different premiss. When Bismarck wrote to Prince Hatzfeldt in 1888 about the security of France and Germany under England's guarantee, he did not need to utter the renunciation of something that would have been politically and socially unacceptable. He would never have accepted conditions that were to Germany's detriment. Stresemann should not overplay the comparison with Bismarck. The Locarno policy gives little cause to do so.'[14]

---

[12] 'The Treaty of Locarno' (Broadcast Address, 3 Nov. 1925), in Stresemann, *Essays and Speeches*, 232–9, here pp. 234–5.

[13] Ibid. 235. Stresemann regularly used the radio, a medium which was a success right from the start of transmission at the end of 1923. The audience figures rose exponentially from this time on: from barely 10,000 listeners on 1 April 1924 to 780,000 on 1 April 1925, 1.6 million on 1 April 1927, 2.8 million on 1 April 1929, and 3.7 million on 1 April 1931. One year later every fourth German household had a radio. Figures are according to Kolb, *Weimar Republic*, 94.

[14] *Neue Preußische Zeitung*, 4 Nov. 1925. See, too, Ernst Niekisch, *Grundfragen deutscher Außenpolitik* (Berlin, 1925), 9–10.

The right clearly recognized that Stresemann was again, just as in the 1924 elections, trying to strike against the DNVP with the help of the Bismarck myth. By popularizing an alternative Bismarck image (that of the 'matter-of-fact statesman'), Stresemann was hoping to deprive the nationalist opposition of one of their strongest weapons in both foreign and domestic policy debates. He was supported in this aim not just by the DVP-allied *Rheinisch-Westfälische Zeitung*, which promoted Bismarck as a 'politician of the peace',[15] but also and above all by the periodical *Deutsche Stimmen*. In an article of September 1925, the Prussian Landtag MP Albrecht Graf von Stolberg-Wernigerode (DVP) railed against the 'wrong views' being spread about Bismarck: 'Those who today call loudest for a new Bismarck believe that he would handle foreign policy with cuirassier boots, break the Treaty of Versailles and avoid any step that does not lead directly to his aim.' This interpretation of the Iron Chancellor was, however, 'false' in all regards because Bismarck 'showed himself to be a political maestro' of 'moderation'.[16]

In the months that followed, Stolberg-Wernigerode became Stresemann's most articulate and active supporter in the struggle for the 'correct' interpretation of Bismarck within the bourgeois camp.[17] In his 1926 book *Zurück zu Bismarck*, Stolberg-Wernigerode strongly criticized the nationalist opposition's claim that with the Treaties of Locarno the government had given up any chance of winning back those territories lost in 1919.[18] The DNVP's political style, Stolberg-Wernigerode claimed, was entirely confrontational, but 'Bismarck's politics have taught us that attack is not a suitable weapon for a statesman. If one has the power to wage war with good hope of success, then, according to Bismarck's example, the matter must be handled such that the enemy attacks. Then he is morally guilty, he becomes isolated and loses the war. Where in the Treaties of Locarno does it say, however, that we may not defend ourselves if we are attacked?'[19]

The aim of all 'patriotically minded' circles—'to restore Germany to a standing that reflects her cultural and economic importance'—was not to be achieved through the power politics and striving for prestige victories which the German Nationalists mistakenly thought Bismarck embodied.[20]

---

[15] *Rheinisch-Westfälische Zeitung*, 1 Apr. 1926, morning edition.

[16] Albrecht Graf zu Stolberg-Wernigerode, 'Der liberale Bismarck', *Deutsche Stimmen*, XXXVII (1925), 357–64.

[17] See, for example, Albrecht Graf zu Stolberg-Wernigerode, 'Was sagt Bismarck den Deutschnationalen über Locarno', *Deutsche Stimmen*, XXXVII (1925), 465–70.

[18] Albrecht Graf zu Stolberg-Wernigerode, *Zurück zu Bismarck* (Berlin, 1926), 7.

[19] Ibid.   [20] Ibid. 12.

Stolberg-Wernigerode pointed out that this position was more akin to the mistakes made by Bismarck's successors in the 1890s, mistakes which had led Germany directly into international isolation and into the First World War.[21] Only a well-balanced, non-aggressive foreign policy—similar to that conducted by Bismarck when Germany stood at the height of its power—was suitable to reestablish the political influence that Germany had possessed under the Iron Chancellor.[22]

For that very reason, Stolberg-Wernigerode insisted, it would 'fundamentally' contradict 'Bismarck's principles if the opposition fights the Locarno-policy'. Stresemann's foreign policy was an attempt 'to manoeuvre along Bismarckian lines under current conditions and according to our power position today. While it is presumptuous to say that the diplomacy of Locarno can be compared to Bismarck's alliance politics, one thing can be maintained with certainty: what the opposition demands with respect to Locarno is the direct opposite of anything Bismarck would have done.'[23]

Stolberg-Wernigerode's efforts to characterize the German Nationalists' criticism of Locarno as a betrayal of Bismarck's *Realpolitik* were taken up by Stresemann. In a speech to the League of German Students on 6 July 1926, Stresemann maintained that he was misunderstood by his domestic political rivals just as Bismarck had been. The future would show, however, that his path was the correct one. Just like Bismarck had said in the Prussian parliament after Königgrätz, he too would be able to say: 'I do not take it amiss that you denied your support for my foreign policy. You could not have known that which I hoped to achieve . . .'.[24]

But what did the German Foreign Minister hope to achieve with his negotiations at Locarno, or with his foreign policy in general? Did he remain, as he had been in the First World War, a nationalist pursuing the goal of expanding Bismarck's Reich, or had he gone beyond his wartime position to a conception of Germany as a powerful but ready-to-compromise member of the European concert of powers?[25]

---

[21] Albrecht Graf zu Stolberg-Wernigerode, 'Außenpolitik im Sinne Bismarcks', *Deutsche Stimmen*, XL (1928), 328–31, here p. 329.

[22] Stolberg-Wernigerode, *Zurück zu Bismarck*, 12.   [23] Ibid. 13.

[24] Stresemann, *Vermächtnis*, vol. 2: *Locarno und Genf*, 336. Stresemann often described his own situation in Bismarck's words. See, for example, his diary entry of 27 March 1925, in Stresemann, *Vermächtnis*, vol. 2: *Locarno und Genf*, 303–4. There is also an undated collection of Bismarck quotations, which the Foreign Minister used in his speeches. See the collection 'Zitate von Bismarck über Politik und Staatskunst', in Stresemann papers, Politisches Archiv des Auswärtigen Amtes, HI 67543 ff.

[25] Both viewpoints have found advocates. Stresemann's early biographers emphasized the way in which he had outgrown his wartime nationalism to become a man of peace and an architect of Franco-German rec-

Evidence suggests that the truth may lie somewhere in the middle. There is little doubt that Stresemann's ultimate goal was the peaceful restoration of Germany as a Great Power. He himself declared this to the Central Committee of his party.[26] Although Stresemann accepted the loss of Alsace-Lorraine, and became increasingly sceptical about the possibility of the *Anschluß* of Austria and the re-acquisition of colonies, he certainly advocated the return of Danzig and the 'Corridor' as well as a revision of the border with Poland in Upper Silesia.[27] An important, if not the decisive, motivation in concluding the Locarno Treaties and initiating a policy of reconciliation with France was Stresemann's expectation that it would have such favourable effects as an early evacuation of the Rhineland, a chance to recover Eupen Malmédy from Belgium, a possible earlier date for the Saar plebiscite, a further easing of reparations, and an accelerated liquidation of Allied military control in Germany.[28]

It would be wrong, therefore, to evaluate Stresemann's foreign policy as a selfless sacrifice of German goals for the sake of closer ties with the other European states. Stresemann's last major speech of 9 September 1929, at the autumn conference of the League of Nations, was very clear on this matter. Just like his French colleague Briand, Stresemann criticized the economic 'Balkanization' of Europe and demanded a European currency and European stamps. While he was pressing for an economically united Europe, he dismissed any idea of a political federation. The nation state, as created by Bismarck, remained the alpha and omega of Stresemann's politics. Stresemann—like all European statesman of his time—*did* pursue a nationalist foreign policy. In German terms after 1919 this meant a revisionist policy. He desired to see Germany restored to her former greatness and once more asserting her 'natural' position in the concert of European powers.

The apparent contradiction between the annexationist of the First World War and the moderate Foreign Minister of the German Republic is thus not as

onciliation. See, for example, Rudolf Olden, *Gustav Stresemann* (Berlin, 1929). Also, Antonia Vallentin, *Gustav Stresemann: Vom Werden einer Staatsidee* (Leipzig, 1929). The 'Stresemann myth' which these books helped to establish was challenged in 1957 by Anneliese Thimme, who argued that he should be seen as a politician pursuing strictly national goals rather than as a European statesman. See Anneliese Thimme, *Gustav Stresemann: Eine politische Biographie zur Geschichte der Weimarer Republik* (Hanover and Frankfurt, 1957). One of Stresemann's most recent biographers, Christian Baechler, has again argued that he had grown beyond his crude nationalist wartime beliefs. Instead, he had become an advocate of a well-balanced European concert of powers. See Christian Baechler, *Gustave Stresemann (1878–1929): De l'imperialisme à la sécurité collective* (Strasbourg, 1996). Similarly, Wright, *Weimar's Greatest Statesman*.

[26] DVP Central Committee meeting on 1 October 1926, in Eberhard Kolb and Ludwig Richter (eds.), *Nationalliberalismus in der Weimarer Republik: Die Führungsgremien der Deutschen Volkspartei*, 2 vols. (Düsseldorf, 1999), here vol. 2: 1926–1933, 665.

[27] Wright, *Weimar's Greatest Statesman*, 359 ff.   [28] Ibid.

fundamental as has often been suggested. The 'conversion of the nationalist Saul to the pan-European Paul', as Hagen Schulze put it, never took place. Bismarck's Reich and its freedom of action in foreign affairs were always central in Stresemann's political thinking.[29] Stresemann realized, however, that a nationalist foreign policy could not be successful if it directly challenged the governments of the victorious powers. This was precisely why he based his policy on an objective appreciation of the constellation of forces in Europe and 'pursued his revisionist policy as an international policy of reconciliation'.[30] Stresemann's understanding of the restrictions on German foreign policy permitted him to become the foremost representative of a policy of peaceful co-operation with the West. He was an enlightened representative of a German *Großmachtpolitik*. As such he became the promoter of a moderate image of Bismarck, a Bismarck who would have supported Stresemann's own foreign policy. A Foreign Minister who instead 'wished to restore everything from sheer passionate feeling, would bring us into conflict with all other powers. It would be good to write a book about . . . Bismarck, in which it was revealed how he made the most careful use of power when he was at the height of his own power, and how he overcame those who could not get enough of it in 1866 and 1870. He wanted to preserve peace in Europe. That would be a better image of him than that which legend conjures . . .'.[31] Stresemann thus portrayed himself as being in line with Bismarck's foreign policy when he rejected all speculations about winning back Danzig, Western Prussia, and Upper Silesia by force.[32] He repeatedly and publicly emphasized that a revision of the conditions of the Treaty of Versailles could only take place successfully through the principle of moderation, the 'main attribute of Bismarck's politics'.[33]

The view that a policy of peaceful co-operation with the West was without any realistic alternative was shared by most Reichstag delegates. Supported by the remaining coalition partners, the DVP, the Centre, and the BVP, as well as by the SPD and the DDP, the Locarno accords and the authorization for entry

---

[29] Schulze, *Weimar*, 275.

[30] Karl D. Erdmann, 'Gustav Stresemann: Sein Bild in der Geschichte', *HZ* CCXXVII (1978), 599–616.

[31] Speech in Stuttgart, 18 April 1926, in Stresemann, *Vermächtnis*, 2. 503–4, here p. 504. See also Stresemann's similar comments at the 1 October 1926 session of the DVP's Central Committee, during which he alluded to Stolberg-Wernigerode's book. Cf. Kolb and Richter (eds.), *Nationalliberalismus*, 2. 665.

[32] On this see Karl D. Erdmann, *Gustav Stresemann: The Revision of Versailles and the Weimar Parliamentary System, Speech Delivered at the German Historical Institute, London* (London and Ashford, 1980), 14. Stresemann confirmed his non-aggressive approach to revisionism by joining the Briand-Kellogg pact in 1928.

[33] Speech in Munich, 18 January 1926, in Stresemann papers, H 160950–2. The meeting at which Stresemann spoke was held under the motto 'Bismarck's spirit—our model!' See the report in *Deutsche Allgemeine Zeitung*, 18 Jan. 1926, morning edition. Attention to the speech was also paid in the *Regensburger Anzeiger*, 19 Jan. 1926, morning edition.

into the League of Nations were passed by a comfortable majority of 291 votes against 174.[34]

The immediate crisis concerning foreign policy was therefore over and on 1 December 1925 Luther and Stresemann signed the Locarno accords in London. However, the domestic crisis provoked by the agreement remained. The loss of the DNVP's support over the issue of the Locarno Treaties left the governing coalition without a dependable majority in the Reichstag. Moreover, the SPD's vote in favour of the Locarno Treaties had not been a vote of confidence in the Luther cabinet. On the contrary, it had been achieved only after repeated assurances that Luther would resign once the treaties had been ratified.[35] In keeping with these assurances, the cabinet submitted its resignation to President Hindenburg on 5 December 1925, after the return of Stresemann and Luther from the signing of the Locarno Pact in London.[36] Once the DDP and Centre had failed in their attempt to form a great coalition government, the President called upon Luther once again to set up a *Bürgerblock* cabinet on 13 January 1926. The second coalition government under Luther only existed for a few months. In early May 1926 Luther countersigned a decree which had been issued by Hindenburg. This decreed that all German embassies, legations, and consulates outside Europe, in addition to designated ones within Europe, were to fly the colours of the old Empire as well as the new flag. The government thereby strayed into the realm of symbolic politics—something more likely to arouse passions than rational responses. In the resulting furore that broke out among the old partners of the Weimar coalition at this insult to the republican standard, Luther's cabinet fell.[37]

On 17 May 1926 Luther's government was followed by another minority government led by his predecessor Wilhelm Marx. The new cabinet's foreign policy was backed by the SPD, as was evident in the public discussion over the Berlin Treaty, which was signed on 24 April 1926 by Gustav Stresemann and the Soviet ambassador to Berlin, Nikolaj Krestinskij.[38] The signatories agreed to maintain neutrality in the case of the other being attacked by a third power. They also agreed not to enter into alliances that might impose economic sanctions on the other party to the treaty. Germany *de facto* promised not to take part in any League of Nations' sanctions against Moscow. Furthermore, the

[34] The German Nationalists voted solidly against the proposals. See RT, 27 Nov. 1925, vol. 388, 4655.

[35] Klaus E. Riesberg, 'Die SPD in der Locarno-Krise Oktober / November 1925', *Vierteljahreshefte für Zeitgeschichte*, XXX (1982), 130–61.

[36] *Schulthess*, LXVI (1925), 188–9.

[37] *Schulthess*, LXVII (1926), 93–9. See, too, Ribbe, 'Flaggenstreit', 175–88.

[38] The Berlin Treaty is printed in *ADAP 1918–1945*, B series: 1925–33 (Göttingen, 1967), here vol. II, 402–3.

treaty provided for an extension of the friendly political and economic ties between the two countries based on the Rapallo Pact of April 1922.[39]

The German–Soviet settlement served to allay Russian fears that Germany had moved into an anti-Soviet camp by concluding the Locarno Treaties. From a German perspective, it assisted in maintaining Germany's diplomatic flexibility and preventing a Franco-Soviet *rapprochement*.[40] Politically, Germany was now integrated into the system of the western states. In military terms, however, she had neither opted for the partners of the security pact nor for the Soviet Union. In relation to domestic politics, the agreement, labelled by the press a 'Reinsurance Treaty' in analogy to the Russo-German agreement of 1887, served to weaken the DNVP's allegation that the 'western bias' after Locarno was a deviation from Bismarck's path. In a radio address of 1 May 1926 Stresemann emphasized that the Berlin Treaty was directed at the same goal as Bismarck's foreign policy, namely to 'uphold peace and friendship' between the Reich and Russia.[41] Privately, however, Stresemann was sceptical of the agreement with Moscow. In mid-June 1925 he noted in his diary: 'We are faced today with very similar decisions [to those faced by Bismarck prior to the conclusion of the Russo-German Reinsurance Treaty] and if the Russia of today were the Russia of those days, the decision would be very simple. But to ally oneself with communist Russia is akin to going to bed with the murderer of one's own people.'[42]

During the negotiation of the Berlin Treaty, the Soviet government had tried to persuade Stresemann to go one step beyond Rapallo and to enter into a formal alliance with the object of reducing Poland to her ethnographical boundaries on both sides. Stresemann resisted this temptation, but conceded Germany's neutrality in the event of a Soviet–Polish conflict. However, German neutrality was limited to the improbable event of Poland being the aggressor against the Soviet Union; the obligation to remain neutral was invalidated if Poland were the victim of Soviet aggression.[43]

Even if the Berlin Treaty did not fulfil the over-optimistic expectations with which it was greeted in Moscow and in influential circles in Germany, it did meet with universal approval in the Reichstag. The almost unanimous ratifica-

[39] On Rapallo see Peter Krüger, 'A Rainy Day, April 16 1922: The Rapallo Treaty and Cloudy Perspectives for German Foreign Policy', in Carole Fink, Axel Frohn, and Jürgen Heideking (eds.), *Genoa, Rapallo, and European Reconstruction in 1922* (Washington, DC, 1991), 49–64.
[40] See Martin Walsdorff, *Westorientierung und Ostpolitik: Stresemanns Rußlandpolitik in der Locarno-ära* (Bremen, 1971), 151–6. See also Edward H. Carr, *German–Soviet Relations between the Two World Wars 1919–1939* (Baltimore, 1951).
[41] Stresemann, *Vermächtnis*, 2. 540.   [42] Stresemann papers, diary entry of 11 June 1925.
[43] Walsdorff, *Westorientierung*, 29.

tion of the Treaty by the Reichstag on 10 June 1926 was a moment of triumph for Stresemann.[44] At a stroke he had invalidated the right's accusation of diplomatic bias towards the West. The Berlin Treaty was proof, so Stolberg-Wernigerode wrote, 'that there was never any bias towards the West. Only those who judged without knowing the full facts could say such a thing.' Stolberg-Wernigerode also countered the demands for a closer alliance with Russia, as had been envisaged in the Reinsurance Treaty, by raising the question as to 'whether Russia is as much a calculable factor as it was in Bismarck's time. This can rightly be denied. It was a mistake of the post-Bismarck era that the alliance with Russia ended. However, it would also not correspond to Bismarck's thinking if we now relied on Russia alone. Still situated in the centre of Europe and surrounded by many enemies we tread Bismarck's path, trying to secure ourselves on all sides. Not Locarno or the Berlin Treaty, but Locarno and the Berlin Treaty—that is the solution.'[45]

The leadership of the German Nationalist opposition, whom Stolberg-Wernigerode was attacking in his article, was indeed put in a difficult position by the Berlin Treaty. Stresemann had fulfilled one of their central foreign policy demands. The DNVP's expert on Eastern Europe, Otto Hoetzsch, even went personally to the Foreign Office to inform Stresemann that it was 'fully justifiable . . . to refer to Bismarck' in the context of the Russian–German 'Reinsurance Treaty'.[46] Yet, at the same time, the Hugenberg wing of the DNVP was anything but ready to publicly acknowledge Stresemann's foreign policy success as such. Hugenberg's newspapers continued their witch hunt against the Foreign Minister. Under pressure from within his party, Count Westarp publicly declared that the Russo-German neutrality agreement would not change the attitude of the DNVP to Stresemann's foreign policy in general. Even if the treaty meant that 'Germany's freedom of action with regard to Article 16' was restored, 'perhaps one reason for our resistance to the League of Nations policies of Herr Luther and Herr Stresemann does no longer exist, but it is in no way the only reason'.[47]

In November 1926, the Pan-German League went one step further. In an open letter to the German Foreign Minister the nationalist group denied Stresemann's right to use the name 'Bismarck' in support of his foreign policy.

[44] RT, 10 June 1926, vol. 390, 7437–8.

[45] Stolberg-Wernigerode, *Zurück zu Bismarck*, 14.

[46] See Stresemann's diary entry, in *Vermächtnis*, 2. 537. Within the cabinet too, the DNVP ministers endorsed Stresemann's policy without objections. See *Akten der Reichskanzlei: Die Kabinette Marx III und IV*, vol. 2, 779 (cabinet meeting of 9 June 1927).

[47] Westarp on 25 April 1925, as quoted in *Korrespondenz der Deutschnationalen Volkspartei*, 27 Apr. 1926.

Only 'a strange Bismarck', the League claimed, would have supported any of Stresemann's policies.[48]

Relations between the nationalist right and Stresemann's party had not always been as difficult as they were during and after the conclusion of the Locarno Treaties. In the summer of 1925, still under the influence of a co-operative effort during Hindenburg's presidential election campaign, both the DVP and the DNVP had commonly supported a bill which sought to realize a project of high symbolic importance: the establishment of 18 January (the day of the 1871 Imperial Proclamation by Bismarck) as a national holiday.[49]

Movies, monuments, and mass rallies: Bismarck in the 'Golden Twenties'

The debate over a universally acceptable date for a national holiday was as old as the Republic itself. Since 1919 the issue had repeatedly led to emotionally charged political debates.[50] When in June 1925, the Luther government presented to the Reichstag a bill to establish Reich Foundation Day (18 January) as a national holiday, emotions again ran high. The former Minister of the Interior, Wilhelm Sollmann (SPD), immediately suggested that 18 January would never be accepted as a national holiday by the majority of people, but rather would be seen as a 'greatly enlarged German Nationalists' holiday'. His criticism, which was accompanied by loud cheering from the SPD faction, was directed against the 'character' of Bismarck's state, a state unable to satisfy the needs of the working classes.[51]

The assessment that 18 January was an inappropriate date for a national holiday was shared by the DDP. Theodor Heuss dismissed the bill as an attempt to start 'a new fight' in the public arena. Heuss also warned DVP delegates, who were supporting the German Nationalists' legislative draft, against the 'dangerous romanticism of seeing that which is past only in its transfiguration. It is only the poor guy who seeks in the past recipes for the future, or who uses it as a crutch in a present for which he is not adapted.'[52]

Obviously, Heuss's interpretation of the bourgeois Bismarck-nostalgia did not meet with enthusiasm from the right. In their replies DVP and DNVP

---

[48] *Alldeutsche Blätter*, 13 Nov. 1926.   [49] RT, vol. 398, document no. 359.
[50] See Fritz Schellack, *Nationalfeiertage in Deutschland von 1871–1945* (Frankfurt, 1990), 133–273.
[51] RT, 12 June 1925, vol. 385, 2220.
[52] RT, 15 June 1925, vol. 385, 2304. See, too, the speech of Ludwig Bergsträßer (DDP), in RT, 15 June 1925, vol. 385, 2326.

MPs accused the left of a 'gross underestimation' of the importance of German history, a history that 'did not only begin on 9 November 1918 or 11 August 1919 or with the publication of the Communist Manifesto'.[53] Furthermore, the opponents of the bill were accused of underestimating public affections for the traditions of Bismarck's Reich; the day on which Bismarck had founded the Reich was 'a holy day for millions of Germans', or so the German Nationalist MP Emil Berndt suggested.[54]

The majority of Reichstag deputies thought otherwise: the DNVP's bill proposal was defeated by 193 votes to 138.[55] The public quarrel over Bismarck's legacy, which reached its first peak after the Hindenburg election campaign in the debate over a universally acceptable national holiday, none the less survived the parliamentary defeat of the DVP and DNVP. Public celebrations on 18 January and 1 April (Bismarck's birthday) retained their central roles in the festive culture of the Weimar right.[56]

Commemoration ceremonies in honour of the Iron Chancellor were preferably held wherever a large Bismarck memorial provided a suitable setting for party rallies and public speeches. Hamburg became one of the centres of the Bismarck cult for that very reason; the Roland-like Bismarck statue prominently standing above the harbour provided an ideal background for all sorts of commemoration marches and speeches. From 1925 onwards the Patriotic Leagues, for example, organized annual torchlight processions on 1 April from Hamburg-Eilenau to the Bismarck monument in St Pauli.[57] Up to 30,000 men and women participated in these annual events.[58] After 1927 the Hamburg 'Bismarck marches' were increasingly overshadowed by violent confrontations between Bismarckians and Communist protesters.[59]

Bismarck celebrations on 1 April were, however, by no means limited to Hamburg. Organized by the German People's Party, the German Nationalist People's Party, or by extra-parliamentary societies such as the Pan-German League, the Stahlhelm, and the Kyffhäuser League, public commemoration events took place wherever there was a Bismarck monument. In nearly all cases, rhetorical praise of the Bismarck era was supplemented by the defamation of the allegedly politically and morally corrupt Republic.

---

[53] Siegfried von Kardorff's speech (DVP), RT, 12 June 1925, vol. 385, 2240–1.

[54] RT, 12 June 1925, vol. 385, 2224–5.   [55] RT, 15 June 1925, vol. 385, 2361.

[56] See Robert Gerwarth, 'Republik und Reichsgründung: Bismarcks kleindeutsche Lösung im Meinungsstreit der ersten deutschen Demokratie 1918–1933', in Winkler (ed.), *Griff nach der Deutungsmacht*, 115–33.   [57] *Hamburger Nachrichten*, 31 Mar. 1925, morning edition.

[58] See, for example, *Hamburger Nachrichten*, 1 Apr. 1926.

[59] See, for example, *Hamburger Nachrichten*, 1 Apr. 1927, evening edition.

But the Bismarck myth did not merely survive in the celebratory oratory of long-established groups and organizations. Nor was it a phenomenon restricted to the older generation. 'Bismarck', so wrote the liberal nationalist Wilhelm Spieckernagel in 1926, 'has become the yardstick of everything political. Today . . . more than ever.'[60] The generation gap between old and young nationalists during the Weimar period was, however, reflected in the fact that the younger generation applied Bismarck's yardstick not just to the present, but also to the later period of Wilhelmine Germany: 'The generation of 1890–1914 denied his work,' Spieckernagel explained. 'With a few notable exceptions, the German bourgeoisie could not muster the courage to oppose the New Course and is therefore jointly culpable for the waste of Bismarck's legacy.'[61]

It was the stated aim of the German Nationalists' Party Youth, the last of the political youth organizations of an established Reichstag party to come into being, to restore Bismarck's legacy in the minds of the younger generation and make it serviceable in the present and future.[62] It was only in 1922, during a meeting in Hanover, that the DNVP decided to unify the as yet uncoordinated local youth groups into a single organization under the leadership of Wilhelm Kube. The organization would promote an ideal image through the adoption of the name 'Bismarck'.[63] Patronage of the youth organization was accepted by Bismarck's grandson Otto, who gave permission to use his surname for the nationalist cause in 'such a way as seems of best advantage to you'.[64]

The Bismarck Youth recruited young men and women between the ages of 14 and 25. It first gained a foothold in the cities and industrial regions, and finally spread into the rural areas of eastern Germany. The best regions for recruiting proved to be those areas with a largely Protestant population: Berlin, Lower Saxony, and Magdeburg, Hesse and Thuringia, Pomerania, Hamburg, and

---

[60] Wilhelm Spieckernagel, 'Zum Geburtstag des Reichsgründers', *Deutsche Stimmen*, XXXVIII (1926), 149–52, here p. 149.   [61] Ibid. 149–50.

[62] The German Nationalists decided to establish a DNVP youth organization at the 1920 party conference in Hanover. See BA (Berlin), R 8005/53, 332–4. On Weimar's political youth organizations in general see Elizabeth Domansky, 'Politische Dimensionen von Jugendprotest und Generationenkonflikt in der Zwischenkriegszeit in Deutschland', in Dieter Dowe (ed.), *Jugendprotest und Generationenkonflikt in Europa im 20. Jahrhundert* (Berlin, 1986), here p. 128. See, too, Wolfgang R. Krabbe (ed.), *Politische Jugend in der Weimarer Republik* (Bochum, 1993).

[63] See Westarp Papers, political correspondence, BA (Berlin), N2329/262. See, too, Gisbert J. Gemein, 'Die DNVP in Düsseldorf', Ph.D. thesis (Cologne, 1969), 127–8. Also: Reinhard Behrens, 'Die Deutschnationalen in Hamburg 1918–1933', Ph.D. thesis (Hamburg, 1973), 106. Finally, Hertha Siemering (ed.), *Die deutschen Jugendverbände* (Berlin, 1923), 212–13.

[64] *Jung-Bismarck Berlin*, 1 Oct. 1921, 1.

Württemberg.[65] By 1928 the Bismarck Youth had roughly 42,000 members, organized in more than 800 local groups all over Germany. This made it the second largest youth organization after the Socialist Workers' Youth (SAJ).[66] The 'Bismarck Youth' was dominated by members from the bourgeoisie and the nobility. The largest regional Bismarck Youth organization, the Bismarck League Berlin, founded in 1920, was a rare exception in this case: more than 80 per cent of the 6,000 members (in 1922) came from a working-class background.[67]

In 1922 Hermann Otto Sieveking, a 32-year-old former combat officer and son of a wealthy Hamburg merchant, took over as chairman of the Bismarck Youth. Under his leadership, the organization gained an increasingly military structure. Local leaders were ordered to ensure that leisure activities became more paramilitary, including regular physical exercises. Sieveking was success-ful in uniting his organization and in transforming it into a paramilitary force for 'national restoration'.[68]

To strengthen their corporate identity, the Bismarck Youth held annual national youth meetings in different cities. The gatherings at Erlangen (1922), Goslar (1923), Braunschweig (1924), Bielefeld (1925), Stettin (1926), and Siegen (1927) were followed in 1928 by a convention in Friedrichsruh, which had a particular importance for the organization as it was the burial place of Otto von Bismarck.[69]

This Seventh Nationalist Youth Meeting had been scheduled by the Bismarck Youth leadership for the end of July 1928 in honour of the thirtieth anniversary of their icon's death. The party leadership intended the meeting to demonstrate its youth organization's strength. This was particularly important because the Reichstag elections of 20 May 1928, for which the Bismarck Youth had heavily campaigned, had ended with a catastrophe for the DNVP. Their share of the vote fell from 20.5 per cent to 14.2 per cent, and the parliamentary faction lost 30 seats, reducing it to 73 members.[70]

In an article for the Bismarck Youth's periodical, *Deutsches Echo*, Sieveking did not deny the fact that his organization had failed to attract sufficient

---

[65] See Wolfgang Krabbe, *Die gescheiterte Zukunft der Ersten Republik: Jugendorganisationen bürgerlicher Parteien im Weimarer Staat 1918–1933* (Opladen, 1995), 171–96.

[66] Figures according to *Hamburger Nachrichten*, 28 July 1928.

[67] Cf. *Das junge Deutschland*, XVI (1922), 197.

[68] See Behrens, 'Die Deutschnationalen', 103, 107, and 110.

[69] See the propaganda poster announcing the Friedrichsruh meeting in German Historical Museum, Berlin, 1987/292.3.

[70] On the election results see Falter, *Wahlen*, 71.

numbers of young people during the election campaign. There was, however, no thought of resignation. Instead, the Bismarck Youth would have to redouble its efforts to attract young people to the German Nationalists' cause.[71] The Bismarck Youth's national meeting in Friedrichsruh was to be attended by Prince Oskar of Prussia and Field Marshal von Mackensen, and would mark the beginning of this increased effort at youth mobilization.[72]

Sieveking claimed that the event would show its ideological opponents 'that there is still a German youth which knows how to act on behalf of the Kaiser and the Reich in the spirit of the Reich's founder. We shall show the world that we are prepared to fight for the idea of monarchism and for a *Volksgemeinschaft* in agreement with our *völkisch* and conservative world views.'[73]

For Sieveking and his followers the re-establishment of the Hohenzollern monarchy in a future 'Third Reich' was the political basis of the organization's efforts.[74] According to *Deutsches Echo* the forthcoming 'Third Reich' to which the Bismarck Youth aspired would once again be a great power on the world stage. Domestically, this Reich was to become a classless and ethnically homogeneous *Volksgemeinschaft*.[75] In the meantime, the members of the Bismarck Youth wished to fight the 'boundless parliamentarianism' of the Weimar Republic 'to the extreme [*bis aufs Messer*]', although a *coup d'état* no longer seemed a viable option after the experiences of the failed Kapp and Hitler putsches.[76]

In order to achieve their political aims and to promote a nationalist fervour among the organization's followers, the Bismarck Youth leadership established a programme of 'moral training' and 'political education'. This included the

---

[71] Hermann O. Sieveking, 'Wir und das Wahlergebnis', *Deutsches Echo*, IV (1928), 124–5.

[72] The attendance figures for this gathering vary considerably. The non-aligned *Zwiespruch* puts the number at just 520 in its critical report. See *Der Zwiespruch*, X (1928), 133. *Deutsches Echo*, however, refuted these figures in a comprehensive report at the beginning of September. See *Deutsches Echo*, IV (1928), 197–213. See also the reports in *Hamburger Nachrichten* and *Der Tag*, which spoke of 3,000 participants: *Hamburger Nachrichten*, 29 July 1928, morning edition; *Der Tag*, 29 July 1928, Sunday edition.

[73] Sieveking's opening speech at the Nationalist Youth Meeting in 1928 as quoted in *Deutsches Echo*, IV (1928), 128. Even Kaiser Wilhelm II sent a telegram to Sieveking. On this and the speeches of von Mackensen and Count Westarp see ibid. 195.

[74] *Deutsches Echo*, IV (1928), 197–213. The restoration of the Hohenzollern monarchy was one of the main goals of the 'Bismarck Youth' from the very beginning and remained so under Sieveking. See for example the correspondence of 6 Jan. 1920 between Kurd Viebig, then president of the German Nationalists' Youth League, and Count Westarp in Westarp Papers, political correspondence, BA (Berlin) N23291/45, 20. See also Sieveking's article in *Deutsches Echo*, II (1926), 198. Finally, *Korrespondenz der DNVP*, 23 Jan. 1925.

[75] Wolfgang R. Krabbe, 'Die Bismarckjugend der Deutschnationalen Volkspartei', *German Studies Review*, XVII (1994), 9–32.

[76] *Deutsches Echo*, I (1925), 312; II (1926), 158; IV (1928), 125. See, too, Lewis Hertzmann, *DNVP: Right-Wing Opposition in the Weimar Republic 1918–1924* (Lincoln, Neb., 1963).

reading of books on Bismarck's rule for both the youth groups of 14–18-year-olds and the activist groups or *Wehrgruppen* of 19–25-year-olds.[77] 'History', as the Bismarck Youth's members were told by *Deutsches Echo*, was the 'source, from which our vital, hope-giving power flows'. To study the key events of the 'great national past' was like a 'reviving bath for the German soul' tortured by the present state of Germany's weakness. Additionally, 'excursions to the places of the unsurpassable, admirable and unforgettable deeds of our fathers and forefathers' were organized for the members of the Bismarck Youth.[78] Among these places of 'historical importance' were the various Bismarck monuments spread all over Germany.

Bismarck monuments were, of course, not just places of pilgrimage for young German nationalists, but also popular excursion destinations for the population at large.[79] For the majority of the conservative and national-liberal bourgeoisie the monuments gave expression to their wish for a return to former greatness. Furthermore, they were considered to be sites of national contemplation which needed to be preserved and increased in number. The largest of Weimar's numerous pressure groups for the construction of further Bismarck memorials was the League for the Erection of a Bismarck National Monument, which was revived in 1925 by several influential industrialists and politicians.[80]

In the short term the League had to restrain its activities because of funding limitations and the continuing occupation of the left bank of the Rhine. This meant that no exact date could be set for the completion of the monument. Consequently the League confined itself momentarily to spreading 'Bismarck's thinking', which the League's first chairman, Max Wallraff, defined as a patriotic belief in the Reich's resurrection.[81]

In order to emphasize the national character of the project, Bismarck societies, which had ceased to exist during the war, were re-founded all over Germany. 'Bismarck's thinking' was to achieve a breakthrough not just in Prussia, but in the whole of Germany. The Third German Bismarck Day on 14 September 1929 was held in the Munich Odeon and attended by prominent Bavarians to allow its proponents to demonstrate 'that the German South is not

---

[77] See Behrens, 'Die Deutschnationalen', 104 (for Hamburg) and Gemein, 'DNVP', 130 (for Düsseldorf).

[78] Willy-Oskar Mundt, 'Geschichtsrückblick als Quelle der Kraft', *Deutsches Echo*, III (1927), 115–16.

[79] See the vast collection of 1920s postcards depicting Bismarck monuments in the archive of the Otto-von-Bismarck-Stiftung (P 1999).

[80] See Dorrmann, 'Bismarck-Nationaldenkmal', 1083–4. See, too, Hauptstaatsarchiv NRW, Düsseldorf, file 'Verein zur Errichtung eines Bismarck-Nationaldenkmals (BND) e.V.', RW 2/4, p. 3.

[81] Cf. Max Wallraf in the League's privately sponsored *Bismarck-Blatt*, Dec. 1928, p. 1.

going to let itself be outdone in its joyful and proud memory of Bismarck by the North and the West'.[82]

As the Munich example indicates, the Bismarck societies enjoyed the support of highly influential contemporaries. Apart from the Bavarian Minister President Heinrich Held, the mayor of Munich Karl Scharnagel, the president of the chamber of commerce Joseph Pschorr, the neo-conservative publicist Oswald Spengler, and the historian Karl Alexander von Müller, were all members of the Munich Bismarck Society.[83] In 1931, this society was able to celebrate the erection of a new Bismarck monument in the Bavarian capital. Designed by Fritz Brehm and financed by the Rhineland industrialist Paul Reusch, the seven-metre-high stone monument was erected next to the German Museum.[84] Apart from encouraging the construction of further Bismarck monuments, the Bismarck societies organized annual celebrations on 1 April as well as lectures about the Iron Chancellor. All these events had the same basic aim: to contrast Bismarck's 'greatness' with the perceived weakness of the Weimar Republic.

A two-part film about Bismarck, which had been planned since 1923, served the same purpose.[85] However, it manifested a completely different approach to the communication of its mythic content. Technical advances and the huge increase in the number of cinemas since the First World War facilitated the dissemination of particular images of history to an ever-growing audience.[86] In the mid-1920s roughly two million Germans went to the cinema on a daily basis. The number of cinemas increased from around 2,300 in 1918 to more than 5,000 in 1930. Historical films were particularly popular, as the enormous successes of Fritz Lang's *Die Nibelungen* (1924) and Anton von Czerépy's *Friedericus Rex* (1922–3) demonstrate.[87]

The Bismarck film project had been initiated by a company under the chairmanship of Otto von Bismarck Jr. Other members of the company's board included Friedrich Wilhelm von Loebell and two prominent heavy industrialists, Fritz Thyssen and Emil Kirdorf.[88] The film, which enjoyed the personal

[82] *Münchener Neueste Nachrichten*, 13 Sept. 1929.

[83] Hauptstaatsarchiv Düsseldorf, file 'Verein zur Errichtung eines BND e.V.', here vol. 33 I.

[84] See Hort, *Bismarck in München*, 164–94. See also Gavriel D. Rosenfeld, *Munich and Memory: Architecture, Monuments and the Legacy of the Third Reich* (Berkeley, Los Angeles, and London, 2000), 113–14.

[85] See Maja Lobinski-Demedts, 'Bismarck im Film', in Machtan (ed.), *National-Mythos*, 156–79. See, too, Robert A. Rosenstone, *Revising History—Film and the Construction of a New Past* (Princeton, 1995), 182.

[86] See Gerhard Schoenberger, 'Das Preußenbild im deutschen Film: Geschichte und Ideologie', in Axel Marquardt and Heinz Rathsack (eds.), *Preußen im Film* (Hamburg, 1981), 9–38, here p. 29.

[87] See, in particular, Helmut Regel, 'Die Friedericus-Filme der Weimarer Republik', in Marquardt and Rathsack (eds.), *Preussen im Film*, 124–34, here p. 71. Also, Siegfried Kracauer, *Von Caligari zu Hitler* (Frankfurt, 1984), 124. See, too, Katherine Roper, 'Friedericus Films in Weimar Society: Potsdamismus in a Democracy', *German Studies Review*, XXVI (2003), 493–514.   [88] BA (Berlin), Filmarchiv, no. 1615.

support of President von Hindenburg, certainly did not intend to show the historical Bismarck with all his strengths and weaknesses. Instead it aimed to propagate 'national values' with which the domestic political conflicts of the 1870s and 1880s should in no way interfere: 'The plot must end with the founding of the Reich in 1871. The following internal struggles and his [Bismarck's] departure would only awaken difficult memories which would divide rather than unify [the Germans] and be counterproductive for its patriotic purpose.'[89]

It was obvious what this 'patriotic purpose' was. The Bismarck films should serve to sharpen the cinema-goers' awareness of the 'current political power-lessness', to 'shake up the spirits of our people . . . and make them conscious of what they have lost'.[90] The lavishly illustrated book which accompanied the film spoke openly of these aims. It also explained why film was chosen as a medium. Its editor, Ludwig Ziehen, maintained that 'newspaper articles and speeches . . . are certainly useful and necessary' in order to anchor Bismarck in the German collective memory. Film, however, 'is more effective for the masses, because it portrays the deeds and successes of the past more vividly'.[91]

The 'masses'' need for a Bismarck film was the subject of a fierce political debate. In June 1925 the project, still in its embryonic form, met with strong criticism from Social Democratic politicians. Among others the chairman of the Berlin SPD, Franz Künstler, suggested that the film, or 'historical document' as he sarcastically coined it, was threatening to become 'the worst form of historical manipulation'.[92]

Dismissive statements such as this fell on deaf ears among the conservatives. The guests at the première in the Berlin Primus-Palast on 23 December 1925, most of them notable figures from society and politics, were, according to the journal *Der Film*, 'delighted' by the film.[93] When 'the old Kaiser, Moltke, Bismarck etc. appeared', *Reichsbote* reported, there was 'tumultuous applause, which finally ended in the audience's standing up and singing of the German national anthem'.[94]

Both the ideological subtext of the film and its reception by its first audience explain why the project was so strongly criticized in left-wing circles.[95] 'One

---

[89] Quoted from a confidential document of the 'Bismarck Film Company'. The document was discovered by *Vorwärts*, which printed it just one day before the 1926 celebrations of the 55th anniversary of the Reich's founding. See *Vorwärts*, 17 Jan. 1926, Sunday edition.

[90] Ludwig Ziehen, *Bismarck: Geleitbuch zum Bismarck-Film* (Berlin, 1926), foreword (not paginated).

[91] Ibid.   [92] RT, 16 June 1925, vol. 386, 2359.   [93] *Der Film*, 24 Dec. 1925.

[94] *Der Reichsbote*, 22 Dec. 1925, as quoted in Lobinski-Demedts, 'Bismarck im Film', 165.

[95] Lothar Machtan, 'Der inszenierte Mythos: Bismarck im Film', in Jost Dülffer and Hans Hübner (eds.), *Otto von Bismarck: Person—Politik—Mythos* (Berlin, 1993), 247–58, quotation on p. 258.

should recognize and be particularly critical about the political intentions behind the production of such a heroic Bismarck film,' *Rote Fahne* warned its readers on 22 December 1925.[96] The film, which showed episodes of Bismarck's life from his youth in the period immediately after the Napoleonic Wars to his time at the Bundestag in Frankfurt, was nothing more than a 'demonstration in "honour" of the Hohenzollerns' bloodhound, the forger of dispatches and grim enemy of the working classes, Otto von Bismarck'. From a political point of view, the film encouraged the belief in 'the absolute mastery of the individual'.[97]

Despite such criticism, the Reich's film classification board classed the film as 'educational for the nation [*volksbildend*]'. A little more than a year later, on 7 January 1927, 'Bismarck, part 2' was promoted as the second great cinematic event of the year after Fritz Lang's *Metropolis*.[98] The 'film of Germany's greatest era'—so ran its subtitle—portrayed Bismarck's life and times from his installation as Prussia's Minister President, the Wars of Unification and the Imperial Proclamation at Versailles, to the triumphal return of German troops through the Brandenburg Gate in Berlin. The reaction of the audience at the première yet again confirmed that the film aroused happy nostalgic feelings: 'There were storms of applause at every scene,' *Deutsche Zeitung* informed its readers. 'This film is what every German wants and needs.' The Primus-Palast, one of the largest cinemas in Berlin, reported that the film was the greatest success since its foundation: 'record sales for every showing'. The Kammer-Lichtspiele in Dresden telegraphed to report the same phenomenon: 'all shows sold out'.[99]

Public enthusiasm for the Bismarck films obliged the left-wing press to take issue with their historical authenticity. *Berliner Tageblatt* objected to the one-sided portrayal of the Reich's founder. It suggested the Bismarck films only served the interests of those who backed the film and were in no way a just representation of Bismarck's historical personality. The directors had not only skipped the 'Bismarck of domestic politics', the 'Junker, a man of patriarchal force, who did not understand the socio-political developments of the century'—but had also tried to exorcize the 'spirit of Locarno' with the 'spirit of Sedan'.[100]

Although the method of dissemination had changed with the myth's transfer onto the big screen, its anti-republican content remained unaltered. Whether the film suggested that Bismarck's solution to the German question was the inevitable result of German history since the Wars of Liberation, or

---

[96] *Rote Fahne*, 22 Dec. 1925.   [97] Ibid. Similarly, *Vorwärts*, 25 Dec. 1925, morning edition.
[98] BA (Berlin), Filmarchiv, no. 1615.   [99] Quotations from *Der Film*, 15 Jan. 1927.
[100] *Berliner Tageblatt*, 8 Jan. 1927, evening edition.

whether the people were reminded in memorial celebrations of the 'proud flight of the German eagle', which had 'set course for the sun' under Bismarck but whose 'pinions were now broken', the effect was the same: the metaphor-rich mystification of the Iron Chancellor served to emphasize the contrast between the 'great days of Bismarck' and the sombre republican present.[101]

Despite the stabilization of the Reich's foreign and domestic situation after 1923, the interpretations of Bismarck remained virtually unchanged. This was true both for the images held up by the bourgeois camp and for the criticism of them by left-wing publicists. When Ernst Feder ridiculed the backwards-looking 'flight from reality' of conservative-nationalist politicians and publicists, and *Vorwärts* protested against the right-wing 'monopolization' of the celebrations of the Reich's founding, they both used arguments which had been repeatedly invoked in various contexts since 1918.[102]

The attitude of leading democrats to Bismarck's controversial domestic policies can be analysed with a similar result. Just as during the debate on the Law for the Protection of the Republic in 1922, so the fiftieth anniversary of the promulgation of Bismarck's anti-socialist legislation became an opportunity to hold up the Republic's liberal spirit and to juxtapose it with Bismarck's repressive measures in the 1870s and 1880s.[103]

The high point of the anniversary year was a mass demonstration in Berlin on 21 October 1928 in commemoration of the first anti-socialist law, which had been passed in the Reichstag on 18 October 1878. The demonstration was organized by the SPD, which had become the strongest political party once again following the Reichstag elections of 1928. Almost 100,000 people gathered in the Lustgarten near the old Hohenzollern palace to decry Bismarck as the repressor of the masses, and to celebrate their victory over his discriminatory legislation. 'Bismarck is dead,' went the slogan on one of the banners, 'but Social Democracy is alive!'[104]

Friedrich Stampfer, editor-in-chief of *Vorwärts*, dedicated the entire front page of his paper to the anniversary. He characterized Bismarck's attempt 'to strangle one of the greatest intellectual movements in the history of mankind

---

[101] Speech of the Dean of Berlin's Friedrich-Wilhelms-Universität, Prof. Dr Pompeckj, in *Reichsgründungsfeier der Friedrich-Wilhelms-Universität zu Berlin am 18. Januar 1926* (Berlin, 1926), 28–30.

[102] Quotations from *Berliner Tageblatt*, 16 Jan. 1926, morning edition, and *Vorwärts*, 10 Aug. 1926, evening edition.

[103] Müller-Koppe, 'Sozialdemokratie', 180–207. A typical commentary is Paul Kampffmeyer's radio broadcast, subsequently printed as 'Aus der Geschichte der Arbeiterbewegung: Das Sozialistengesetz', *Vorwärts*, 20 Oct. 1928, morning edition.

[104] *Vorwärts*, 19 Oct. 1928. A detailed account of the events can be found in *Vorwärts*, 22 Oct. 1928, morning edition.

with snares of legal paragraphs' as a complete failure, as manifested by the SPD's success in the most recent Reichstag elections of 1928.[105]

The SPD's landslide electoral success of 1928 had indeed contributed significantly to the increase in self-confidence among the supporters of the Republic. The Grand Coalition government under Hermann Müller displayed its optimism for the Republic's future on Constitution Day (11 August) 1929. In Berlin popular celebrations were organized and sponsored by the national government. Free classical concerts were offered to the public, sports events took place in the Berlin park of Hasenheide, and fireworks and flight shows over the city were designed to entertain the masses.[106] The celebrations on 11 August were considered by the democratic press to be indicative of the consolidation of democracy. *Berliner Tageblatt*, for example, reported a torchlight procession in Berlin, in which more than 100,000 people participated on 11 August 1928: 'Here walks . . . the people: married couples with their kids, young men with girls in their arms, men and women of all social spheres and professions . . . Whoever has seen this has not only witnessed an organized torchlight march but the celebrations and the democratic confession of a whole people.'[107]

The self-assuredness of this event as well as the SPD's celebrations on 21 October 1928 were deliberate provocations to which the Weimar right reacted immediately. The SPD's criticism of Bismarck, 'the founder of German social policy', was described as 'wild propaganda' from a party whose only interest seemed to lie in exacerbating class hatred.[108] *Der Tag*, which hardly seemed to be surprised by the 'witch-hunt against the Reich's founder', emphasized the legitimacy of Bismarck's efforts to destroy the SPD. He had realized that 'their spirit of urban *Untermenschentum* ruined the youngest, strongest, and most numerous part of our nation and thus threatened the Reich with destruction'.[109]

The radical left, too, criticized the Social Democratic demonstration strongly, albeit on completely different grounds. The KPD organized a counter-demonstration on 21 October 1928, where it promoted the view that it was the Communist Party, not the Weimar SPD, which could rightfully claim to represent those who had suffered under Bismarck's legislation. The 'bourgeoisified' SPD, on the other hand, would have adopted the methods of the police state during the revolution of 1918–19, methods against which their predecessors in the workers' movement had fought vigorously.[110]

[105] *Vorwärts*, 21 Oct. 1928, Sunday edition.   [106] *Berliner Tageblatt*, 12 Aug. 1928, morning edition.
[107] *Berliner Tageblatt*, 13 Aug. 1928.   [108] *Neue Preußische Zeitung*, 22 Oct. 1928.
[109] *Der Tag*, 21 Oct. 1928, Sunday edition.
[110] See the front-page article, 'Vor fünfzig Jahren und heute! Nur die KPD verteidigt die Traditionen der proletarischen Vorkämpfer aus der Zeit des Sozialistengesetzes', *Rote Fahne*, 18 Oct. 1928.

8. SPD demonstration in Berlin's Lustgarten to commemorate the 50th anniversary of Bismarck's anti-socialist legislation, 21 October 1928.

Bismarck zu Hermann Müller: „Ich bin mit Ihnen zufrieden, Müller. Bebel hätte den Panzerkreuzer niemals gebaut!"

9. Chancellor Hermann Müller (SPD) humbly receives Bismarck's congratulations for building the 'Cruiser A': a caricature in *Rote Fahne* (21 October 1928) designed to illustrate the SPD's betrayal of socialist values.

Behind the KPD's attack on the SPD was the quarrel over the construction of the Cruiser 'A', which had been approved by Marx's bourgeois government before the 1928 general elections. The Cruiser 'A' had been immensely important for the left-wing parties during the Reichstag election campaign of 1928. The KPD, under Ernst Thälmann's leadership, demanded free meals for children at primary school instead of a new warship. The SPD had also campaigned with the slogan 'Children's meals, not warships'. Consequently disapproval in the party, and above all in the KPD, was great when it became apparent that the new SPD-led coalition government was forging ahead with the cruiser's construction.[111] This provided a useful slogan for the KPD. 'No class conscious worker demonstrates with the cruiser-SPD!' ran the combative headlines in *Rote Fahne* on the day before the demonstrations of 21 October.[112]

[111] See Winkler, *Schein der Normalität*, 541 ff.   [112] *Rote Fahne*, 20 Oct. 1928.

The anniversary of Bismarck's anti-socialist legislation was thus only a pretext for rhetorical attacks against the government by the KPD. Slogans like 'From Bismarck to Müller. From police sabre to armoured car! The system of suppressors remains, the methods have just been modified' or 'Bloodhound Noske, Bismarck's pupil' soon revealed the KPD's true target.[113] The events on and around 21 October 1928 were further proof that the political chasm between the Social Democrats and the Communists was no less than that between the democratic left and the political right. Beneath the level of high politics, where there had been a certain degree of stabilization since 1923, fundamental differences of ideology remained. The consequence of this was the absence of any basis on which a democratic consensus could be established, such a consensus being a vital prerequisite for a true socio-political stabilization. It was not as if the need for an identity-forging democratic myth to bind the Germans to their state was not clearly acknowledged. 'The Republic needs a foundation myth,' *Frankfurter Zeitung* announced in 1929 when it suggested making Constitution Day, 11 August, Germany's national holiday.[114] This proposal was backed by many Republicans, who made a great effort to free 11 August from its glamourless image. Friedrich Stampfer, for example, argued in *Vorwärts* that the Weimar Constitution 'has given the German people the opportunity to continue its existence in a nation-state after the hopeless collapse of the old state'.[115] *Reichsbanner* seconded: 'We have seen the greatest collapse in German history and we have wandered through the darkest years of our existence. The Republic has prevented the downfall of the Reich. The Republic has dealt with a decade of bitter distress. . . . The Republic has saved Germany; it will lead her and the German people to freedom and to new heights.'[116]

However, efforts to make Constitution Day the German national holiday always failed in the face of nationalist and Communist opposition. Even in the phase of 'relative stability' ('relative' when set against the stormy beginning and end of the Weimar Republic) a basic lack of consensus remained the most characteristic feature of Weimar Germany's political culture. The Republic was consequently ill-prepared when in 1929 storm clouds gathered over Weimar Germany. Two quite different events in particular created an atmosphere in which the key elements of the Bismarck myth—anti-parliamentarianism and the belief in the necessity of heroic leadership—were to gain a sudden explosive relevance. The first of these was the plebiscite over the Young Plan; the second was the world economic depression.

---

[113] *Rote Fahne*, 21 and 23 Oct. 1928.   [114] *Frankfurter Zeitung*, 10 Aug. 1929.
[115] *Vorwärts*, 11 Aug. 1929.   [116] *Reichsbanner*, 10 Aug. 1929.

8

Towards the Abyss: Bismarck and the Dissolution of the Weimar Republic

Years of radicalization: Bismarck between the Young Plan and the sixtieth anniversary of the Reich's foundation

On 2 October 1929, the nationalist periodical *Deutsches Echo* confronted its readers with a full-page announcement demanding support for the plebiscite against the Young Plan:[1]

> The nationalist front has entered into the decisive struggle for German freedom. Under the disastrous leadership of this government and the short-sighted parole to reduce the burden for this generation, serf-like tributes will be weighed down upon the German youth and unborn generations. This irresponsible gamble with the future of the German people is precisely what the newly created nationalist front hopes to prevent by putting the Law against the Enslavement of the German People to a national referendum. The struggle for the German referendum is of central importance for the German youth. It is the self-evident task of every Bismarckian to canvass beyond his own circle in order to ensure the success of the referendum. It is a matter of saving for the German future that part of Bismarck's Empire and Bismarck's spirit which has been rescued from the criminal revolution![2]

The campaign for the so-called 'Freedom Law', which drew on the pretext of preserving and restoring the Bismarckian inheritance, roused the public to a hitherto unknown pitch of emotion in late 1929.[3] The campaigners' attempt to

---

[1] The Young Plan of May 1929 replaced the Dawes Plan of 1924. It fixed the final sum of German reparation payments at 112 billion Goldmarks, and, for the first time, established a concrete duration of the payment thereof. Even though the Young Plan was favourable in comparison to the Dawes Plan, the German right vigorously rejected the idea of having to pay instalments to the Allies for another sixty years. On the Young Plan, see in particular Philipp Heyde, *Das Ende der Reparationen: Deutschland, Frankreich und der Youngplan 1929–1932* (Paderborn, 1998).

[2] *Deutsches Echo*, 2 Oct. 1929.

[3] Paragraphs 1 and 2 of the 'Freedom Law' were directed against the 'war guilt lie' and asked the government to annul the appropriate articles of the Versailles Treaty. Paragraph 3 rejected the acceptance of any new burdens and duties *vis-à-vis* external powers. The height of demagoguery, however, was paragraph 4 (included on Hugenberg's insistence), which threatened the Chancellor, ministers and plenipotentiaries,

mobilize every form of anti-democratic resentment naturally included the invocation of Bismarck; no other mythical figure was able to condense and illustrate the key elements of right-wing oppositional ideology more forcefully than the Iron Chancellor. And no other 'hero' of German history was more present in the German collective memory. As Max Wallraf pointed out in a speech held at the Third German Bismarck Day in Munich on 14 September 1929, the Iron Chancellor was omnipresent in German politics: 'Each and every day his impressive figure stands above the chaos and the distress of our time.'[4]

That Bismarck was instrumentalized in a campaign against the reparation policies of the Republic was in itself hardly surprising. More importantly, however, the anti-Young Plan campaign strongly contributed to the radicalization of the public discourse on Bismarck. Although the plebiscite was ultimately defeated on 22 December 1929 with only 13 per cent of the electorate voting in favour of it, the campaign greatly agitated the public and widened the ideological gaps which had always been reflected in the various attitudes towards the Iron Chancellor. In the heated atmosphere created by the fiercest anti-republican campaign Weimar had ever witnessed, the Bismarck myth acquired a far more explosive topicality as a weapon against the 'system' than had been the case during the previous years of relative stabilization.

Even more decisive for the rapid deterioration of the political climate in Weimar Germany were the effects of the world economic crisis.[5] On 24 October 1929, Wall Street's 'Black Friday', the share prices on the New York Stock Exchange dropped dramatically and continued to do so over the following days. The economic effects of 'Black Friday' quickly reached the other side of the Atlantic and they hit Germany particularly hard. The country's economy was heavily dependent upon short-term foreign loans, especially from the United States. In the light of the financial crisis these loans were now being withdrawn.[6] The number of unemployed—which was already comparatively high during the earlier years of the Weimar Republic—rose sharply from the

---

who signed agreements such as the Young Plan, with long jail terms. On this see the detailed account of right-wing agitation against the Young Plan by Volker Berghahn, 'Das Volksbegehren gegen den Young-Plan und die Ursprünge des Präsidialregimes 1928–1930', in Dirk Stegmann *et al.* (eds.), *Industrielle Gesellschaft und politisches System: Beiträge zur politischen Sozialgeschichte: Festschrift für Fritz Fischer zum siebzigsten Geburtstag* (Bonn, 1978), 431–46, here p. 446.

[4] Wallraf as quoted in *Münchener Neueste Nachrichten*, 13 Sept. 1929.

[5] On this see Jürgen Falter, 'Unemployment and the Radicalization of the German Electorate 1928–33', in Peter Stachura (ed.), *Unemployment and the Great Depression in Weimar Germany* (London, 1986), 187–207.

[6] See Harold James, 'Economic Reasons for the Collapse of the Weimar Republic', in Ian Kershaw (ed.), *Weimar: Why did German Democracy fail?* (London, 1990), 30–57.

end of 1929: from 1.3 million in September 1929 to 3.2 million (4.5 million including short-term unemployment) in January 1930.[7]

If the direct economic effects of the world economic crisis were harsh for Germany, the psychological consequences were no less disastrous. Feelings of insecurity extended far beyond those who were immediately affected economically. The prevalent doomsday atmosphere allowed the enemies of the Republic successfully to unleash their uninhibited agitation against Weimar by portraying the crisis as a consequence of the democratic 'system'. As a result of the economic and political crisis after 1929 mistrust of the multi-party state and the parliamentary system in general infiltrated wide sections of the population.[8] In a situation in which more and more people considered the parliamentary system bankrupt it proved to be relatively easy for the right-wing enemies of democracy to mobilize latent resentments towards public institutions and the ruling parties. Again it was Bismarck who was used to illustrate and popularize anti-parliamentary sentiments. The economist Edgar Salin, for example, accused the Republic in 1930 of being incapable of settling Germany's economic problems. He suggested that the political and economic strength of the Reich during the first years of its existence had stemmed from the 'unpretentious, awe-inspiring person of the old Kaiser and the towering, heroic figure of the Iron Chancellor'.[9]

The executive committee of the League for the Erection of a Bismarck National Monument argued along similar lines. In early 1930 the committee publicly demanded—in the name of Bismarck—that the German people should overcome the 'petty discord of the parliament' and restore the 'unity of the people, of the nation, and of the Empire'.[10] With the onset of the depression, the League gave up all claims to political neutrality. After the death of Gustav Stresemann in 1929 (Stresemann had been a member of the League's executive committee), the League increasingly transformed itself into a platform to promote anti-republican ideas. The organization was now exclusively run by dedicated anti-democrats such as Friedrich von Berg (chairman of the German Nobility's Council), Prince Otto von Bismarck Jr., the former Field Marshal von Mackensen, the Stahlhelm leader Franz Seldte, Fritz Thyssen, and Hermann Otto Sieveking.[11] In early 1930 these men felt that times had never

---

[7] In September 1931, the number of unemployed rose to 4.3 million, then to 5.1 million in September 1932. At the beginning of 1933, 6 million Germans were unemployed, in comparison to 12 million employed. On these figures, see Kolb, *Weimar Republic*, 106.

[8] On this see Schulze, *Weimar*, 321.

[9] Edgar Salin, *Die deutschen Tribute: Zwölf Reden* (Berlin, 1930), 10–11 and 50–1.

[10] *Bismarck-Blatt*, May 1930, 1.

[11] See the list of board members published in *Bismarck-Blatt*, July 1931, 4.

been more favourable to their ultimate objective of replacing the Republic with a political regime based on the ideas underlying Bismarck's constitution of 1871. Even though the idea of overcoming parliamentary democracy in favour of a more authoritarian political system had been an essential component of the Bismarck myth ever since 1918, the narrative gained force in the context of the parliamentary crisis which would lead to the dissolution of the grand coalition government under Hermann Müller on 27 March 1930.[12] Only hours after Chancellor Müller had submitted the resignation of his cabinet, Hindenburg entrusted the conservative Centre MP and highly decorated former combat officer Heinrich Brüning with the task of forming a new government. The next day Brüning and Hindenburg agreed to form the first 'presidential cabinet', a government which was largely independent of parliament and had its basis in the emergency powers defined in Article 48 of the Weimar Constitution.[13]

Yet, despite the emergency rights available to the Brüning government, the Chancellor and his aides had little cause for optimism. The economic situation they were facing was devastating. Brüning's stringent deflationary policies designed to convince the Western Allies of Germany's willingness to pay reparations (despite her inability to do so) led to soaring levels of unemployment and ever-growing dissatisfaction within the population.[14] After the September 1930 general elections, Brüning was additionally confronted with a hostile Reichstag, in which the two most radical parties, the NSDAP and the KPD, were strongly represented.[15]

In the parliament's opening session on 17 October 1930, Gregor Strasser, one of the 107 National Socialists in the newly elected Reichstag, emphasized that his party's success was a result of the Nazis' irreconcilable opposition to the Republic. He accused the Weimar 'system' of having transformed Bismarck's 'proud' Reich within only twelve years into a state in which 'corruption and crime' were the most conspicuous characteristics.[16]

---

[12] *Schulthess*, LXXI (1930), 91. On the fall of the Müller government see Winkler, *Weimar*, 366–71.

[13] See William L. Patch, *Heinrich Brüning and the Dissolution of the Weimar Republic* (Cambridge, 1998), 72.

[14] On Brüning's economic policy see Harold James, *The German Slump: Politics and Economics 1924–1936* (Oxford, 1986). On the so-called 'Borchardt controversy' about Brüning's handling of the economic depression see Jürgen Baron von Kruedener (ed.), *Economic Crisis and Political Collapse: The Weimar Republic 1924–1933* (New York, Oxford, and Munich, 1990). See, too, Knut Borchardt, *Wachstum, Krisen, Handlungsspielräume der Wirtschaftspolitik* (Göttingen, 1982).

[15] The National Socialists had managed to increase their votes from just over 800,000 in May 1928 to 6.4 million in 1930. The Communists, too, benefited considerably from the depression, though not as dramatically as the Nazis: the KPD increased their votes from 10.6% to 13.1% and their Reichstag seats from 54 to 77. All the other parties lost votes. Cf. Falter, *Wahlen*, 72.

[16] Strasser in RT, vol. 444, 17 Oct. 1930, 56–64, quotation on p. 57.

In view of such accusations, it was necessary for the Brüning government to introduce measures to improve its public image. In order to convince the German voters of the 'patriotic' character of the government's policies, a ceremony was held on 18 January 1931 commemorating the sixtieth anniversary of Bismarck's founding of the Reich. In November 1930, the Reichswehr Minister Wilhelm Groener had advocated an 'especially festive' commemoration ceremony to mark the anniversary. Given the precarious economic situation, Groener argued in a letter to Chancellor Brüning, it was essential that 'the Reich government seizes every opportunity to remind the German people of the heroic deeds in its national history'.[17]

Immediately after the government's intention to celebrate the sixtieth anniversary of Bismarck's unification of Germany in the Reichstag had become publicly known, critical voices were to be heard from the democratic left. The head of the Prussian government, Otto Braun, believed that the sole purpose of the ceremony was to 'hold high the memory of the glorious Kaiserreich'.[18]

Braun's assessment was somewhat misleading—the 1931 Reichstag commemoration ceremony in honour of the Reich's founding had little to do with any restorative ideas. There can be no doubt that Brüning wanted to transform the Weimar system by reducing parliamentary input with respect to budgetary affairs. However, there is little evidence for his later assertion in 1970, that the peaceful reintroduction of the monarchy founded on a broad popular support was the focal point of his policies as Chancellor.[19] Instead, as the Minister of the Interior, Joseph Wirth, noted in a cabinet meeting, it was the intention of the government to foil foreseeable monarchist and nationalist celebrations of the Reich's founding with a central festive act organized by the state—in fact the largest celebration of Bismarck's unification of Germany in the history of the Weimar Republic—and thereby to claim the legacy of the Iron Chancellor for itself.[20] In accordance with this goal, the Minister of the Interior ordered flags to be raised on all public buildings for 18 January 1931.[21] In

---

[17] See Groener's letter to Brüning, 5 Nov. 1930, in BA (Berlin), R 43 I , no. 567, p. 159. On Groener see Johannes Hürter, *Wilhelm Groener: Reichswehrminister am Ende der Weimarer Republik (1928–1932)* (Munich, 1993).

[18] See Otto Braun's confidential letter of 18 September to the Prussian Ministry of the Interior, BA (Berlin), R 43 I, no. 712, pp. 181 and 182.

[19] See Heinrich Brüning, *Memoiren 1918–1934* (Stuttgart, 1970), 453–54. See, too, Andreas Rödder, 'Dichtung und Wahrheit: Der Quellenwert von Heinrich Brünings Memoiren und seine Kanzlerschaft', *HZ* CCLXV (1997), 77–116.

[20] Cabinet minutes of 17 December 1930, in *Akten der Reichskanzlei: Die Kabinette Brüning I und II*, vol. I: *30. März 1930 bis 10. Oktober 1931*, ed. Tilman Koops (Boppard, 1982), 743–5.

[21] See 'Rundschreiben des Reichsinnenministers an alle Behörden des Reiches', 6 Jan. 1931, in BA (Berlin), R 43 I, no. 567, p. 183.

addition, wreaths were laid at the sarcophagus of Bismarck in Friedrichsruh by order of the Reich cabinet.[22]

The ceremony in the Reichstag emphasized the importance of commemorating the founding of the Reich at a time of national peril.[23] According to the most senior parliamentarian in the Reichstag, Wilhelm Kahl (DVP), the memory of 18 January 1871 reminded every German of their obligation to take current political decisions 'in the spirit of our past'.[24] This appeal was endorsed by Chancellor Brüning, who added that the historical 'apogee' of 1871 should remind the nation in these dire days to follow the path to German renewal. The current government would 'not lose faith in a better German future, and will devote all its strength to fulfil its role as the augmenter of the blessings of peace for the German Reich in the fields of national well-being, freedom, and moral fortitude in accordance with the proclamation of 1871. For this goal, for the Reich and its people, we are prepared to sacrifice all our energy. Therefore, in remembrance of our great Chancellor Bismarck, we give testimony in the call: long live our beloved fatherland!'[25]

Brüning's speech was motivated by his intention to appropriate Germany's 'glorious' past for the cabinet's own political ends. Measured against this aim the commemoration ceremony of 18 January 1931 was clearly a 'failure', as the conservative *Kreuzzeitung* pointed out the next day.[26] Instead, the event provided a welcome opportunity for the KPD and NSDAP to hone their profiles as radical opponents of the Weimar Republic. Both parties had turned down the Reich President's invitation to attend the commemoration ceremony in the Reichstag, although their reasons could hardly have been more different. The KPD wanted to display through its absence the 'indifference' with which the working people regarded the 'squabbling' amongst the middle-class parties over Bismarck's legacy.[27] At the same time, the KPD took the SPD's participation in the ceremonies as a reason to once more indulge in the polemic against the Social Democratic leadership. The SPD's ability to feel 'enthusiasm'

---

[22] By means of a press release the Reich government ensured that this became known to a wider public. See BA (Berlin), R 43 I, no. 567, p. 192.

[23] Ibid., p. 188.

[24] Kahl as quoted in *Schulthess*, LXXII (1931), 17–18. Kahl had given a similar speech in 1898 at a memorial service for Bismarck in the Berlin Kroll Opera. See Wilhelm Kahl, *Bismarck lebt: Gedächtnisrede bei der allgemeinen Trauerfeier in Berlin am 7. August 1898* (Freiburg im Breisgau, 1898).

[25] See Brüning's speech in BA (Berlin), R 43 I, no. 567, pp. 193–4 as well as the comments in *Germania*, 19 Jan. 1931, evening edition.

[26] *Kreuzzeitung*, 19 Jan. 1931, evening edition. On the numerous (non-state-sponsored) celebrations organized by right-wing oppositional groups (Kyffhäuser League, Stahlhelm, Patriotic Leagues, etc.), see the report of 'Wolff's Telegraphisches Büro', in BA (Berlin), R 43 I, no. 567, pp. 197–205.

[27] *Rote Fahne*, 20 Jan. 1931.

for the old Prussian colours of black, white, and red (with which the plenary chamber of the Reichstag had been decorated for the commemoration ceremony) demonstrated the extent to which they had forgotten their roots, the struggle against 'Chancellor Bismarck and the socialist laws'. Instead, their participation in the commemoration ceremony provided further evidence that the SPD had entered an 'alliance' with the middle-class 'fascists'.[28] In the eyes of the KPD, this view was confirmed by the SPD's decision to tolerate the Brüning government.[29]

The vitriolic tone displayed by *Rote Fahne* indicated once again how deep the divide between the moderate and radical left had become since the summer of 1928, when the Sixth World Congress of the Communist International in Moscow had set the course for a more uncompromising left-wing policy. According to the new dogma established in Moscow, the Social Democrats and their ideology of class co-operation were the main enemy of the working classes in the revolutionary civil war.[30]

The NSDAP, on the other hand, declared that their absence from the commemoration ceremony was an expression of their protest against the political instrumentalization of the Reich's founder by politicians who had committed 'treason' against Bismarck's legacy.[31] The National Socialists' position was partly a result of a meeting between Hitler and Brüning on 5 October 1930 which had revealed their fundamental political differences. When Hitler demanded an immediate moratorium on reparations and at least three cabinet posts in return for parliamentary support of Brüning's policies, the Chancellor refused immediately.[32] Consequently, the Nazis' rhetorical attacks against the cabinet, often formulated with reference to Bismarck, became noticeably more aggressive. *Deutsche Zeitung*, for example, credited a National Socialist student leader with the words that the German people's current path 'through the hell of Weimar' would ultimately lead to salvation, and thus to the 'Third Reich'. Bismarck would thereby serve as a guiding star: 'He is with us on our way into the Third Reich of the Germans: Bismarck!'[33]

---

[28] *Rote Fahne*, 20 Jan. 1931.

[29] On this see Rainer Schaefer, *SPD in der Ära Brüning: Tolerierung oder Mobilisierung? Handlungsspielräume und Strategien sozialdemokratischer Politik 1930–1932* (Frankfurt, 1990), 65–72.

[30] Secondary literature on the radicalization of the KPD after 1928 is extensive. See, for example, Hermann Weber, *Die Wandlung des deutschen Kommunismus: Die Stalinisierung der KPD in der Weimarer Republik*, 2 vols. (Frankfurt, 1969), here I. 195–9. See, too, Winkler, *Schein der Normalität*, 661 ff. On Thälmann's view of the SPD as 'social fascists', Eve Rosenhaft, *Beating the Fascists? The German Communists and Political Violence 1929–1933* (Cambridge, 1983), 72.

[31] *Völkischer Beobachter*, 20 Jan. 1931. Equally, *Der Angriff*, 19 Jan. 1931.

[32] Brüning, *Memoiren*, 192 ff.

[33] *Deutsche Zeitung*, 18 Jan. 1931, morning edition.

The NSDAP, however, was not the only right-wing organization which stood in firm opposition to the Brüning cabinet. The DNVP and its youth organization (which from 1 April 1929 was named 'Bismarck League' rather than 'Bismarck Youth') also dedicated themselves explicitly to the fight against Brüning's policies.[34] The Bismarck League's leader, Hermann Otto Sieveking, accused the government of continuing the 'traditional politics of enslavement and *Erfüllung* [policy of unconditional fulfilment of the reparations and disarmament clauses of the Treaty of Versailles]'.[35] There was a certain logic in this accusation: Brüning's policy was indeed comparable to the measures Joseph Wirth had already taken in 1921–2 in order to convince the Western Allies of Germany's willingness to pay reparations despite her inability to do so. Both Wirth and Brüning chose this path in order to bring about a revision of the Versailles Treaty system. To Sieveking and others who promoted a confrontational (and allegedly 'Bismarckian') 'foreign policy of strength', this approach seemed fundamentally misguided. Bitterly disappointed by the Chancellor's foreign policy, Sieveking declared that a 'national renewal' was impossible under Brüning. The consequence to be derived from this 'insight' was clear and simple: the system of Weimar and Versailles, which was already reeling in its 'death throes', had to be 'swept away'.[36]

The Stahlhelm leader Franz Seldte also felt that the time had come for decisive political change. According to Seldte, who used the occasion of the sixtieth anniversary of the Reich's foundation for a speech in Magdeburg (which was subsequently published in nationalist papers as an 'appeal' to the German people), it was imperative to overcome the 'un-German *Zwischenreich*' as embodied in the Weimar Republic. The end of Weimar was no longer a distant ideal: 'The Stahlhelm regards this as certain: there is a vision of the coming state and a plan to build it. Our select class of leaders is prepared and there is an iron will of the new German state to attack . . . .'.[37]

---

[34] For the name change of the 'Bismarck Youth' into 'Bismarck League' see *Deutsches Echo*, V (1929), 94.

[35] *Deutsches Echo*, VII (1931), 147–9.

[36] Ibid. Sieveking himself never got to experience the end of the Weimar Republic which he had demanded. On 4 September 1931 he died of blood poisoning at the age of 40. See *Deutsches Echo*, VII (1931), 194 ff. His successor was the 47-year-old Herbert von Bismarck. On this, see *Deutsches Echo*, VII (1931), 220. For a broader evaluation of radicalization within the German youth after 1929/1930 see Larry E. Jones, 'Generational Conflict and the Problems of Political Mobilization in the Weimar Republic', in id. and James Retallack (eds.), *Elections, Mass Politics, and Social Change in Modern Germany* (Washington, DC, and Cambridge, 1992), 347–69. See, too, Irmtraud Götz von Olenhausen, 'Die Krise der jungen Generation und der Aufstieg des Nationalsozialismus: Eine Analyse der Jugendorganisationen der Weimarer Zeit', *Jahrbuch des Archivs der Deutschen Jugendbewegung*, XII (1980), 53–82.

[37] See, for example, *Deutsche Tageszeitung*, 18 Jan. 1931, Sunday edition. On Seldte see Volker R. Berghahn, *Der Stahlhelm: Bund der Frontsoldaten 1918–1935* (Düsseldorf, 1966), 69 ff.

Seldte's speech on Reich Foundation Day 1931 expressed a key demand of right-wing agitation: the Republic should be replaced by a non-democratic, authoritarian regime—the 'Third Reich'.[38] In terms of content, Seldte's speech offered little new, even though it served to emphasize the inseparable connection between anti-democratic sentiments and the Bismarck myth. However, the open threat of a *coup d'état* by the chairman of the largest German veterans' organization during a commemoration service revealed the new radical quality of the Bismarck myth. While it had always been a political weapon to delegitimize the Republic, the Bismarck myth had not yet *explicitly* been linked to concrete plans to overthrow the state of Weimar.

The new political explosiveness of the Bismarck myth alarmed democratic circles. *Germania*, for example, a paper which was no stranger to polemic and threatening gestures from the right, reacted indignantly to Seldte's speech. It emphasized that Bismarck's unification of the Reich was regarded by German Catholics as a pivotal event in German history. Hostility towards the Republic, however, which was all too often associated with ceremonies commemorating Bismarck's achievements, was not shared by political Catholicism: 'This Reich in which we live today is not a *Zwischenreich*, and indeed not—as the Stahlhelm declares in its abusive publication—an "un-German *Zwischenreich*" which should be replaced by a mythical "Third Reich".' It had 'unfortunately become fashionable in certain circles' to 'contrast in a negative light' the Republic with Bismarck's Reich. Although there were obvious differences 'between then and now', for example, differences 'between prosperity and poverty, between power and impotence . . . there is no difference with respect to our determination to deploy all forces for the benefit of our Reich and our national future, now as then'.[39]

Germania's forceful rejection of Seldte's speech was designed to counter the Bismarckians' fierce agitation against the Republic on 18 January 1931. In the light of the economic depression and subsequent political radicalization, however, it is reasonable to assume that very few people were willing to 'deploy all forces for the benefit of the Reich' as long as this Reich was a Republic. Germany was in the middle of a major crisis and the inability of Weimar

[38] The 'idea of the Reich' experienced a remarkable renaissance in the political rhetoric of the early 1930s. It combined romantic notions of a glorious past with anti-democratic, anti-Western, and anti-Communist sentiments. See Lothar Kettenacker, 'Der Mythos vom Reich', in Karl H. Bohrer (ed.), *Mythos und Moderne: Begriff und Bild einer Rekonstruktion* (Frankfurt, 1983), 261–89. Also Herfried Münkler, 'Das Reich als politische Macht und politischer Mythos', in id., *Reich-Nation-Europa: Modelle politischer Ordnung* (Weinheim, 1996), 11–59. For Catholic concepts of the 'Reich' see Klaus Breuning, *Die Vision des Reiches: Deutscher Katholizismus zwischen Demokratie und Diktatur 1929–1934* (Munich, 1969).

[39] *Germania*, 18 Jan. 1931, morning edition. See, too, *Vorwärts*, 18 Jan. 1931, morning edition.

10. Hitler poses in front of a Bismarck portrait after his release from Landsberg in 1924.

democracy to solve this crisis encouraged the Bismarckians in their belief that the 'decisive phase of the struggle' against the Republic had begun.[40] This assumption proved to be correct and Bismarck was to play a key role in the final act of Weimar Germany's history. More and more Germans were longing for a 'new Bismarck' in the face of the political and economic situation after 1929. And no one exploited the desire for a Bismarck-like 'redeemer' with the same demagogic skill as the leader of the largest right-wing opposition party, Adolf

[40] *Bismarck-Blatt*, July 1930, 52.

Hitler. His ability to use the Bismarck myth as a propaganda device would prove to be one of the conditioning factors in his rise to power.

Bismarck, Hitler, and the rise of National Socialism

In February 1939, six years after his 'seizure of power' and the dissolution of the Weimar Republic, the German Chancellor Adolf Hitler attended the launching of the battleship *Bismarck*. In his speech in Hamburg harbour, the Führer explained his reasons for naming Europe's largest battleship after the founder of the Reich: 'Of all men who can lay claim to having paved the way to the new Reich [meaning the 'Third Reich'], one figure stands in awe-inspiring solitude: Bismarck.'[41]

Hitler's claim was entirely tenable to the extent that the Führer did not refer to the historical personality of the first Reich Chancellor but to the Bismarck *myth*. Apart from Frederick the Great, the Iron Chancellor was the historical figure invoked most often in Hitler's speeches in order to lend support to the Führer's position.[42] Hitler's political references to Bismarck (for which there is evidence from the early 1920s) served a number of purposes, the most important of which was to emphasize the overriding role of leader figures in Germany's past, present, and future.

It has often been pointed out that after 1925 the NSDAP differed from all other political movements and parties in the Weimar Republic in that it submitted completely to the will of its 'charismatic leader'.[43] It was therefore the only party whose inner organizational structure reflected the public demand for strong leadership.[44] However, the Führer principle had not always been the focal point of the party's ideology and organization. In the early years of the National Socialist movement—and even, as Albrecht Tyrell has argued, up until 1923—Hitler publicly described himself as the 'drummer' of the national cause, rather than as the predestined leader of the German people.[45] Nevertheless, there are indications that Hitler understood the strong public desire for charismatic leadership in the years before his failed putsch of 1923 and that to

---

[41] *Hamburger Tageblatt*, 14 Feb. 1939, evening edition.

[42] On the role of Frederick II in Hitler's world-view and Nazi propaganda, see Konrad Barthel, *Friedrich der Große in Hitlers Geschichtsbild* (Wiesbaden, 1977).

[43] The first to apply Weber's concept of 'charismatic leadership' to Hitler was Joseph Nyomarkay, *Charisma and Factionalism in the Nazi Party* (Minneapolis, 1967).

[44] See Dietrich Orlow, *The History of the Nazi Party*, vol. 1: *1919–1933* (Pittsburgh, 1969), 8–10.

[45] Albrecht Tyrell, *Vom 'Trommler' zum 'Führer': Der Wandel von Hitlers Selbstverständnis zwischen 1919 und 1924 und die Entwicklung der NSDAP* (Munich, 1975).

him Bismarck was synonymous with such leadership. In April 1922, for example, on the occasion of a National Socialist 'Bismarck festival', Hitler praised the Iron Chancellor extensively and stated: 'We must follow in his footsteps.' Only then would the party succeed in 'gaining the support of the millions . . . And when that time has come, then we will want to say: we bow before you, Bismarck!'[46]

At this stage Hitler did not specify what qualified Bismarck as a model for the National Socialist movement. Most of his comments suggest that he did not want to promote a return to the political structures of Bismarck's Reich. But Hitler had recognized the intense public demand for a saviour-like charismatic leader, the creator of a new Reich. He consciously appealed to the idea that only a strong personality of Bismarckian proportions would be able to bring about the kind of political change which could lead Germany out of its present misery. Bismarck had created the German Reich single-handedly, a Reich which was 'the most powerful embodiment of German power and mastery . . . A single head, towering above all, had restored freedom of development to the German genius in a battle against the mediocrity of the majority. If we were to dispense with Bismarck in our history only wretched mediocrity would fill the most glorious period for our people in centuries.'[47]

At no time before 1923–4 did Hitler unambiguously claim 'Bismarckian qualities' for himself. The failed putsch in Munich, however, made Hitler believe that he was a martyr of the nationalists' cause and changed his self-perception remarkably: being the 'drummer' of the nationalist-*völkisch* movement was no longer enough for him.[48] During his high treason trial at the Munich People's Court in 1924 this became particularly evident. Hitler accepted full responsibility for the attempt to overthrow the Weimar Republic. None the less, he denied that he had committed high treason, since the 'crime of November 1918' had not been expunged and a constitution based on this 'crime' could have no validity. He then defended himself by referring to the constitutional conflict prior to 1871, insisting that often enough history had been made by great Germans *against* majority decisions.[49] By positing a

---

[46] Adolf Hitler, *Sämtliche Aufzeichnungen, 1905–1924*, ed. Eberhard Jäckel (Stuttgart, 1980), 599.

[47] Adolf Hitler, *Hitler's Secret Book*, introd. Telford Tailor, translated from German into English by Salvator Attanasio, 2nd edn. (New York, 1962), 124.

[48] On this see Ian Kershaw, *Hitler: 1889–1936: Hubris* (London, 1999), 183–5. On 5 August 1923, Hitler still maintained that he was only preparing the ground for the coming Führer. See *Sämtliche Aufzeichnungen*, no. 554, p. 966. During his trial, however, he suggested that he himself was the one to fulfil the role of the leader. Ibid., no. 606, pp. 1107–8; no. 622, p. 1188; no. 625, pp. 1210 and 1215.

[49] On the constitutional conflict see Ernst R. Huber, *Deutsche Verfassungsgeschichte seit 1789*, vol. 3: *Bismarck und das Reich*, 3rd edn. (Stuttgart, 1988), 305–67.

kinship between his own high treason and Bismarck's breach of the constitution, he suggested that in both cases seemingly illegal means had been adopted for better ends: 'What did Bismarck actually commit in the constitutional conflict? He ignored the constitution, the parliament, and the stifling majority . . . and ruled purely by recourse to the means of power of the state, ruled with the support of the army, the body of officials and the crown. How was Bismarck described in the entire press of the opposition? As a violator of the constitution, as a person guilty of high treason!' Bismarck's action had, however, been legitimized by the success of the German troops at Sedan and by the results of this military victory. For only because of this deed had 'the German people reached unity . . . its highest fulfilment and its greatest freedom'.[50]

The Munich People's Court, chaired by Judge Georg Neithardt, was obviously predisposed to Hitler's arguments. On 1 April 1924 the court condemned him and his three co-conspirators to the minimum sentence of five years' imprisonment and imposed a comparatively low fine of 200 Reichsmark. Hitler's imprisonment at Landsberg, which in fact ended in December 1924, provided him with the opportunity to study Nietzsche, Ranke, Treitschke, Marx, and Bismarck's *Thoughts and Reminiscences*.[51]

The basis of Hitler's special interest in history was ambivalent. He and other leading representatives of the 'movement' certainly believed in the mythical past of the German people and its particular world mission.[52] Joseph Goebbels, for example, noted in his diary that he shared the German people's 'longing for the one man, just as the earth longs for rain in the summer'. The German people would have to return to 'strength, enthusiasm, and restless devotion. These are all miraculous things. But isn't a miracle the only thing which can save us

---

[50] Cf. *Der Hitler-Prozess 1924: Wortlaut der Hauptgerichtsverhandlung vor dem Volksgericht München I*, ed. Lothar Gruchmann and Reinhard Weber, part 4: *19.–25. Verhandlungstag* (Munich, 1999), here: *23. Verhandlungstag*, 1574. The same theme appears in a speech by Hitler on 9 November 1927. See: 'Die Toten des 9. November 1923', in *Hitler: Reden, Schriften, Anordnungen, Februar 1925 bis Januar 1933*, vol. 2: *Vom Weimarer Parteitag bis zur Reichstagswahl, Juli 1926–Mai 1928*, part 2: *August 1927–Mai 1928*, ed. Bärbel Dusik (Munich, 1996), 542.

[51] On this see the memoirs of Hans Frank, party lawyer and later Governor-General of occupied Poland: Hans Frank, *Im Angesicht des Galgens: Deutung Hitlers und seiner Zeit auf Grund eigener Erlebnisse und Erkenntnisse* (Munich, 1953), 43. Apart from Bismarck's *Thoughts and Reminiscences*, Hitler read several books on the Iron Chancellor and his time in office. In *Mein Kampf*, he described how he found two illustrated books devoted to the Franco-Prussian War of 1870–1 in his father's library. They became his 'favourite books'. Finally, Hitler received a copy of *Fürst Bismarcks gesammelte Reden* in 1935, according to the bookplate signed by Hitler's personal secretary, Martin Bormann. Hitler marked certain sections in this book, particularly those in which Bismarck commented on conflicting party interests, questions of leadership, and relations with Russia and the SPD. On this see Herbert D. Andrews, 'Hitler, Bismarck and History', *German Studies Review*, XIV (1991), 511–36.

[52] See Frank-Lothar Kroll, *Utopie als Ideologie: Geschichtsdenken im Dritten Reich* (Paderborn, 1998), 66.

now? God, show the German people a miracle! A miracle!! One man!!! Bismarck, wake up!'[53]

As Hitler made clear in *Mein Kampf*, however, 'history' had a primarily instrumental purpose for the movement.[54] To Hitler, history was important both as a political weapon against his opponents and as a means to justify his own political beliefs.[55] Hitler's preoccupation with Bismarck's *Thoughts and Reminiscences* assisted him in defining his own role in the historical development of Germany. And in Landsberg, he realized what this role was. He was not merely the 'drummer' of the nationalist cause; he was the predestined leader himself, the Bismarck of his time.[56]

In *Mein Kampf*, which was praised in nationalist circles as the 'most significant political publication since Bismarck's *Thoughts and Reminiscences*', Hitler's representation of himself as a 'second Bismarck' received only fleeting expression.[57] Soon after Landsberg, however, Hitler began to suggest that he would fill the void which the Iron Chancellor had left in 1890. Immediately after the end of his imprisonment, for example, he posed for a photograph with a Lenbach portrait of Bismarck in the background.[58]

Hitler's writings and speeches suggest that he began to use the Bismarck myth for his own ends once he had discovered that he himself was the one to lead 'his' people. In Hitler's *Second Book*, written in 1928 but only published posthumously, this became particularly evident.[59] According to Hitler's admiring statements, Bismarck's *kleindeutsch* solution to the German question was the 'highest achievement' which could have been expected 'within the limits of the possible of that time'. Bismarck in his old age was therefore able to look back upon a mission fulfilled. However, his 'finished life work' did not signify the 'end of the life of the German nation'. In Hitler's view it had been the 'task of the post-Bismarck period' to pursue an ethnic policy [*Volkstumspolitik*] and

---

[53] See Goebbels' diary entry of 4 July 1924, in Joseph Goebbels, *Die Tagebücher von Joseph Goebbels: Sämtliche Fragmente*, ed. Elke Froehlich, 5 vols. (Munich, 1987), here 1. 94.

[54] Adolf Hitler, *Mein Kampf*, translated from German into English by James Murphy, 2nd edn. (London, 1939), 110.

[55] Ibid.

[56] Kershaw, *Hubris*, 212–19. Also Sabine Behrenbeck, *Der Kult um die toten Helden: Nationalsozialistische Mythen, Riten und Symbole 1923–1945* (Vierow, 1996), 96.

[57] Quotation from Adolf Bartels, 'Adolf Hitlers "Mein Kampf"', *Deutsches Schrifttum*, XIX (1927), 1–2. In his book, Hitler praised Bismarck's qualities as a statesman and denounced his 'bungling successors' as incompetent. See Hitler, *Mein Kampf*, 132.

[58] See the photograph in Rudolf Herz, *Hoffmann & Hitler: Fotografie als Medium des Führer-Mythos* (Munich, 1994), 100.

[59] On the significance of Hitler's *Second Book* see Martin Broszat, 'Betrachtungen zu "Hitlers Zweitem Buch"', *Vierteljahreshefte für Zeitgeschichte*, VI (1961), 417–30.

furthermore, to solve the acute problem of sustaining the German people through the acquisition of *Lebensraum*—living space in the East.[60]

According to Hitler, it was precisely this task which the post-Bismarckian era had failed to fulfil. Instead, social and political disintegration had prevailed and increased up to 1914. Responsibility for the growing social fragmentation after 1871 could not be ascribed to Bismarck, but to his 'incompetent' successors and the various political opposition groups of the Kaiserreich: the Centre Catholics, the Progressive Liberals, and the Socialists in particular. The same political groups had then prevented a German victory in the Great War and founded the despised Weimar Republic upon the ruins of 'Bismarck's proud Reich'.[61]

Hitler was convinced that the Iron Chancellor had understood the 'destructiveness' of socialism and that he had tried to eradicate the evil forces threatening 'his' Reich from within. He had, however, chosen the wrong method to achieve this goal. 'In his anti-socialist laws', Hitler argued, Bismarck 'put up desperate resistance against the destructive mission of the Marxist dogma. It had no effect. Not only because his successors lacked the energy in following the course Bismarck had charted, and because they abandoned this course, no, because the means of conflict themselves were not up to the task. By using political means of police force, an attempt was made to break the backbone of an ideological doctrine which was anchored in the masses and found their positive response.'[62] According to Hitler, the 'breaking' of the Marxist world-view and its representative organizations was only possible by countering 'Bolshevism' with an ideology of equal resolution and determination. Bismarck had not been able to rely upon a collective ideology as strong as National Socialism. This, Hitler argued, was why the anti-socialist laws had failed and why socialism in Germany had not thus far been destroyed.[63] For Hitler, an essential part of his own self-appointed historical mission was to make up for this missed opportunity.

In *Mein Kampf,* Hitler set out the ideological programme with which he hoped to confront socialism. His programme contained two fundamental ideas, both of which were derived from a vulgarized form of Social Darwinism:

---

[60] Quotations in this paragraph are taken from *Hitler's Secret Book*, 54 ff.

[61] Hitler, *Mein Kampf,* 534.

[62] Hitler on 14 April 1926, in *Hitler: Reden, Schriften, Anordnungen, Februar 1925 bis Januar 1933*, vol. 1: *Die Wiederbegründung der NSDAP, Februar 1925–Juni 1926*, ed. Clemens Vollnhans (Munich, 1992), 377–8.

[63] Ibid. See also Hitler's speech at a NSDAP rally in Delmenhorst on 25 May 1932, in *Hitler: Reden, Schriften, Anordnungen, Februar 1925 bis Januar 1933*, vol. 5: *Von der Reichspräsidentschaftswahl bis zur Machtergreifung, April 1932–Januar 1933*, part 1: *April 1932–September 1932*, ed. Klaus A. Lankheit (Munich, 1996), 131–5, here p. 133.

the racial doctrine, and the quest for living space. These two components provided the basis for Hitler's anti-Semitic and expansionist world vision, his concept of a permanent, merciless struggle between races for *Lebensraum*. The fight for *Lebensraum* could only be won by a people which maintained and defended its 'racial purity'.[64] In other words, Germany would have to conquer new 'living space' in the East and it would have to 'remove' the Jews. These were Hitler's ultimate objectives and the political aims which Germany's political leaders after Bismarck had failed to pursue.

Hitler believed that the implementation of these goals allowed him to invoke Bismarck's definition of politics as the 'art of the possible'. According to Hitler this phrase numbered among those most frequently misinterpreted by his contemporaries. He complained bitterly about the politicians who currently used the phrase in order to justify their 'policy of weakness' towards the Western allied powers.[65] In this context Hitler explicitly criticized Gustav Stresemann and his foreign policy of *rapprochement*: 'If Bismarck had ever imagined that fate would have damned him to endorse with this utterance ['politics is the art of the possible'] the statesmanlike qualities of Herr Stresemann, he would have surely omitted the utterance, or in a very small note he would have denied Herr Stresemann the right to refer to it.'[66]

Hitler emphasized that both Bismarck's intentions and his methods had been fundamentally different from those of Stresemann. Bismarck 'utilized every opportunity and worked through the diplomatic art as long as it promised success; he threw the sword into the scales if force alone was in a position to bring about a decision'. In other words, Bismarck had been convinced that in pursuing a particular goal all means were to be exploited in order to guarantee the undertaking's success. This and nothing else, Hitler insisted, was the legitimate interpretation of Bismarck's statement that 'politics is the art of the possible'.[67]

In accordance with this interpretation, Hitler felt historically justified in taking advantage of all means at his disposal for Germany's new ascent to world power status. In order to recapture Germany's 'freedom', he was willing to run the same degree of risk as the 'greats' to perform exceptional historical deeds: 'Was Frederick the Great's decision, for instance, to participate in the first

---

[64] See Eberhard Jäckel, *Hitlers Weltanschauung: Entwurf einer Herrschaft*, 4th rev. edn. (Stuttgart, 1991), 29 ff. and 55 ff.

[65] *Hitler's Secret Book*, 153.   [66] Ibid. 87 and 135.

[67] Ibid. 153. On Hitler's interpretation of '*Realpolitik*', see also Broszat, 'Betrachtungen zu "Hitlers Zweitem Buch"', 420–2. Already in *Mein Kampf*, Hitler repeatedly referred to this Bismarckian quote. See Hitler, *Mein Kampf*, 182 and 226–7.

Silesian War not linked with a risk? Or did Germany's unification by Bismarck entail no dangers? No, a thousand times no!'[68] By taking risks similar to those Frederick II and the Iron Chancellor had taken in their days, Hitler promised to bring what they had begun to a triumphant conclusion. In the eyes of the German public, the National Socialist 'blood and soil' ideology should appear as the extension of Bismarck's ideas, adapted to the present situation. 'If Bismarck were to return with his political comrades,' Hitler declared in January 1931, 'they would all stand on our side today!'[69]

The question remains as to why Hitler was more successful in assuming the role of a 'new Bismarck' after 1929 than he was in the earlier days of the movement. The NSDAP had not undergone a fundamental programmatic change, even though Hitler was keen to tone down his radicalism in the years after the failed putsch. In the Reichstag elections of 1928, the Nazi Party did not manage to outgrow its role as an insignificant splinter party. Historical research focusing on the rise of the NSDAP has always been eager to emphasize the multiple reasons for Hitler's electoral successes from the late 1920s onwards.[70] However, with respect to the factors enabling Hitler to perform the role of a 'new Bismarck', few were as important as the failure of the Austro-German customs union project in the summer of 1931. It was this second failed attempt of the Republic to compensate for its supposed lack of legitimacy via a *großdeutsch* enlargement which enhanced Hitler's credibility as the only politician with the necessary resolution to overcome the Versailles Treaty and to complete Bismarck's work with the establishment of a Greater German Reich.

The customs union project, which was high up on the political agenda from late 1930, was the clearest expression of a reversal in German foreign policy. The dreadful state of domestic politics and the National Socialists' electoral successes encouraged the government to abandon Stresemann's *Verständigungspolitik*, as well as the idea of a far-reaching economic and political integration of Europe as formulated in the Briand Plan of May 1930.[71]

With the Austro-German customs union project, Brüning and Stresemann's successor as Foreign Minister, Julius Curtius, hoped to achieve the first concrete step in the gradual revision of the *kleindeutsch* borders as determined by

---

[68] See *Hitler's Secret Book*, 119.

[69] Hitler's speech in Coburg on 18 January 1931, in *Hitler: Reden, Schriften, Anordnungen, Februar 1925 bis Januar 1933*, vol. 4: *Von der Reichstagswahl zur Reichspräsidentschaftswahl, Oktober 1930–Juni 1931*, part 1: *Oktober 1930–Juni 1931*, ed. Constantin Goschler (Munich, 1996), 175–6, here p. 176.

[70] See the detailed account in Kershaw, *Hubris*, 313 ff.

[71] On the Briand Plan see Antoine Fleury (ed.), *Le Plan d'Union fédérale européenne: Perspectives nationales, avec documents* (Frankfurt, 1998). On the reversal of German foreign policy, see Peter Krüger, *Die Außenpolitik der Republik von Weimar*, 2nd edn. (Darmstadt, 1993), 529.

the treaties of Versailles and St Germain.[72] At the same time, the customs union was designed to lessen the pressure resulting from domestic politics and economic crisis through a prestigious foreign policy success. At least in this respect, the customs union project was quite similar to the SPD's commitment to *Anschluß* in 1919. Like Ebert and Löbe in 1919, Brüning and Curtius assumed that the establishment of a customs union would immediately reduce the domestic political pressure on their government. They knew that, despite the Allies' ban on *Anschluß* in 1919, the idea of *Großdeutschland* had never ceased to enjoy the broadest non-partisan support within the German public.[73] 'Geopoliticians' such as Karl Haushofer, neo-conservatives like the editor of *Die Tat*, Hans Zehrer, and democrats such as Paul Löbe and Wilhelm Heile, all equally favoured the idea of a customs union with Austria because they considered it a prerequisite for a later political unification.[74] German industry, too, was pressing for the customs union, hoping that Austria's traditional connections with south-eastern Europe would be beneficial to their businesses.[75] The liberal journalist Werner Christiansen thus described a broad consensus among the German public when he noted that 'the customs union will give rise to the *Anschluß* . . . just as a hundred years ago the *Zollverein* has prepared the way for the unified German state created by Bismarck'.[76]

The Reich cabinet eventually committed itself to the customs union on 18 March 1931 after long negotiations with Vienna, and despite the anticipation of unfriendly French reactions in the Wilhelmstraße.[77] Few, however, expected

[72] Andreas Rödder, *Stresemanns Erbe: Julius Curtius und die deutsche Außenpolitik 1929–1931* (Paderborn and Munich, 1996), 186–226.

[73] In addition to the Austro-German *Volksbund*, founded in the immediate post-war-period, another influential association, the Austro-German *Arbeitsgemeinschaft*, was established in 1925 to promote the idea of *Anschluß*. On the *Arbeitsgemeinschaft* and its prominent members see BA (Berlin), R 8011/10. On the positive publicity which the founding of the *Arbeitsgemeinschaft* received, see BA (Berlin), R 8011/1. Finally, Gerhard von Branca, *Die Deutsch-österreichische Arbeitsgemeinschaft* (Munich, 1927).

[74] See Wilhelm Heile's article in *Berliner Tageblatt*, 15 Aug. 1925 as well as Gustav Stolper, 'Die Vision Mitteleuropas', *Die Hilfe*, XXXV (1929), 402. For the same view from nationalist sources, see Karl Haushofer, 'Mitteleuropa und der Anschluß', in Friedrich Kleinwächter and Heinz von Paller (eds.), *Die Anschlußfrage in ihrer kulturellen, politischen und wirtschaftlichen Bedeutung* (Vienna, 1930), 150–3. Hans Zehrer, 'Die Ideen der Außenpolitik', *Die Tat*, XXI (1929), 109.

[75] Since the beginning of 1927 the 'Reichsverband der Deutschen Industrie' and the German 'Industrie- und Handelstag' held joint meetings with their Austrian counterparts in order to prepare for economic unification. On this see Suval, *Anschluss Question*, 108. For a contemporary assessment of the economic importance of the *Anschluß* question see Bruno von Enderes, *Die wirtschaftliche Bedeutung der Anschlußfrage* (Leipzig, 1929).

[76] Werner Christiansen, 'Ueber die Zollunion zum Anschluß', *Die Hilfe*, XXXVII (1931), 249–51, here p. 251.

[77] Cabinet minutes of 18 March 1931, in *Akten der Reichskanzlei: Die Kabinette Brüning*, 2. 969–71. The government's public announcement of the customs union project is reprinted in *Schulthess*, LXXII (1931), 88–90.

the severity with which Paris responded to the Austro-German customs union plans. To counter the German initiative, the Quai d'Orsay dramatically increased its financial pressure on the weaker partner, Austria.[78] Paris was able to exploit the fact that, at the time, France was the only large European nation with the resources to float large international loans. Vienna, shaken by the consequences of the Great Depression and in desperate need of international financial aid, started enquiring confidentially in April 1931 as to whether the French government would grant them a loan. When Austria's largest financial institution, the Rothschild-owned *Credit-Anstalt*, had to announce its insolvency on 12 May 1931 the whole Austrian economy was on the verge of collapse. The bankruptcy of the *Credit-Anstalt* immediately affected German banks, too, whose financial stability was already shaky before American loans were withdrawn in 1929. In the summer of 1931, the German bank crisis reached its critical peak.[79]

On 3 September 1931, Curtius and his Austrian colleague Schober were forced to assure the European Affairs Committee of the League of Nations that all plans for the establishment of a customs union between the two countries had been abandoned. Two days later, the Permanent Court of International Justice in The Hague announced, in a narrow decision of 8 to 7 votes, that the Austro-German customs union was incompatible with the principles laid down in Article 88 of the Treaty of St Germain and with the accords of the Geneva Protocol of 4 October 1922.[80]

The failure of the customs union provoked indignation across the entire political spectrum in Germany. Even in liberal circles, the outcome of Geneva and The Hague was seen as the 'worst conceivable defeat' and as proof of Germany's current inability to 'conduct an independent policy on the world stage'.[81] Meanwhile, it fell to the political right to ascribe the diplomatic defeat to the lack of 'national' will in the Brüning government and the general incapacity of the democratic state to pursue an active foreign policy.[82] The neo-

---

[78] See Haim Shamir, *Economic Crisis and French Foreign Policy 1930–1936* (Leiden, 1989), 8–10 and 27–34.

[79] On the German banking crisis see James, *German Slump*, 283–323. See, too, Edward W. Bennett, *Germany and the Diplomacy of the Financial Crisis 1931* (Cambridge, Mass., 1962), 59–74.

[80] *Schulthess*, LXXII (1931), 573–5. See, too, Krüger, *Außenpolitik*, 535.

[81] Werner Christiansen, 'Die deutsche Niederlage—was nun?', *Die Hilfe*, XXXVII (1931), 873–7, quotations on pp. 873–4. A summary of the German public's reactions to the failure of the customs union can be found in *Egelhaafs Historisch-politische Jahresübersicht* (1931), 60.

[82] See, for example, *Neue Preußische Zeitung*, 4 Sept. 1931 as well as the edition of 6 Sept. 1931. Interestingly, after the Second World War, both Curtius and Brüning denied any personal responsibility for the customs union project and its failure. See Julius Curtius, *Bemühung um österreich: Das Scheitern des Zollunionsplans von 1931* (Heidelberg, 1951), 34 as well as Brüning, *Memoiren*, 265.

conservative periodical *Die Tat* evaluated the failure of the customs union project as the 'most bitter defeat in German foreign policy since the Battle of the Ruhr'. The abandonment of vital national interests as embodied in the customs union project could not be justified to the public as '*Realpolitik*'. In fact, Curtius's 'surrender' in Geneva had been nothing less than a declaration of bankruptcy on the part of the 'ailing' Weimar system.[83] Once again, it was argued, it had become evident that the vision of a *großdeutsch* Reich dominating central Europe could only be realized after the elimination of the Treaty of Versailles *and* the Weimar state, both of which allegedly stood in the way of Germany's 'rebirth' in the forthcoming 'Third Reich'.[84]

The immediate political consequences of the failure of the customs union plans were less severe than anticipated by the right, but nevertheless noticeable. Curtius's position as Foreign Minister had become untenable and, on 3 October, Brüning urged his Foreign Minister to resign. Less than a week later, on 9 October, the Chancellor conceded to the demands of Schleicher and Hindenburg to include more nationalist politicians in his cabinet.[85]

In his subsequent government declaration of 13 October 1931, Brüning demonstrated strength. Two days earlier the extreme right, at its convention in Bad Harzburg, had severely criticized the Reich Chancellor because of his lack of success in domestic and foreign policy.[86] The Chancellor, however, declared his resolution not to wilt in the face of criticism from the right-wing opposition. He would rather be branded as 'traitor to the fatherland' than retreat from his chosen path. He could take heart in the 'beneficent precedents in the history of the Prussian and German people. At first these men, who did not lose their nerve and had the courage to pursue an unpopular policy, were scorned and ridiculed. After things had turned out for the best, however, these personalities were monopolized as examples of national conviction.'[87]

Brüning's obvious reference to Bismarck provided Hitler with a welcome cue. On 16 October 1931, *Völkischer Beobachter* published a letter Hitler had written to the Reich Chancellor. In this letter Hitler appealed to Brüning, as

[83] *Die Tat*, 1931.

[84] See Stefan Brauer, *Grundpositionen der deutschen Rechten 1871–1945* (Tübingen, 1999), 117–39. Also Hans Fenske, ' "Das 'Dritte Reich": Die Perversion der Reichsidee', in Bernd Martin (ed.), *Deutschland in Europa: Ein historischer Rückblick* (Munich, 1992), 210–30.

[85] See cabinet minutes of 10 Oct. 1931, in *Akten der Reichskanzlei: Die Kabinette Brüning*, vol. 3, 1823, n. 1. Brüning took over the office of Foreign Minister himself; Reichswehr Minister Groener also became Minister of the Interior as successor to the Centre politician and previous Reich Chancellor Wirth; the highly conservative State Secretary Joel was promoted to Minister of Justice.

[86] See *Schulthess*, LXXII (1931), 224–9.

[87] RT, 13 Oct. 1931, vol. 446, 2074.

the successor to 'the great founder of the Reich', to learn from the mistakes of the recent past, and to break with the 'dominant political ideas and tendencies of the Weimar system'. Hitler demanded that Brüning resort to more radical means in pursuing national interests, such as the project of a customs union with Austria. If, however, Brüning continued to collaborate with the Social Democrats, then, according to Hitler, success for his government would remain elusive. Bismarck, to whom the Chancellor had referred in his speech, had in contrast to Brüning 'created the preconditions which enabled him to push through his political programme'. Hitler advised the Reich Chancellor to follow the example set by Bismarck.[88]

A month before, Hitler had received 'thunderous applause' from his party followers when he cast ironic aspersions on the government's hope that a powerful *großdeutsch* Reich would arise out of the customs union with Austria. When Bismarck resolved to pursue the path leading from the *Zollverein* to the North German Federation (*Norddeutsche Bund*) and finally to the German Reich, Hitler argued, he had not relied on the parliament but rather on the military strength of his armed forces: 'Bismarck implemented his unification policy with the aid of the Prussian army. Brüning implements his policy with a rag-bag assortment [*Gemengsel*] of Social Democrats, Centrists [*Zentrümlern*], members of the German People's Party, with an elite composed of pacifists and democrats . . . He who has such forces behind him cannot pursue a policy of national reawakening!'[89]

It was moments like these during which Hitler displayed the uniqueness of his demagogic talent. Like no other politician of his time, he knew how to exploit the failure of the customs union project for his own purposes. Hitler linked his criticism of the system with the staging of his own person as the only politician with the necessary power of will to 'complete' what Bismarck had begun. What Hitler's message conveyed to the German people after the foreign policy defeat of the Brüning government in Geneva was unmistakable: only a leader of Bismarck's dimensions could bring about a revision of *both* Versailles: the *kleindeutsch* solution of 1871 and the peace settlement of 1919. This was exactly what Hitler promised to achieve. He never intended to 'restrict' himself to a revision of the Austro-German border. For the time being, however, Hitler only claimed to be the guardian of Bismarck's legacy, and the man who would overcome the *kleindeutsch* limitations of Bismarck's Reich.

---

[88] 'Offener Brief Hitlers an Heinrich Brüning, 14. Oktober 1931', in *Hitler: Reden, Schriften, Anordnungen, Februar 1925 bis Januar 1933*, vol. 4 B: *Von der Reichstagswahl bis zur Reichspräsidentenwahl*, part 2: *Juli 1931–Dezember 1931*, ed. Christian Hartmann (Munich, 1996), 138–48.

[89] 'Rede auf dem Gautag der Thüringer NSDAP in Gera, 6. September 1931', ibid. 78–9.

The idea of the *Anschluß* and its concomitant slogans, such as '*Heim ins Reich*'—originally the title of a periodical published by the largely Social Democratic Austro-German People's League—was not the only *Zeitgeist* tendency that Hitler absorbed into his own world-view. Hitler's ideological 'borrowing' was in fact systematic. None of the ideas put forward by him was original. What he offered the Germans in terms of a political programme was a crude mixture comprising the populist ideas and ideologies which were brewing in the post-war intellectual atmosphere.[90]

Hitler absorbed popular *Zeitgeist* tendencies and projected them onto the coming 'Third Reich'—a slogan invented by the neo-conservative author Arthur Moeller van den Bruck in 1923.[91] The Nazis adopted the catchphrase of the 'Third Reich', which seemed ideal to represent both their concept of a radical break with Weimar democracy and the re-establishment of historical continuity. Combined with other important reasons for supporting the NSDAP (such as fear of Marxism, frustrated career ambitions, and the erosion of social prestige and professional security) it was the utopia of this coming 'Third Reich', allegedly freed from social, economic, and political tensions, which appealed to many voters in times of economic and political despair.[92] Hitler equally benefited from the widely entertained hope for a strong political leadership which would encapsulate the traditions of German history and which would commit itself to the idea of fulfilling the unique 'world mission' of the German people. Whoever could satisfy this seemingly paradoxical but nevertheless widespread thirst for continuity *and* change could be sure of finding wide approval from the electorate.[93]

Hitler and other high-ranking Nazis consciously appealed to the people's desire for the restoration of continuity. In a campaign rally in April 1932—shortly before the Prussian *Landtag* elections—Joseph Goebbels insisted that 'National Socialism has every right to claim that it embodies the idea of Prussia. Wherever in Germany we National Socialists may stand, we are Prussians.

---

[90] On this see, for example, Verhey, *Spirit of 1914*, particularly 213 ff. See, too, Nobert Götz, 'Ungleiche Geschwister. Die Konstruktion von nationalsozialistischer Volksgemeinschaft und schwedischem Volksheim', Ph.D. thesis (Berlin, 1999), 87 ff.; Chickering, '*We men who feel most German*', 37. Also, Karl Lange, 'Der Terminus Lebensraum in Hitlers Mein Kampf', *Vierteljahreshefte für Zeitgeschichte*, XIII (1965), 426–37. Finally, Woodruff D. Smith, *The Ideological Origins of Nazi Imperialism* (New York and Oxford, 1986), 224–30.

[91] Arthur Moeller van den Bruck, *Das dritte Reich*, ed. Hans Schwarz, 3rd edn. (Hamburg, 1931).

[92] Thomas C. Childers, *The Nazi Voter: The Social Foundations of Fascism in Germany, 1919–1933* (Chapel Hill and London, 1983), 264–5.

[93] See Martin Broszat, 'Soziale Motivation und Führerbindung des Nationalsozialismus', *Vierteljahreshefte für Zeitgeschichte*, XVIII (1970), 392–409. On the importance of historical continuity and the impact of a 'hero cult' for the National Socialist movement, see Behrenbeck, *Kult um die toten Helden*.

The idea we promote is Prussian. What we fight for is the modernized version of those ideals pursued by Frederick William I, Frederick the Great, and Bismarck.'[94]

At the same time, the NSDAP used the Bismarck myth to express its unrivalled opposition to the Weimar Republic. During the campaign for the Reichstag elections, Hitler never tired of pointing out that the parties of the November Revolution had presided over the unparalleled demise of every aspect of German life. Even before the electoral campaign for the July general elections began, Hitler combined this theme with the Bismarck myth: 'Thirteen years have passed [since the revolution]. Thirteen years were enough for Bismarck to transform the Prussia of Olmütz into the Prussia of the German Reich founding. It was enough time for him to bring Germany out of its state of disunity and lead it to a beautiful and prosperous future. A system which has ruled as unrestricted as the current one rules in Germany must be able, after thirteen years, to point to some successes.'[95]

The general election results of 31 July 1932 indicated that similar beliefs were held by vast sections of the German population. With a total turnout of 84.1 per cent, the highest in a Reichstag election in the Weimar Era, the NSDAP managed to gain a share of 37.4 per cent of the popular vote. That was an increase of 19.1 per cent from the previous Reichstag elections and, accordingly, the number of National Socialist Reichstag mandates rose from 107 to 230.[96]

Even though the NSDAP enjoyed cross-class support, they had been particularly successful in mobilizing previous non-voters and those who in previous elections had voted for the two liberal parties, the DNVP, or for the splinter parties.[97] Evidence suggests that many of Hitler's supporters came from political circles in which the Bismarck cult enjoyed its greatest adherence. Between 1930 and 1933, the NSDAP proved to be particularly popular in Hindenburg's strongholds in the presidential elections of 1925, regardless of the social structure of the constituency. Equally, the NSDAP received fewer votes wherever Hindenburg had been unsuccessful in 1925.[98] Whoever had hoped in 1925 that Hindenburg would become a 'second Bismarck' now turned to Hitler.[99]

---

[94] Goebbels, as quoted in Manfred Schlenke, 'Nationalsozialismus und Preußen / Preußentum', in Otto Büsch (ed.), *Das Preußenbild in der Geschichte* (Berlin and New York, 1981), 247–64, here p. 248.

[95] Hitler's speech in Delmenhorst on 25 May 1932, in *Hitler: Reden, Schriften, Anordnungen, Februar 1925 bis Januar 1933*, vol. 5: *Von der Reichspräsidentschaftswahl bis zur Machtergreifung, April 1932–Januar 1933*, part 1: *April 1932–September 1932*, ed. Klaus A. Lankheit (Munich, 1996), 131–5, here p. 132. On the Olmütz Punctuation of 29 November 1850, see Heinrich Lutz, *Zwischen Habsburg und Preußen. Deutschland 1815–1866* (Berlin, 1994), 386–9. [96] Falter, *Wahlen*, 44.

[97] See Jürgen Falter, *Hitlers Wähler* (Munich, 1991), 369. [98] Ibid. 357–60.

[99] See Falter, *Wahlen*, 46, and id., 'The Two Hindenburg Elections of 1925 and 1932: A Total Reversal of Voter Coalitions', *Central European History*, XXIII (1990), 225–41.

The Bismarckians' receptiveness to Hitler was also evident in the case of the German Nationalists' Bismarck League, which in the 1930s lost more and more members to the NSDAP's Hitler Youth. Horst Wessel, for example, the famous Berlin SA leader who was murdered in 1930 and was later stylized as a 'hero of the Nazi movement', had started his political career in the DNVP's Bismarck Youth before converting to National Socialism.[100] Even Otto von Bismarck Jr., who had been an honorary member of the Bismarck Youth, and his younger brother Gottfried joined the Nazi: Party in the early 1930s.[101]

Within the industrial elite, too, promoters of the Bismarck myth were particularly quick to profess their sympathy for Hitler. Fritz Thyssen and Emil Kirdorff were among the first leading industrialists to support Hitler openly.[102] Both Thyssen and Kirdorff had sat on the board of the Bismarck Film Company and both were members of the executive committee of the League for the Erection of a Bismarck National Monument. It is likely that Hitler was aware of this connection because he played the 'Bismarck card' when giving his famous speech in the Düsseldorf Industry Club on 26 January 1932. Hitler promised to re-establish the 'unity of will' which the German nation had shown in Bismarck's time. The audience greeted his words with considerable applause.[103]

The close affinity between the Bismarck myth and the belief in Hitler as a new 'saviour' was no secret to his contemporaries. Confronted with the increasing number of calls for a 'second Bismarck', the chief editor of *Weltbühne*, Carl von Ossietzky, had already reflected upon the connection between Bismarck and Hitler in early 1931. Hitler's success in presenting himself as a national redeemer aroused a feeling of incomprehension in the 1935 Nobel Peace laureate. Ossietzky emphasized that despite all due criticism of his domestic policy, Bismarck had been one of the most important figures of the past century (*'eine Jahrhundertgestalt'*). 'But', he continued, 'who is Adolf Hitler? How intellectually deprived a people must be to see a leader, a personality worthy of emulation, in this absurd poltroon! How big their psychological incapacity must be, how impoverished their instinct for the genuine and the false! Well, Hitler will never proclaim the "Third Reich", Hitler will meet his end . . . .'[104]

---

[100] See Jay W. Baird, *To Die for Germany: Heroes in the Nazi Pantheon* (Bloomington, Ind., 1990), 75 ff.
[101] See Malinowski, *Vom König zum Führer*, 500.
[102] Kirdorf became a member of the NSDAP in 1927. Thyssen was a sympathizer of Hitler's movement since the early 1930s. On this see Henry Ashby Turner, Jr., *German Big Business and the Rise of Hitler* (New York and Oxford, 1985), 91 and 145–6.
[103] Ibid. 204–19. See, too, Reinhard Neebe, *Grossindustrie, Staat und NSDAP 1930–1933: Paul Silverberg und der Reichsverband der Deutschen Industrie in der Krise der Weimarer Republik* (Goettingen, 1981), 119 ff.
[104] Carl von Ossietzky, 'Zur Reichsgründungsfeier', *Die Weltbühne*, XXVII (1931), 79–81.

Despite the Nazis' landslide success in the first Reichstag elections of 1932, it seemed as if Ossietzky's prediction would come true. Hindenburg was still not willing to go beyond offering the 'Bohemian corporal' the post of vice-chancellor in a cabinet led by Papen. And the grave electoral setbacks which the NSDAP experienced in the second Reichstag elections of 1932 (as well as the similarly disappointing results of the local elections in Thuringia on 4 December 1932) strengthened the conviction among many contemporaries that Hitler's political demise was only a question of time.[105]

This assumption proved to be premature. On the evening of 29 January 1933, Franz von Papen informed Hindenburg that if Hitler was appointed as Chancellor, 'reliable' conservative politicians (among them three leading members of the League for the Erection of a Bismarck National Monument, Count Schwerin von Krosigk as Minister of Finance, Hugenberg as Economics Minister, and Seldte as Minister of Labour) would determine the character of his cabinet. On these grounds, the Reich President was willing to relinquish his reservations with regard to Hitler's appointment as Reich Chancellor.[106] On the morning of 30 January 1933, Hitler, who appeared to be 'framed in' by the 'Bismarckians', swore his oath of allegiance to the Weimar Constitution.[107]

Hitler's appointment as Chancellor of the Reich was by no means the inevitable outcome to the multi-dimensional German state crisis which had begun with the collapse of Hermann Müller's Grand Coalition government on 27 March.[108] Nor was it the necessary result of Weimar Germany's battle over the past, even if right-wing circles suggested in 1933 that the 'Bismarckian' tradition had emerged victoriously from this conflict. Hitler was only appointed as Chancellor because Hindenburg and his camarilla urgently needed a broad popular basis for their authoritarian politics. In this respect, the popular support which the National Socialists enjoyed made the appointment of Hitler as

---

[105] Compared to the previous Reichstag elections on 31 July, the NSDAP lost over 2 million votes in November 1932. Their share sank from 37.3% to 33.1%, and the number of Reichstag mandates from 230 to 196. See Falter, *Wahlen*, 74. For an analysis of the election results see Thomas C. Childers, 'The Limits of National Socialist Mobilisation: The Election of 6 November 1932 and the Fragmentation of the Nazi Constituency', in id. (ed.), *The Formation of the Nazi Constituency 1919–1933* (London and Sydney, 1986), 232–59. On the election results in Thuringia see Falter, *Wahlen*, 96. The end of Hitler was predicted, for example, by *Simplicissimus* in its edition of January 1933. In the *Weltbühne*, similar predictions can be found. See the anonymous article, 'Die größte Firma', *Die Weltbühne*, XXIX (1933).

[106] On the context see Henry Ashby Turner, Jr., *Hitler's Thirty Days to Power: January 1933* (Reading, Mass., 1996).

[107] See Mommsen, *Weimar*, 526 ff.

[108] See Ian Kershaw, 'Der 30. Januar 1933: Ausweg aus der Staatskrise und Anfang des Staatsverfalls', in Heinrich August Winkler (ed.), *Die deutsche Staatskrise 1930–1933: Handlungsspielräume und Alternativen* (Munich, 1992), 277–84.

head of government *possible*. Even though a majority of Germans had voted against Hitler in the Reichstag elections of 6 November 1932, he was still the leader of the strongest political party.

Of the manifold causes of the rise of the National Socialist movement to become the strongest party in Germany, there can be no doubt that the public's longing for a saviour-like 'Führer', which had intensified throughout the 1920s, featured prominently. By the late 1920s, as a result of the growing political and economic crisis of the depression era, the public's perception of Weimar democracy as a total failure allowed the idea of charismatic leadership to move from the wings of politics to centre stage. It did not escape Hitler's attention that Bismarck was widely perceived as the ultimate model of such a heroic leadership. As the well-respected Munich historian Karl Alexander von Müller had already exclaimed in 1929, it was Bismarck's image 'which appears in front of us, when we hope' for the 'future leader'.[109] When this future leader of the German people emerges, Müller concluded, 'he will greet the man we memorize today as his relative and predecessor'.[110]

In precisely this respect, the Bismarck myth helped to create a political climate which smoothed the way for Hitler's success. Hitler was cunning enough to seize the political opportunities which were latent in the Bismarck myth. With genuine virtuosity Hitler appealed to existing myths and used them for his own purposes. In so doing, he narrowed the gulf between large parts of middle-class Germany and his own political movement, as is evident from the immediate reactions to Hitler's appointment. Lieutenant-General Richard Kaden, for example, commented on the events of January 1933 with the words:

How clearly the turn of fate of our people on 30 January confirms the old empirical principle, that only the leader, the single personality, never the masses, can bring liberation. . . . We saw that in Bismarck, now we see it again in Hitler, whose flaming battle cries, in combination with national sentiment and social understanding, have stirred up and united the masses.[111]

How little Hitler's Chancellorship would actually have in common with Bismarck's rule should have been obvious to anyone who had read *Mein Kampf* or who had listened to any of Hitler's speeches. Hitler made no secret of his

---

[109] Karl Alexander von Müller at the 'Third German Bismarck Day' in Munich, 14 September 1929, as quoted in: *Bismarck-Blatt*, Jan. 1930, 3–8.
[110] Karl Alexander von Müller, 'Bismarck und die heutige Zeit', in *Bismarck-Blatt*, Jan. 1930, 3–8, here p. 8. See, too, the similar speech given by the former Reichstag president, Max Wallraf, at the 'Fourth German Bismarck Day' in Bingen (Rhineland) in September 1931. The speech is printed in *Bismarck-Blatt*, Nov. 1931.
[111] Richard Kaden, *In der alten Armee: Lebenserinnerungen aus Frieden und Krieg* (Groitzsch, 1933), 311.

unshakable determination to radically break with all of the parliamentary and constitutional traditions which had also characterized Bismarck's Reich. For the moment, however, the critical reasoning of a minority, who warned against analogies being drawn between Hitler and Bismarck or between '1871' and '1933', faded into the background. Heinrich Mann's verdict that Hitler's references to Frederick the Great and Bismarck could not legitimize his political actions, since neither one of the two would have accepted him as German Chancellor, found no echo whatsoever in public debate after 30 January 1933.[112] Instead, the dominant voices were those celebrating the 'seizure of power' as a victory of the 'ideas of 1871'. In accordance with this general sentiment, the majority of Germans greeted Hitler as the man who would continue and complete the work of Bismarck. For some of them it took twelve years to realize that the 'Bismarckians' had won a Pyrrhic victory and that Hitler was in fact the man who would destroy the Reich that Bismarck had created in 1871.

---

[112] Heinrich Mann, *Der Hass: deutsche Zeitgeschichte* (Amsterdam, 1933), 79 and 90–2. See, too, Thomas Mann's diary entry of 8 September 1933, in Thomas Mann, *Tagebücher 1933–1934*, ed. Peter de Mendelssohn (Frankfurt, 1977), 173.

9

Epilogue: Bismarck between the 'Seizure of Power' and Reunification (1933–1990)

Bismarck under the swastika

Two months after Hitler's appointment as German Chancellor, the historian Otto Westphal triumphantly proclaimed the end of an era. The period during which 'Bismarck's enemies' had ruled over Germany was irrevocably over. Westphal concluded his talk at Göttingen's Historical Society by emphasizing that Germany was currently witnessing a 'revolution and a re-creation of Bismarck's Reich at the same time, a revolutionary transformation with deep historical sympathies'.[1]

Westphal's interpretation of 30 January 1933 as a victory of the 'Bismarckian' tradition over the 'spirit of 1918' indicates how successful Nazi propaganda was in nurturing conservative illusions about the true character of the 'Third Reich'. In early May 1933, both the *Frankfurter Illustrierte* and *Münchner Neueste Presse* reported in lengthy features that construction works at the Bismarck National Monument in Bingen had begun thanks to the Führer's initiative.[2] Hitler had in fact no responsibility at all for the building work. In 1932, Max Wallraf's successor as chairman of the League for the Erection of a Bismarck National Monument succeeded in securing Hindenburg's patronage of the organization. It was on his assurances that the construction works for the Bismarck National Monument in Bingen started on 30 January 1933—a coincidence which Nazi propaganda knew how to exploit.[3]

Shortly afterwards, on 5 March 1933, Hitler gave another example of his skilful demagogic use of historical myths when he announced a new flag decree over the radio. In conjunction with the swastika banner, the black, white, and red colours of the Bismarckreich would once again become the national flag of

---

[1] Otto Westphal, 'Bismarck und Hitler', *Vergangenheit und Gegenwart*, XXIII (1933), 469–81, here p. 481.
[2] Dormann, 'Bismarck-Nationaldenkmal', 1083.
[3] On the beginning of the construction works in Bingen, see Hauptstaatsarchiv Düsseldorf, file 'Verein zur Errichtung eines BND', vol. 8, p. 375.

the German Empire. 'These flags', so Hitler suggested, 'combine Imperial Germany's glorious past and the powerful rebirth of the German nation. United they shall symbolize the power of the state and the internal unity of all German nationalist circles.'[4]

The flag change was a prelude to the festive opening of the new Reichstag on 21 March 1933. Joseph Goebbels, the recently appointed Propaganda Minister of Hitler's cabinet, had chosen the place and date of the 'Day of Potsdam' for symbolic reasons. On 21 March 1871, Bismarck had opened the first sitting of the German Reichstag. Furthermore, the Garrison Church at Potsdam was the burial place of Frederick the Great. Both the day and the setting were therefore ideal to demonstrate National Socialism's attachment to Prusso-German history. The ceremony itself was a solemn commemoration of Prussia's glory. Veterans of the old Prussian army marched by the Garrison Church, which had been decorated with black, white, and red banners. The high point of the day was the meeting of Hindenburg and Hitler on the steps of the Garrison Church. The Führer went up to the uniformed Reich President, shook his hand, and bowed in respect over the coffin of Frederick the Great.[5]

The 'Day of Potsdam' did not fail to serve its intended purpose. In reflecting upon 21 March 1933, the historian Johannes Haller, for example, declared with relief that 'the beginning has been made. We have left the false path and found again the right way . . . Today he [Hitler] stands where Bismarck stood once, the inheritor, the continuer, and, should God wish it, the completer of his [Bismarck's] works. When the old Field Marshal, the Prussian soldier, and the youthful Chancellor, the South German son of the people, shook hands by the sarcophagus of Frederick the Great . . . then the seed which Bismarck sowed grew, the tree, which he had planted, and which had been struck by lightning, began to bloom once again.'[6]

Haller's judgement was premature. Bismarck's Germany was not 'resurrected' on 21 March 1933. The new rulers only appropriated the myths surrounding Germany's past in order to give their rule the appearance of historical legitimacy. This 'wooing' of Prusso-German history was as much a 'central element of the seizure of power and consolidation period' as were the violent

---

[4] Schulthess, LXXIV (1933), 56–66.

[5] On the 'Day of Potsdam' see the article by Werner Freitag, 'Nationale Mythen und kirchliches Heil: Der "Tag von Potsdam"', *Westfälische Forschungen*, XLI (1991), 379–430.

[6] Johannes Haller, 'Zum 1. April 1933', in id., *Reden und Aufsätze zur Geschichte und Politik* (Stuttgart and Berlin, 1934), 376–81, here p. 381. See, too, Bernd Faulenbach, 'Die "nationale Revolution" und die deutsche Geschichte: Zum zeitgenössischen Urteil der Historiker', in Wolfgang Michalka (ed.), *Die nationalsozialistische Machtergreifung* (Paderborn, Munich, Vienna, and Zurich, 1984), 357–71.

attacks against the political enemies of National Socialism.[7] Between 30 January and early March 1933 alone, 51 opponents to the new regime were killed and hundreds were injured in street fights.[8] The overall pogrom atmosphere increased after the Reichstag fire of 27 February 1933.[9] Only one day later, the Hitler cabinet announced two emergency decrees: one 'for the Protection of the Nation and the State' and another to counter 'Treason against the German Nation'. Important civil rights were suspended 'temporarily'. The 'Reichstag Fire Decree' (as it was commonly referred to) was nothing less than 'the proclamation of the permanent state of emergency' in Germany.[10] Along with leading Communist party functionaries like Ernst Thälmann and the editor of *Rote Fahne*, Werner Hirsch, numerous left-wing intellectuals (such as Carl von Ossietzky, Erich Mühsam, and Egon Erwin Kisch) were arrested.

In the following months, the process of eliminating the 'internal enemies of the Reich' continued to go hand in hand with repeated assurances of the historical legitimacy of the 'Third Reich'. Only a week after the Enabling Law had been passed by the Reichstag on 23 March 1933 with a comfortable majority of 444 (out of 642) votes, Bismarck's birthday on 1 April provided an ideal opportunity to exploit the Bismarck myth for National Socialism.[11] In a nationwide broadcasted speech of 1 April 1933 held at the Bismarck Memorial on the banks of Lake Müggel in Berlin, Joseph Goebbels underlined the similarities between Germany's current leader and his historical 'model', the Iron Chancellor: 'Bismarck was the great political revolutionary of the nineteenth century, Hitler is the great political revolutionary of the twentieth century. . . . We want to promise the great dead man and his name: the Reich is in safe hands with us!'[12]

While Goebbels spoke on the parallels between Hitler and Bismarck, the first co-ordinated action of the Nazi regime against Jewish-owned businesses was taking place. Under the slogan 'Germans! Defend yourselves! Do not buy

---

[7] Karl Dietrich Bracher, 'Das Ende Preußens', in Karl Dietrich Erdmann (ed.), *Preußen: Seine Wirkung auf die deutsche Geschichte* (Stuttgart, 1985), 281–307, here p. 298.

[8] Figures taken from Jost Dülffer, *Nazi Germany 1933–1945: Faith and Annihilation*, translated from the German by Dean Scott McMurry (London, 1996), 32.

[9] On the Reichstag fire, see, for example, Hans Mommsen, 'Der Reichstagsbrand und seine politischen Folgen', *Vierteljahreshefte für Zeitgeschichte*, XII (1964), 351–413.

[10] Karl Dietrich Bracher, *The German Dictatorship: The Origins, Structure, and Effects of National Socialism*, translated from German into English by Jean Steinberg (London, 1971), 197.

[11] On the passing of the Enabling Law, see RT, 23 Mar. 1933, vol. 457, 45. See, too, Karl Dietrich Bracher, 'Stufen der Machtergreifung', in id. *et al.* (eds.), *Die Nationalsozialistische Machtergreifung: Studien zur Errichtung des totalitären Herrschaftssystems in Deutschland 1933/34*, 2nd edn. (Cologne, 1962), 31–368, here pp. 144 ff.

[12] Goebbels as quoted in *Berliner Lokal-Anzeiger*, 2 Apr. 1933. Another large commemoration event, jointly organized by the Nazis, the Stahlhelm, the BVP, and the DNVP, was held at the Rottmannshöhe near Lake Starnberg (Bavaria). See *Völkischer Beobachter* (Munich edition), 3 Apr. 1933.

from Jews!', the NSDAP called for a nationwide boycott of Jewish shops on 1 April 1933.[13] Goebbels' speech in Berlin was designed to underscore the historical mission of the 'Third Reich', its legitimate right to fight all 'internal enemies' including the Jews. At the same time, the references to Bismarck and other 'heroes' of Prusso-German history served to appease Hitler's German Nationalist partners, whose ministers in the government had objected not only to the boycott of Jewish shops and institutions, but also to the increasing street violence instigated by the SA in the first weeks after 30 January 1933.[14]

It was not long before Hitler gave up his strategic conciliatory policy towards the conservatives who were to become the next victims of the process of *Gleichschaltung*. Within a couple of months, the whole pluralistic parliamentary system of Weimar—including nationalist organizations and parties—was replaced by a one-party state.[15] On 27 June 1933, the leadership of the German Nationalist Front (formerly the DNVP) announced its affiliation with the NSDAP in a 'friendship agreement'.[16] 'Voluntary' assimilation and official bans on parties and organizations went hand in hand. The leader of the Berlin Bismarck League, Georg Haever, tried to rescue his organization's independence by expressing his unreserved support for the new regime. In a personal letter to Hitler, Haever offered his organization's 'help in the great task of building the new Reich'.[17] His assurances of loyalty were of no use. On the basis of the emergency decree 'for the Protection of the Nation and the State' of 28 February 1933—originally issued to counter the alleged threat of Communist insurrections—the Bismarck League was dissolved and its assets confiscated.[18]

National Socialist rule was further consolidated by the establishment of the one-party state on 14 July 1933 and the subsequent elimination of internal party opposition in the 'Night of the Long Knives' of 30 June 1934.[19] Once this was

---

[13] On this see Goebbels, *Tagebücher*, 2. 400–1. (1–2 Apr. 1933). For a detailed account of the boycott on 1 April 1933, see Saul Friedländer, *Nazi Germany and the Jews: The Years of Persecution 1933–39* (London, 1997), 20–4. See, too, Avraham Barkai, *Vom Boykott zur 'Entjudung': Der wirtschaftliche Existenzkampf der Juden im Dritten Reich 1933–1943* (Frankfurt, 1987), 26 ff.

[14] On the German Nationalists' objections to the boycott, see AdR, *Kabinett Hitler*, as well as Friedländer, *Nazi Germany*, 20. On the Bismarck myth and its role in the 'appeasement' of the conservative right, see Lothar Gall, 'Die Deutschen und Bismarck', 532. Similarly, Machtan (ed.), *National-Mythos*, 56.

[15] Bracher, *German Dictatorship*, 214 ff.

[16] See Friedrich Freiherr von Gaertringen, 'Die Deutschnationale Volkspartei', in Erich Mathias and Rudolf Morsey (eds.), *Das Ende der Parteien 1933* (Düsseldorf, 1960), 543–652, here p. 652.

[17] BA (Berlin), R43 I/2655.

[18] See Gaertringen, 'Deutschnationale Volkspartei', 610–11. See, too, Arno Klönne, *Jugend im Dritten Reich* (Munich, 1990), 20.

[19] See Immo von Fallois, *Kalkül und Illusion: Der Machtkampf zwischen Reichswehr und SA während der Röhm-Krise 1934* (Berlin, 1994), 104 ff. On the consolidation of the Nazi regime in general, see Kershaw, *Hubris*, 597 ff.

achieved, the old nationalist myths were pushed into the background. Bismarck, so it seemed, had fulfilled his role for Germany's new rulers.[20] In the summer of 1934, shortly after the Röhm purge, the Pan-German League's Bismarck celebrations were declared illegal and the work on the Bismarck National Monument in Bingen was stopped, never to be resumed.[21] In the same year, the Bismarck memorial in Munich, which had only been erected in 1931, was moved from the Ludwig Bridge to a less prominent spot.[22]

To be sure, Bismarck did not disappear completely from public life. However, the myth was appropriated by an all-embracing totalitarian regime which could not allow the historical mission of its own quasi-religious leader to be overshadowed by the deeds of other 'great men' in German history. Both Bismarck and Frederick the Great were consequently reinvented as Hitler's spiritual predecessors, whose work was about to be completed by the 'greatest leader of all times'. This quasi-official reading of history found its first expression in a postcard printed in millions on the occasion of Hitler's forty-fourth birthday on 20 April 1933.[23] Three men—each with his own caption—were pictured on the postcard: Frederick the Great 'brought about Prussia's powerful position through his military successes, the protection of acquisitions, improvement of the army and the legal system, reorganizing the administration and establishing new settlement areas, and thus laid the foundations for the German Reich'. Otto von Bismarck 'founded first the North German Federation and then the German Reich, created the Triple Alliance with Austria and Italy, acquired colonies and thus made Germany into a great power'. Adolf Hitler finally 'put an end to the destruction of the German Reich by Marxism and Bolshevism, restored German national self-belief, re-awoke the spirit of Potsdam and completed Bismarck's work—the unified nation-state'.[24]

Large historical exhibitions in Berlin in the mid-1930s, such as 'Eternal Germany' (a presentation of 'immortal' German books such as Bismarck's *Gedanken und Erinnerungen*, and Hitler's *Mein Kampf*) or 'The German Face

[20] Wilhelm Mommsen, 'Der Kampf um das Bismarck-Bild', *Universitas*, V (1950), 273–80, here p. 275. Also Emil Franzen, 'Das Bismarck-Bild in unserer Zeit', *Neues Abendland*, V (1950), 223–30. See, too, Zmarzlik, *Bismarckbild*, particularly pp. 18, 21–2, and 35.

[21] See Freisel, *Bismarckbild der Alldeutschen*, 98. See, too, the protocol of the last executive committee meeting on 30 December 1936, in Hauptstaatsarchiv Düsseldorf, file 'Verein zur Errichtung eines BND', vol. 6 I, 323.

[22] Rosenfeld, *Munich and Memory*, 114.

[23] See Manfred Schlenke, 'Nationalsozialismus und Preußen: Legitimation durch Tradition', in id. (ed.), *Preußische Geschichte: Eine Bilanz in Daten und Deutungen*, 2nd edn. (Freiburg and Würzburg, 1991), 262–7, here p. 266.

[24] Machtan (ed.), *National-Mythos*, 50.

over the Centuries' (a collection of portraits of 'great Germans'), adopted a similar historical schema of rupture and recovery: the German ascent had begun with Hermann's battle against Rome and was continued under Frederick the Great and Bismarck. After the temporary low point of German history, marked by Bismarck's dismissal in 1890 and the Weimar Republic, continuity had been re-established through the 'national rebirth' of 1933.[25]

The transformation of Weimar Germany's pluralistic historical discourse into the officially regulated historical narratives of Nazi Germany was also reflected in school textbooks, which soon adopted a *mélange* of traditional nationalist images of Bismarck combined with specifically National Socialist views. School textbooks dating from the Nazi period interpreted Bismarck as an outstanding German genius who had realized the 'centuries-old' desire of the Germans for national unity.[26] The parliament and its 'Jewish infiltrated' parties, on the other hand, were portrayed as the greatest obstacles to Bismarck's policies. By eliminating the party political system, Adolf Hitler had consequently removed the most important reason for Germany's internal fragmentation.[27]

Karl Dietrich Erdmann, who was to become one of the most influential historians in the Federal Republic, strongly supported this view in a history textbook for grammar and senior schools.[28] Erdmann and many of his colleagues thus performed a crucial role for Germany's new rulers: historiography was used to justify and legitimize the Nazis' world-view.[29]

The official image of Hitler as the man who had completed Bismarck's work could be promoted even more convincingly after the *Anschluß* of Austria in March 1938.[30] In *Völkischer Beobachter*, the Austro-German historian Heinrich Ritter von Srbik proclaimed that Bismarck's unfulfilled historical mission was now completed: 'Bismarck's greatness is not diminished when we . . . consider

[25] Hans-Ulrich Thamer, 'Geschichte und Propaganda: Kulturhistorische Ausstellungen in der NS-Zeit', *Geschichte und Gesellschaft*, XXIV (1998), 349–81, here 352 ff.

[26] On this see the detailed analysis provided by Schridde, *Bismarckbild im Geschichtsunterricht*, 54–67.

[27] Ibid. 64.

[28] See the appropriate passages of *Erbe der Ahnen* as printed in Martin Kröger and Roland Thimme, *Die Geschichtsbilder des Historikers Karl Dietrich Erdmann: Vom Dritten Reich zur Bundesrepublik* (Munich, 1996), 120–9.

[29] On the involvement of German historians in the legitimization of the Nazi regime, see, for example, Karen Schönwälder, *Historiker und Politik: Geschichtswissenschaft im Nationalsozialismus* (Frankfurt and New York, 1992). A contemporary example is the monograph by Wilhelm Mommsen, *Politische Geschichte von Bismarck bis zur Gegenwart 1850–1933* (Frankfurt, 1935) in which—according to the author himself—a new (National Socialist) view of history is being adopted.

[30] See Hitler's 'Proclamation to Germany', issued on 12 March 1938, as quoted in *The Speeches of Adolf Hitler, April 1922–August 1939*, ed. Max Domarus, translated from German into English by Norman H. Baynes (Oxford, 1942).

his [Bismarck's] Reich only as a highly important step in the development of the German people and in the history of the German Empire.'[31]

Srbik's enthusiasm over the *Anschluß* was typical of the public response in the Reich. More than 99 per cent of the population of Germany and Austria had voted for their countries' 'reunification'. However unrealistic this figure might be—the conditions under which the plebiscite of April 1938 was held can hardly be described as democratic—there is every reason to assume that the *Anschluß* was popular.[32] In the eyes of many of his fellow countrymen, the Führer had finally fulfilled Bismarck's legacy.

The completion of his 'highest historical mission' enabled Hitler to step out of Bismarck's shadow.[33] A few months after the *Anschluß*, the 'founder of the Greater German Reich' travelled to Friedrichsruh to visit the grave of the 'creator of the *kleindeutsch* Reich'. On 13 February 1939, Hitler laid a laurel wreath on Bismarck's sarcophagus.[34] The following day, the Führer attended the launching of the *Bismarck*, Germany's largest battleship, in Hamburg. He explained his reasons for choosing the battleship's name to the 50,000 invited guests—including the majority of cabinet members and many senior military officers—by saying: 'As Führer of the German people and Chancellor of the Reich I can give this ship no finer name from our history than the name of the man who as a true knight, without fear and without reproach, was the creator of that German Empire whose resurrection from the direst misery and whose wonderful enlargement has been granted to us by Providence.'[35]

With the outbreak of the Second World War in September 1939, Bismarck disappeared almost entirely from National Socialist propaganda. The only exception was Wolfgang Liebeneiner's two-part Bismarck film of 1940–2.[36] Some leading Nazis were, in fact, rather sceptical about the 'educational' value of these films. The National Socialist chief ideologist, Alfred Rosenberg, was

---

[31] *Völkischen Beobachter*, 10 Apr. 1938.

[32] See Hellmuth Auerbach, 'Volksstimmung und veröffentlichte Meinung in Deutschland zwischen März und November 1938', in Franz Knipping and Klaus-Jürgen Müller (eds.), *Machtbewußtsein in Deutschland am Vorabend des Zweiten Weltkrieges* (Paderborn, 1984), 273–93.

[33] *Hitler: Reden und Proklamationen, 1932–1945*, ed. Max Domarus, 2 vols. (Wiesbaden, 1973), here 2. 830.

[34] The German News Agency's report about this visit is published ibid., 1077.

[35] Hitler's speech as quoted in *The Times*, 15 Feb. 1939. *Völkischer Beobachter*'s front-page account of Hitler's historical interpretation of Bismarck was entitled 'Wegbereiter des neuen Reiches', *Völkischer Beobachter*, 15 Feb. 1939. See, too, Herbert D. Andrews, 'Hitler, Bismarck and History', *German Studies Review*, XIV (1991), 511–36.

[36] See Boguslaw Drewniak, *Der deutsche Film 1938–1945* (Düsseldorf, 1987), 198–9. See, too, John E. Davidson, 'Working for the man, whoever that may be: The Vocation of Wolfgang Liebeneiner', in Robert C. Reimer (ed.), *Cultural History through a National Socialist Lens: Essays on the Cinema of the Third Reich* (New York, 2000), 240–67, here p. 255. Also Machtan, 'Der inszenierte Mythos', 247–58.

'highly doubtful' as to whether the second part of the Bismarck film, *Die Ent-lassung*, should be released at all. In a letter to Hitler in early 1942, Rosenberg questioned 'whether now is the time to confront the German people with the problem of the Reinsurance Treaty [and] the unfortunate politics of Kaiser Wilhelm'.[37] To Rosenberg and others, the Bismarck myth was not suitable for ideological wartime mobilization, and it is telling that the Bismarck monument in Frankfurt (Main) was melted down for arms production soon after the outbreak of World War II.[38]

While the Nazis increasingly abandoned Bismarck as a political propaganda device, the founder of the Reich was rediscovered by the German anti-Hitler resistance. From the Moscow-based National Committee of Free Germany (NKFD) to the conservative-nationalist military resistance, highly heterogeneous opposition groups appropriated Bismarck for their own political ends.[39] The vice-president and co-founder of the NKFD, Bismarck's great-grandson Heinrich von Einsiedel, for example, used Bismarck's name extensively in his struggle against Nazi Germany. Only a few weeks after his capture during the advance of the Sixth Army against Stalingrad in September 1942, Einsiedel signed a leaflet to be dropped behind the German lines, in which he reminded his fellow countrymen of his great-grandfather's warnings of the possible consequences of a war against Russia.[40]

After the German defeat at Stalingrad in January 1943, the historical-political use of Bismarck in Soviet war propaganda increased, thereby confirming the importance which was attributed to this myth by those responsible for Moscow's ideological warfare against Nazi Germany. In the written and oral propaganda of the NKFD and the Moscow-based German Officers' League (BDO), German soldiers were reminded of the beneficent results of good Russo-German relations in the Bismarckian Era and asked to compare them with the misery caused by Hitler's megalomania. On 18 January 1944, the seventy-third anniversary of Bismarck's foundation of the Reich, Otto Korfes, a major-general in the Sixth Army defeated at Stalingrad, told his compatriots on the radio station *Freies Deutschland* that 'Germany fell into the misfortune

[37] Rosenberg, as quoted in Drewniak, *Der deutsche Film*, 198–9.

[38] The monument was melted down in April 1940. See *Frankfurter Rundschau*, 6 June 1995.

[39] On the diversified German resistance movement, see Michael C. Thornsett, *The German Opposition to Hitler: The Resistance, the Underground, and Assassination Plots 1938–1945* (London, 1997). See, too, Jürgen Schmädeke and Peter Steinbach (eds.), *Der Widerstand gegen den Nationalsozialismus: Die deutsche Gesellschaft und der Widerstand gegen Hitler* (Munich, 1994).

[40] Heinrich Graf von Einsiedel, *Tagebuch der Versuchung 1942–1950* (Frankfurt, Berlin, and Vienna, 1985), 37. See, too, the Russian leaflet 'Dieser Mann [Hitler] führt Deutschland der Katastrophe entgegen' ['This man leads Germany into the catastrophe'].

of the First World War because we deviated from Bismarck's clever and cautious policies. The gamble by which Adolf Hitler forced the German Reich into this war is an act, which Bismarck would class as a crime against the nation. Every German should be aware of the gap which separates the demagogy of Adolf Hitler from the statesmanlike intelligence and thoughtfulness of Otto von Bismarck.'[41]

Korfes' positive references to Bismarck were less surprising than one might think. Before starting his military career and while still an undergraduate at Berlin University, Korfes had been one of the favourite pupils of Professor Otto Hoetzsch, a German Nationalist expert on Bismarck and a constant defender of good bilateral relations between Soviet Russia and Germany. Korfes had been educated in a social and intellectual environment which had endorsed the Bismarck myth since the 1890s. The same holds true for the conservative opponents of Hitler within the German *Wehrmacht*. Just like Korfes, the men associated with the attempted overthrow of 20 July 1944 drew on Bismarck as a representative of a 'better Germany' in their criticism of Hitler's regime. In early July 1944, barely three weeks before the attempted assassination of Hitler by Claus von Stauffenberg, one of the leading figures of the conservative resistance, Ulrich von Hassel, visited Bismarck's estate in Friedrichsruh. On this occasion Hassel noted in his diary:

It was almost unbearable. I was close to tears most of the time at the thought of the work destroyed. Germany, situated in the middle of Europe, is the heart of Europe. Europe cannot live without a sound, strong heart. During recent years I have studied Bismarck, and his stature as a statesman grows constantly in my estimation. It is regrettable what a false picture of him we ourselves have given the world—that of the power-politician with cuirassier's boots—in our childish joy over the fact that at least someone had made Germany a name to reckon with again. In his own way he knew how to win confidence in the world; exactly the reverse of what is done today. In truth, the highest diplomacy and great moderation were his real gifts.[42]

Hassel's statement must be seen in the broader context of the German conservative resistance's political ambitions. Most of those who participated in the assassination plot of July 1944 had originally welcomed Hitler's establishment of an authoritarian regime in Germany in 1933, because they succumbed to the illusion of some form of resurrection of the old Bismarckian Empire. The 'men of 20 July 1944' did not turn against Hitler to re-establish parliamentary

[41] Korfes, as quoted in Wegner-Korfes, *Bismarck und Rußland*, 227–8.
[42] Ulrich von Hassel, *The von Hassel diaries 1938–1944: The Story of the Forces against Hitler inside Germany as recorded by Ambassador Ulrich von Hassel, a Leader of the Movement* (London, 1948), 316–17.

democracy in Germany. Instead, they intended to create a corporate state based on conservative political values similar to those endorsed in Bismarck's constitution of 1871. Facing the defeat of the German Empire, Hassel, Stauffenberg, and others wanted to save Bismarck's Reich from total destruction. What drew them into opposition was the gradual realization that the man whom they had celebrated as a 'second Bismarck' in 1933 was not re-creating and strengthening, but destroying the Reich which Bismarck had founded in 1871.[43]

In the meantime (and parallel to the declining relevance of the Bismarck myth for National Socialist wartime mobilization), Nazi war propaganda invoked memories of the Wars of Liberation against Napoleon and reminiscences of the mythical figure of Frederick the Great.[44] In the face of the collapse of the *Wehrmacht*, Frederick embodied hopes for a repetition of the 'Miracle of the House of Brandenburg' of 1762, when the death of the Tsarina and the subsequent abandonment of the anti-Prussian coalition by Russia brought about Prussia's unexpected rescue from a disastrous defeat in the Seven Years War. The way in which the King of Prussia held out grimly during the Seven Years War after the crushing defeat at Kunersdorf (1759) was celebrated as a modern-day lesson from history.[45] In the last phase of the Second World War, Frederick served as a historical 'proof' that resolution and sheer willpower could triumph over an enemy with a distinct material advantage.

It was not merely for propaganda purposes that the Nazis referred to Frederick as historical model.[46] The National Socialist ruling elite itself believed in the myth. Goebbels, for example, engrossed himself in the study of Thomas Carlyle's *Geschichte Friedrichs des Großen*, which was published in a new popular edition in 1943.[47] In the spring of 1945, he read out appropriate passages from the book to his depressed Führer. Goebbels interpreted the death of the American President Franklin Roosevelt on 12 April 1945 as a repeat of the 'Miracle of the House of Brandenburg' even though it was clear that the Allied Powers would not abandon their pursuit of Germany's unconditional surrender.[48] Ironically,

---

[43] On the motifs of the resistance and the assassination plot, see among others Theodore S. Hamerow, *On the Road to the Wolf's Lair: German Resistance to Hitler* (Cambridge, Mass., 1997); Hermann Graml *et al.* (eds.), *The German Resistance to Hitler* (London, 1970). Finally, Joachim C. Fest, *Plotting Hitler's Death: The German Resistance to Hitler 1933–1945*, trans. Bruce Little (London, 1997).

[44] On the film 'Kolberg', see David Welch, *Propaganda and the German Cinema 1933–1945*, 2nd rev. edn. (Oxford, 2001), 189–98.   [45] Behrenbeck, *Kult um die toten Helden*, 546–7.

[46] Examples of the dissemination of the myth through official propaganda channels can be found in Herfried Münkler, 'Nationalsozialismus und Preußen/Preußentum: Bericht über ein Forschungsprojekt', in Otto Busch (ed.), *Das Preußenbild in der Geschichte: Protokoll eines Symposiums* (Berlin and New York, 1981), 247–64, particularly pp. 253 ff.

[47] Thomas Carlyle, *Friedrich der Große*, translated from English into German by Kurt Linnebach (Berlin and Amsterdam, 1943).

[48] Joachim Fest, *Der Untergang: Hitler und das Ende des Dritten Reiches* (Berlin, 2002), 26. See also Helmut Heiber, *Joseph Goebbels*, 3rd edn. (Munich, 1988), 328–9.

leading National Socialists eventually became victims of the mythical illusions which they had previously used to secure their own position of power.

The gradual revision of the Bismarck myth in Western Germany

When the Second World War ended in May 1945 Bismarck's Reich was in ruins. Hitler's war had killed millions of people and left most of Germany's larger cities and industrial centres wrecked by carpet bombing and street fighting. After the unconditional surrender of the *Wehrmacht*, first at Reims on 7 May 1945 and two days later at a formal ceremony in Berlin-Karlshorst, the Allied authorities established their rule throughout Germany.

The time seemed ripe for a deconstruction of nationalist historical narratives. The crushing defeat of the 'Third Reich' and the excessive crimes committed in the name of the German nation during the Second World War (which became known to the wider public in the course of the 1946 Nuremberg trials) made it difficult for conservative circles to revive nationalist myths.[49] After 1945, unlike the aftermath of 1918, legends about the army being 'stabbed in the back' by 'Bismarck's enemies' had little chance of gaining wide public support. This was not merely the result of Allied press censorship. The failure of the bomb plot in July 1944, Germany's total military defeat, and the concrete experience of occupation prevented any conspiracy theories from coming into existence.

Instead of the re-emergence of nationalist myths, the need for historical reorientation as a precondition for a change in Germany's political culture was clearly articulated: 'What and how we remember', the Heidelberg philosopher Karl Jaspers wrote in the first edition of the periodical *Die Wandlung*, 'will be a decisive factor in our further development'.[50] An essential part of this historical reorientation was an examination of when and why Germany's historical development had taken the fateful turn which led to Hitler. For Jaspers this question was easy to answer: it was Bismarck who had laid the foundations upon which Hitler's Reich had been built.[51]

---

[49] Rainer M. Lepsius, 'Das Erbe des Nationalsozialismus und die politische Kultur der Nachfolgestaaten des "Großdeutschen Reiches"', in id., *Demokratie in Deutschland: Soziologisch-historische Konstellationsanalysen* (Göttingen, 1993), 229–45, here p. 235.

[50] *Die Wandlung*, I (1945/46), 3–6, here p. 5.

[51] Karl Jaspers, *Die Schuldfrage* (Heidelberg, 1946). See, too, Barbro Eberan, *Luther? Friedrich 'der Große'? Wagner? Nietzsche? . . . ? . . . ? Wer war an Hitler schuld? Die Debatte um die Schuldfrage 1945–1949* (Munich, 1983).

11. 'This man leads Germany towards catastrophe.' Bismarck warns the
Germans that Hitler will destroy his Reich in a Russian war propaganda
leaflet dropped behind the German lines in December 1941.

Similar, though more carefully articulated ideas, were put forward by
Friedrich Meinecke. In his 1946 book, *Die deutsche Katastrophe*, Meinecke
stated that the 'staggering course of World War I and still more of World War
II makes it impossible to pass over the query whether the germs of the later evil
were not really implanted in Bismarck's work from the outset. It is a query
which courageous and unfettered historical thinking must pose in regard to

every great and apparently beneficent historical phenomenon in which a degeneration takes place. One then breathes the atmosphere of the tragedy of history, of human and historical greatness, and also the problematical uncertainty which will ever hover around Bismarck and his work . . .'.[52] The 'road to survival', Meinecke concluded, would require historical reorientation: 'The work of Bismarck's era has been destroyed through our own fault, and we must go back beyond its ruins to seek out the ways of Goethe's era.'[53]

Meinecke's plea for an abandonment of 'Bismarckian values' in favour of a return to the 'cosmopolitanism' of the Goethe era coincided with more comprehensive attempts to revise Bismarck's image.[54] A milestone in this respect was the Bismarck biography written by Erich Eyck, a German lawyer who had been forced into exile by the National Socialists.[55] Eyck's biography, written in England, drew on the spirit of left-liberal criticism of Bismarck's domestic policies articulated in the 1920s. Without questioning Bismarck's political genius as a statesman and diplomat, Eyck accused him of having negatively influenced the political value system of his fellow Germans. Eyck suggested that Bismarck had laid the foundations for the corruption of German nationalism through his lack of respect for liberalism and democracy and through his authoritarian leadership style.[56] Eyck's criticism was taken to the extreme in Robert Saitschick's book *Bismarck und das Schicksal des deutschen Volkes*, which suggested that the founder of the Reich had introduced a tradition of militarism and a leadership cult which had led directly to the Third Reich.[57]

Even though criticism of Bismarck was much stronger in the immediate post-war era than it had ever been before, the revisionism of Meinecke, Eyck, and others was hardly representative of West German society. As far as the majority of Germans were concerned, there was no *Stunde Null*, no immediate democratic 'rebirth' of the German nation and no historical reorientation. The

---

[52] Friedrich Meinecke, *The German Catastrophe: Reflections and Recollections*, translated from the German by Sidney B. Fay (Cambridge, Mass., 1950), 13. [53] Ibid. 115.

[54] See in particular the introduction to Lothar Gall (ed.), *Das Bismarck-Problem in der Geschichtsschreibung nach 1945* (Cologne and Berlin, 1971), 9–24. See also Hans Hallmann (ed.), *Revision des Bismarck-Bildes: Die Diskussion der deutschen Fachhistoriker 1945–1955* (Darmstadt, 1972). Finally, Andreas Dorpalen, 'The German Historians and Bismarck', *The Review of Politics*, XV (1953), 26.

[55] Erich Eyck, *Bismarck: Leben und Werk*, 3 vols. (Zurich, 1941–4). The English translation is entitled *Bismarck and the German Empire*, 2 vols. (London, 1950).

[56] Eyck rejected the traditional conservative interpretation of Bismarck upon which Arnold Oskar Meyer's biography of Bismarck—written prior to 1945, but only published after the end of the Second World War—was based. See Arnold Oskar Meyer, *Bismarck: Der Mensch und der Staatsmann*, 2nd edn. (Stuttgart, 1949). The first edition was destroyed by fire during a bombing raid in 1944. The different images of Bismarck in Eyck's and Meyer's biographies were discussed at length in *Der Spiegel*, 13 Apr. 1950, 20 ff.

[57] Robert Saitschick, *Bismarck und das Schicksal des deutschen Volkes: Zur Psychologie und Geschichte der deutschen Frage* (Munich, 1949).

political climate in Western Germany in the late 1940s and 1950s was far more nationalist than the pro-Western foreign policy of the Adenauer Era suggests.[58] Glorifying novels such as Rudolf Baumgardt's *Bismarck* (1951) sold extremely well.[59] In schools and universities, many of those who had collaborated with the 'Third Reich' were either reinstated or had not been removed in the first place. Conservative historians continued to dominate academic discourse and they decisively rejected the theory of a negatively connoted German *Sonderweg* from Bismarck to Hitler. Hans Rothfels, who had been driven from his professorship in Königsberg by the Nazis in 1934, was among those who heavily criticized Eyck for his 'demonization' of Bismarck. In his 1947 review of Eyck's biography of Bismarck, Rothfels insisted that the first German Chancellor had tamed rather than promoted extreme nationalism.[60] Bismarck, Rothfels argued in one of his other numerous publications on the Iron Chancellor, had known how to prevent the threatened confrontation of European nationalisms and how to maintain the equilibrium between European alliances.[61]

However impassioned the historical debates of the late 1940s and 1950s may have been, they nevertheless differed fundamentally from the uncompromising clash of historical narratives during the Weimar Era in one decisive respect: in Weimar, Bismarck had been used as a historical reference point for right-wing circles to call into question the Republic's historical right of existence. This was never the case in the second post-war era of the twentieth century. Regardless of all the ideological differences which certainly prevailed after 1945, there was at least a far-reaching consensus that 'there could be no "return to Bismarck" in any sense of the words'.[62] To be sure, up until the late 1950s Western Germany's dominant political parties were united in their determination to re-establish the German nation-state within the borders of 1937.[63] The idea of a single, indivisible nation was upheld by the inter-party Committee for an Indivisible Germany (*Kuratorium Unteilbares Deutschland* or KUD), which was founded in reaction to the suppressed uprising of East German workers on 17 June 1953.[64] However, the idea of reunification was never linked to the hope for

---

[58] See Heinrich August Winkler, *Der lange Weg nach Westen*, vol. 2: *Deutsche Geschichte vom 'Dritten Reich' bis zur Wiedervereinigung* (Munich, 2000), 169–70.

[59] Rudolf Baumgardt, *Bismarck* (Munich and Vienna, 1951). See, too, the book review in *Der Spiegel*, 2 Jan. 1952, 32.

[60] See Hans Rothfels' review of Eyck's biography in *The Review of Politics*, IX (1947), 362–80.

[61] See the introduction to Hans Rothfels (ed.), *Bismarck und der Staat*, 2nd edn. (Stuttgart, 1953) as well as his essay collection *Bismarck: Vorträge und Abhandlungen* (Stuttgart, 1970).

[62] Wilhelm Mommsen, 'Der Kampf um das Bismarck-Bild', *Universitas*, V (1950), 273–80, here p. 280.

[63] *The Bonn Constitution: Basic Law for the Federal Republic of Germany* (New York, 1949), 5 and 56.

[64] Edgar Wolfrum, 'Der Kult um den verlorenen Nationalstaat in der Bundesrepublik Deutschland bis Mitte der 60er Jahre', *Historische Anthropologie*, V (1997), 83–114. On the 'KUD', see id., *Geschichtspolitik in*

a Bismarck-like 'saviour' which (predominant as it was during the Weimar Republic) no longer seemed appropriate after the experience of Hitler's rule. It was all too evident that the man who in 1933 the majority of Germans had regarded as a 'second Bismarck' had unleashed the Second World War and bore the responsibility for the destruction of the German Empire.

Once again, the Bismarck myth had undergone a change of content. Instead of promoting the vision of a coming Führer, 'Bismarck' reappeared as a synonym for what had been lost as a result of Hitler's war: the unified German nation-state. From 1945, and particularly after the founding of the two German states (the Federal Republic and the GDR) in 1949, Bismarck became an indispensable component of political speeches about the 'German question' in the Federal Republic.[65] At the first annual meeting of the Committee for an Indivisible Germany on 11 and 12 June 1955 in Braunschweig, for example, the Göttingen historian Hermann Heimpel emphasized in front of 5,000 listeners that the restoration of the '*kleindeutsch* Bismarckreich' was the ultimate goal of his struggle for reunification.[66]

Like Heimpel, the local FDP of North Rhine and Westphalia aligned its hopes for reunification with Bismarck's name. In 1958 they publicly suggested that a monument to German unity be built on the Elisenhöhe near Bingerbrück—the very site where the Bismarck National Monument should have been erected according to plans from the Wilhelmine era and the Weimar Republic.[67]

In the mid-1960s, the federal government under Ludwig Erhard (CDU) continued to stand unanimously behind the interpretation of Bismarck as a warrant of German reunification. In the Bundestag's ceremony on 1 April 1965 to commemorate Bismarck's 150th birthday, Chancellor Erhard insisted that in the face of Germany's division Bismarck would remain 'the symbol of the Germans' desire to be one nation'.[68] At the same time, however, Erhard was eager to emphasize that his government's aim of reunification did not

der Bundesrepublik Deutschland: Der Weg zur bundesrepublikanischen Erinnerung 1948 bis 1990 (Darmstadt, 1999), 108–9. See, too, Leo Kreuz, *Das Kuratorium Unteilbares Deutschland: Aufbau, Programmatik. Wirkung* (Opladen, 1980).

[65] On the founding of the GDR and the FRG see Christoph Kleßmann, *Die doppelte Staatsgründung: Deutsche Geschichte 1945–1955*, 5th rev. edn. (Göttingen, 1991).

[66] Hermann Heimpel, as quoted in Christoph Meyer, *Die deutschlandpolitische Doppelstrategie: Wilhelm Wolfgang Schütz und das Kuratorium Unteilbares Deutschland* (Landsberg, 1997), 122.

[67] Dorrmann, 'Bismarck-Nationaldenkmal', 1087.

[68] Ludwig Erhard's speech as printed in *Gedenkfeier zum 150. Geburtstag des Reichskanzlers Fürst Otto von Bismarck*, ed. German Foreign Office (Bonn, 1965). See, too, the commemorative speech in the Bundestag by Hans Rothfels, 'Otto von Bismarck—Persönlichkeit und Werk', *Das Parlament*, 7 Apr. 1965, and id., 'Zum 150. Geburtstag Bismarcks', *Vierteljahreshefte für Zeitgeschichte*, XVIII (1965), 225–35.

contradict the Federal Republic's commitment to democracy and western integration. In his carefully worded speech, which was edited and published by the German Foreign Office, the Chancellor stated that the Federal Republic was not at all about to combine 'our desire for reunification with the idea of an Empire along Bismarck's model'.[69]

Erhard's clarification was not only directed towards the Federal Republic's Western Allies, who might well have been irritated by the Chancellor's speech. It was also designed to counter a left-wing change of paradigms within western German society which was well on its way in the mid-1960s. When Erhard gave his 'Bismarck speech' in the Bundestag, his interpretation of Bismarck as a 'warrant of German reunification' was in fact more disputed than ever. In 1959, Karl Jaspers had distinctly rejected the present relevance of Bismarck's historical deeds in his acceptance speech for the German Publishers' Peace Prize. Jaspers' speech, held in the Frankfurt Paulskirche in the presence of President Theodor Heuss, culminated in the words: 'Today, in an entirely different world order with new world powers, the Bismarck state is history. If we live as if it [Bismarck's Reich] could once again become reality, then we let the ghosts of the past drink the life-blood of the present and hinder us from recognizing the real dangers and great possibilities of the future.'[70] As opposed to Bismarck, who had achieved German unity on the sacrifice of political freedom, the Federal Republic should recognize that the principle of political freedom was far more important than its desire for reunification.[71]

By 1965, Jaspers' views had found an ever-growing number of supporters. Immanuel Geiss, a young historian from Hamburg, wrote in *Vorwärts* on 1 April 1965: 'We, the younger generation, who no longer wish to have anything to do with heroes and hero worship, have a right to examine Bismarck's historical persona critically and sceptically, coolly and without emotions. Enough incense is being burnt in his honour these days, and many patriots will—either publicly or in private—shed sorrowful tears of patriotic mourning' over the loss of Bismarck's Reich. However, the Bismarck cult of the older generation would 'pose the greatest obstacle to a realistic world view, the lack of which has been one of the most important factors for the catastrophes of both World Wars'.[72]

---

[69] Ludwig Erhard's speech as printed in *Gedenkfeier*.

[70] Karl Jaspers, 'Wahrheit, Freiheit und Friede' in id., *Karl Jaspers: Reden zur Verleihung des Friedenspreises des deutschen Buchhandels*, ed. Hannah Arendt (Munich, 1958), 9–26.

[71] Jaspers, in *Frankfurter Allgemeine Zeitung*, 17 Aug. 1960. Equally, Karl Jaspers, *Freiheit und Wiedervereinigung: Über Aufgaben deutscher Politik* (Munich, 1960).

[72] *Vorwärts*, 31 Mar. 1965.

Geiss's statements are an indication of the gradual change in the Federal Republic's political culture, a change which had much to do with the so-called 'Fischer controversy'.[73] Although the Fischer controversy ostensibly focused on the question of Germany's responsibility for the First World War, it was nothing less than a struggle over the comprehensive revision of twentieth-century German historiography. Up until the early 1960s the distinction between the 'good' traditions of the Bismarckian Empire and the bad traditions of the 'Third Reich' had remained a constituent part of the (West) German historical self-image. The Nazi dictatorship was accordingly marginalized as a terrible 'accident' in German history.[74] In 1961, the historian Fritz Fischer questioned the empirical basis for the 'legend of innocence' in the start of the First World War with his monograph *Griff nach der Weltmacht*.[75] On the 26th German *Historikertag* in October 1964, Fischer's interpretation received strong support, although influential conservative historians such as Gerhard Ritter, Karl Dietrich Erdmann, and Egmont Zechlin rejected the 'left-wing' paradigm change in German historiography and the idea of a negatively connoted *Sonderweg* vigorously.[76] In an article for *Berliner Tagesspiegel* on 1 April 1965, Ritter decisively contradicted the theory of a continuous line between Bismarck and Hitler:

We must not always be blind to the truly great and the successful in our history and concentrate on the shadows and dirty spots in it. We do bitter injustice to ourselves and our ancestors, if we only regard German history through a darkening lens, if we consider it only as a prelude to Hitler's Reich. Those who have lived during the old empire and then through the Nazi period will regard any comparison between the second and the so-called Third Reich as the most hideous slander.[77]

---

[73] See Immanuel Geiss, 'Die Fischer-Kontroverse: Ein kritischer Beitrag zum Verhältnis zwischen Historiographie und Politik in der Bundesrepublik', in id., *Studien über Geschichte und Geschichtswissenschaft* (Frankfurt, 1972), 108–98. See, too, Wolfgang Jäger, *Historische Forschung und politische Kultur in Deutschland: die Debatte über den Ausbruch des Ersten Weltkrieges* (Göttingen, 1984). Finally, Arnold Synottek, 'Die Fischer Kontroverse: Ein Beitrag zur Entwicklung historisch-politischen Bewußtseins in der Bundesrepublik', in Immanuel Geiss and Bernd Jürgen Wendt (eds.), *Deutschland in der Weltpolitik des 19. Jahrhunderts* (Düsseldorf, 1973), 19–47.

[74] Cf. Thomas Herz and Michael Schwab-Tapp, *Umkämpfte Vergangenheit: Diskurse über den Nationalsozialismus seit 1945* (Opladen, 1997), 11 ff. See, too, Jeffrey Herff, *Divided Memory: The Nazi Past in the Two Germanys* (Cambridge, Mass., 1997).

[75] Fritz Fischer, *Griff nach der Weltmacht: Die Kriegszielpolitik des kaiserlichen Deutschland 1914/18* (Düsseldorf, 1961).

[76] On the *Sonderweg* theory, see Bernd Faulenbach, ' "Deutscher Sonderweg": Zur Geschichte und Problematik einer zentralen Kategorie des deutschen geschichtlichen Bewußtseins', *Aus Politik und Zeitgeschichte*, XXXIII (1981), 3–21. See, too, David Blackbourn and Geoff Eley, *The Peculiarities of German History: Bourgeois Society and Politics in Nineteenth-Century Germany* (Oxford, 1984).

[77] Gerhard Ritter, 'Bismarck und die deutsche Einheit', *Tagesspiegel*, 1 Apr. 1965. For similar views, see Theodor Schieder, 'Bismarck: Zur Wiederkehr seines Geburtstages vor 150 Jahren', *Geschichte in Wissenschaft und Unterricht*, XVI (1965), 197–207.

Ritter found support in his struggle against the theory of a German *Sonder-weg* from prominent CDU politicians such as the speaker of the Bundestag, Eugen Gerstenmaier. In his book *Neuer Nationalismus? Von der Wandlung der Deutschen*, Gerstenmaier asked his fellow Germans to develop a more positive attitude towards 'their' history: 'If we [Germans] want to survive as a nation, we must once again begin to know who we are and what we want.' Unless a positive sense of national identity were to become part of the German historical consciousness, he continued, 'we will, already in this century, be reduced to a perhaps quite well functioning, but historically and nationally quite unimportant part of a European consumer society or perhaps to a provincial appendage to the American industrial society . . . In such a state of consciousness a reunification of our people and thus the natural and imperative self-realization of the Germans as a nation would no longer be possible.'[78] In accordance with these demands, Gerstenmaier wrote an open letter addressed to Bismarck, in which he claimed that 'no right thinking person', regardless of 'whether he stands in critical opposition to you for one reason or another will go along with . . . the statement that there is a direct line leading from Luther via Frederick the Great and Bismarck to Hitler. . . . This accusation brings you close to a criminal, with whom you have nothing in common.'[79]

Nevertheless, there were clear signs that the conservative glorification of Bismarck as the 'father of the German nation-state' was losing ground; and the strident tone with which Gerstenmaier and Ritter defended their view was one of them. Bismarck started to lose his importance as a political 'guiding star' in a society increasingly satisfied with 'their' Federal Republic. In 1955, 45 per cent of West Germans had considered the era of the Bismarckreich to be the best in German history. Only 2 per cent, on the other hand, thought that Germany had never enjoyed better times than the present.[80] In the 1960s, this perception slowly began to change. The growing satisfaction with democracy among the population of the Federal Republic can above all be attributed to economic reasons. What is generally referred to as the *Wirtschaftswunder* or 'economic miracle' was the beginning of a thirty-year period of prosperity—the longest in German history.[81] Economic growth facilitated the incorporation of refugees from the former East German provinces into West German society just as it helped to reconcile the West German public to the reality of German division.[82]

---

[78] Eugen Gerstenmaier, *Neuer Nationalismus? Von der Wandlung der Deutschen* (Stuttgart, 1965), 6–10.
[79] *Die Welt*, 27 Mar. 1965. [80] *Jahrbuch der öffentlichen Meinung 1947–1955*, 201.
[81] See Hartmut Kaelble, *Der Boom 1948–1973* (Opladen, 1992).
[82] See Gerold Ambrosius, 'Flüchtlinge und Vertriebene in der westdeutschen Wirtschaftsgeschichte', in Rainer Schulze (ed.), *Flüchtlinge und Vertriebene in der westdeutschen Nachkriegsgeschichte* (Hildesheim,

Furthermore, a younger generation proved unwilling to uncritically accept the outdated value system and myths of their parents' generation. When the city council of Göttingen, dominated by a majority of Social Democrats and Free Democrats, ordered the demolition of the Bismarck monument on 1 April 1965 in what was a deliberately provocative act, it could count on the support of its student-dominated constituency.[83] The student movement of the second half of the 1960s contributed decisively to the change of political climate in the Federal Republic. Radical as it was in its extreme form, the student movement created an atmosphere in which challenges to the images of history of the older generation gained broad support.[84]

Above all, however, it was the *Neue Ostpolitik* of the social-liberal coalition under Chancellor Willy Brandt which undermined the pre-existing view of history and the traditional concept of German national identity.[85] The 1970 treaties with Moscow and Warsaw meant an end to thoughts of re-establishing Germany within its 1937 borders. In the Eastern Treaties the Federal Republic recognized the Oder–Neisse frontier as Germany's unalterable eastern border. In 1972, these agreements were followed by the Basic Treaty or *Grundlagenvertrag* between the Federal Republic and the GDR, in which the two states agreed to develop good neighbourly relations with each other on the basis of equal rights and to respect each other's frontiers as inviolable.[86]

It was during the conclusion of the Eastern Treaties that the final historical-political battle was fought over Bismarck in the Bonn Republic. The decisive turning point in the public controversy about Bismarck's relevance for the politics of the Federal Republic came in 1971. In a live TV speech on 18 January 1971, the hundredth anniversary of Bismarck's Imperial Proclamation at Versailles, President Gustav Heinemann (SPD) announced that the past one hundred years of German history 'do not only include one Versailles, but two, 1871 and 1919. They also include Auschwitz, Stalingrad, and the unconditional

1987), 216–27. See, too, Dierk Hoffmann, 'Die Integration von Flüchtlingen und Vertriebenen nach 1945: Interdisziplinäre Ergebnisse und Forschungsperspektiven: Ein Forschungskolloquium des Instituts für Zeitgeschichte', *Vierteljahreshefte für Zeitgeschichte*, XLVI (1998), 551–4.

[83] On the deconstruction of the Bismarck memorial in Göttingen see *Die Welt*, 31 Mar. 1965. A similar attempt, undertaken by the Bavarian Party, to remove the Bismarck monument from the Bosch Bridge in Munich failed in 1948. See Rosenfeld, *Munich and Memory*, 114.

[84] See Anthony J. Nicholls, *The Bonn Republic: West German Democracy, 1945–1990* (London, 1997), 207; Klaus Schönhoven, 'Aufbruch in die sozialliberale Ära: Zur Bedeutung der 60er Jahre in der Geschichte der Bundesrepublik', *Geschichte und Gesellschaft*, XXV (1999), 123–45.

[85] See the detailed analysis provided by Peter Bender, *Die 'Neue Ostpolitik' und ihre Folgen: Vom Mauerbau bis zur Vereinigung*, 3rd rev. edn. (Munich, 1995).

[86] The most important parts of this agreement are reprinted in *Politics and Government in the Federal Republic of Germany 1944–1994: Basic Documents*, ed. Carl-Christoph Schweitzer *et al.*, 2nd edn. (Providence, RI, 1995), 62–5.

surrender of 1945.'[87] The 'Iron Chancellor', continued Heinemann, while sitting in front of Anton von Werner's famous painting of the Imperial Proclamation of 1871, did not belong in the 'black, red, and gold family gallery'. Bismarck was not part of the liberal tradition upon which the Federal Republic had been founded. On the contrary, he who 'draws a direct line from the Wars of Liberation via the Wartburg and Hambach, the Frankfurt Paulskirche, and Rastatt . . . up to Sedan and Versailles, creates a wrong picture of history'.[88]

Heinemann's speech on the centenary of the Imperial Proclamation at Versailles marked a central turning point in the debate about the German past. Never before had a German head of state attacked the Iron Chancellor in a comparably pointed manner. And never before had such criticism found the support of a vast majority of Germans. Even though the former Chancellor Georg Kiesinger (CDU) immediately voiced his 'lack of understanding' of the President's speech, the positive public response was much stronger than any such criticism.[89]

It was impossible for political commentators to overlook the changes in Germany's political culture that had occurred in the 1960s. In the *Frankfurter Allgemeine Zeitung*, which had glorified the founder of the Reich only six years before, criticism of Bismarck was now clearly articulated. Karl Otmar Freiherr von Aretin argued on 16 January 1971 that even if Bismarck could not be held responsible for the development of the Reich up until 1945 there were at the very least considerable lines of continuity in German political thinking. Bismarck's 'constant toying with the idea of ridding himself of the unco-operative Reichstag by a *coup d'état*' had inspired the conservative elites during the dissolution phase of the Weimar Republic—with far-reaching consequences.[90]

In *Die Zeit* three leading academics of different generations—Theodor Schieder, Karl Dietrich Bracher, and Peter Count Kielmannsegg—expressed their opinion on Bismarck's Reich. Their contributions mirrored the growing willingness of German intellectuals to abandon the Bismarckian Empire as a model for Germany's future. For both Schieder and Kielmannsegg, Bismarck's unified German nation-state was merely 'an episode which did not last'.[91] The

---

[87] Gustav W. Heinemann, *Zur Reichsgründung 1871: Zum hundertsten Geburtstag des ersten deutschen Reichspräsidenten Friedrich Ebert*, ed. Bundeszentrale für politische Bildung (Bonn, 1971). See, too, Sebastian Schubert, 'Abschied vom Nationalstaat? Die deutsche Reichsgründung 1871 in der Geschichtspolitik des geteilten Deutschlands von 1965 bis 1974', in Winkler (ed.), *Griff nach der Deutungsmacht*, 230–65.

[88] Heinemann, *Reichsgründung*. See, too, Matthias Rensing, *Geschichte und Politik in den Reden der deutschen Bundespräsidenten 1949–1984* (Münster and New York, 1996).

[89] On Kiesinger's comments see *Neue Züricher Zeitung*, 19 Jan. 1971, and *Die Welt*, 18 Jan. 1971.

[90] *Frankfurter Allgemeine Zeitung*, 16 Jan. 1971.

[91] *Die Zeit*, 15 Jan. 1971.

division of Germany was accepted as part of the new world order. Karl Dietrich Bracher went even further in his departure from the 'Bismarckian tradition': the 'destruction of the state of 1871' was 'the premiss and starting point for a new German state altogether'. The 'second, finally successful democracy in Germany is unimaginable, impossible without the ultimate failure of the Reich of 1871'.[92]

Statements such as these were indicative of the fundamental changes of historical consciousness in the Federal Republic. In 1952, 36 per cent of West Germans had classed Bismarck as the 'greatest' German (far ahead of Hitler (9 per cent), Frederick II (7 per cent), and Konrad Adenauer (3 per cent)). By 1956, only 25 per cent of the population thought of the Iron Chancellor as the greatest figure in German history. In the following years Bismarck's popularity tailed off even further. In 1967, shortly after Adenauer's death, only 17 per cent of Germans considered Bismarck the 'greatest' German, as opposed to 60 per cent for Adenauer.[93]

The historical-political caesura of the late 1960s and early 1970s was profound. For the first time in the history of the German nation-state, Bismarck was no longer associated with a political order for which a majority of Germans was striving. Instead, Bismarck was confined to history and ceased to be a political model for the Federal Republic.

The primacy of politics over history: Bismarck in the GDR

Post-war images of Bismarck were not only subject to gradual changes in the Federal Republic, but also in the GDR. In contrast to the pluralistic Federal Republic, however, the numerous changes in the GDR's quasi-official image of Bismarck did not occur through public controversies or debates. Instead, historical interpretations were dictated by a state which instrumentalized historical traditions both for domestic political integration and for the *Systemkonflikt* with the 'imperialist' Federal Republic.[94]

Up until the early 1950s, historical perceptions of the Iron Chancellor in the Soviet zone were dominated by a quasi-official 'misery theory' which had found its classic expression in Alexander Abusch's 1946 book *Irrweg einer*

---

[92] Ibid.

[93] The older those questioned were, the greater the proportion of votes for Bismarck. On these statistics, see *Jahrbuch der öffentlichen Meinung 1965–1967*, 144–5.

[94] See Martin Sabrow, *Verwaltete Vergangenheit: Geschichtskultur und Herrschaftslegitimation in der DDR* (Leipzig, 1997).

Nation. Abusch, who had worked in the press office of the KPD's headquarters during the Weimar Republic, argued that there was a direct line of continuity from Bismarck and Prussian militarism to Hitler.[95] According to Abusch, Bismarck's legacy was 'a tradition of violence, deception and demagoguery' upon which Hitler built. Abusch acknowledged that Hitler was far more radical than Bismarck. However, Hitler only 'completed Bismarck's struggle against the workers' party and every democratic movement'.[96]

In July 1952 Walter Ulbricht officially abandoned the 'misery theory'. In a speech at the Second SED Party Conference on 9 July 1952, Ulbricht exhorted the East Germans not to neglect their patriotic consciousness: 'Everyone understands how important the study of German history and the promotion of all German tradition is to the struggle for Germany's national unity, especially in the face of the efforts of the American occupying powers to wipe out the memory of our people's great achievements.'[97] Initially, Bismarck's unification of Germany was not promoted as one of these 'great achievements' from which the GDR could draw its historical legitimacy. Instead the SED's historical propaganda focused on Communist resistance to Hitler, the 1848 revolution, and the Wars of Liberation against Napoleon.[98]

The reason for Ulbricht's historical-political paradigm change was clear. As long as the westward integration of the Federal Republic was incomplete, the GDR attempted to mobilize the West Germans against the Adenauer regime with nationalist slogans and to push for a unified and socialist German nation-state.[99] Even after the construction of the Berlin Wall in 1961, the SED continued to suggest that Germany would ultimately be united in a socialist state.[100] In attempting to create historical legitimacy for this aim, the SED made reference to precisely the man Alexander Abusch had assigned as Hitler's spiritual predecessor in his book *Irrweg der Nation* only a few years earlier: Bismarck. An article which appeared on 2 April 1965 in the SED's newspaper, *Neues Deutschland*, suggested that the Bismarckian inheritance of 'political good sense' had not just been neglected during the Kaiserreich and under the Nazis, but also by

---

[95] Alexander Abusch, *Der Irrweg einer Nation: Ein Beitrag zum Verständnis deutscher Geschichte* (Berlin, 1946).

[96] Ibid., 130.

[97] Ulbricht as quoted in Wolfrum, *Geschichtspolitik in der Bundesrepublik*, 47.

[98] See Harald Bluhm, 'Befreiungskriege und Preußenrenaissance', in Rudolf Speth and Edgar Wolfrum (eds.), *Politische Mythen und Geschichtspolitik: Konstruktion—Inszenierung—Mobilisierung* (Berlin, 1996), 71–95. See, too, Herfried Münkler, 'Das kollektive Gedächtnis der DDR', in Dieter Vorsteher (ed.), *Parteiauftrag: Ein neues Deutschland: Bilder, Rituale und Symbole der frühen DDR* (Berlin, 1996), 458–68.

[99] Eberhard Kuhrt and Henning von der Löwis, *Griff nach der deutschen Geschichte: Erbaneignung und Traditionspflege in der DDR* (Paderborn, 1988). See, too, Schubart, 'Abschied vom Nationalstaat?', 242–5.

[100] See 'Article 8' of the GDR's 1968 constitution as printed in *Deutsche Verfassungen*, ed. Rudolf Schuster, 2nd edn. (Munich, 1992), 359.

the Bonn Republic, a state obsessed with 'revanchism' and the acquisition of nuclear weapons. In this respect, Bonn had much 'to learn from Bismarck and his great and powerful character'. As long as the Federal Republic would not learn from 'Bismarck and his historic achievements' it had 'no right to leadership in Germany'.[101]

The GDR's nationalist rhetoric came to an abrupt end with the Federal Republic's *Neue Ostpolitik*. In the early 1970s, the GDR abandoned its *gesamtdeutsch* policy and attempted to resolve the German question through the concept of a 'socialist nation GDR'.[102] In October 1974, the reunification clause was deleted from the GDR constitution, which now declared that the GDR was 'forever and irrevocably allied with the USSR'. All references to the 'German nation' were expunged. The GDR was no longer a 'socialist state of the German nation', but rather a 'socialist state of the workers and peasants'.[103]

The constitutional change of 1974 was the culmination of a process which had begun in 1971, when the GDR adopted a policy of *Abgrenzung* from the Federal Republic. This reversal of policy was the result of both internal and external factors. In May 1971 Walter Ulbricht was replaced as chairman of the SED by Erich Honecker, a party functionary with more loyalty to Moscow than Ulbricht. Additionally, following the 1968 military intervention in Czechoslovakia, the Soviet Union strove to integrate its bloc more closely, in order to create greater internal cohesion, and to reinforce its hegemony. The beginning of the Honecker era was therefore marked by an abandonment of Ulbricht's hopes for reunification and the subsequent revision of the GDR's official interpretation of history.[104] In this context, the SED reversed its formerly positive attitude towards Bismarck. On the occasion of the hundredth anniversary of Bismarck's unification of Germany, the East German historian Ernst Diehl denied any connection between the GDR and Bismarck. In *Neues Deutschland* Diehl wrote: 'Today, one hundred years after the foundation of the Reich an incontrovertible situation has arisen . . . in the centre of Europe. Any policy which truly aims at détente in Europe must proceed from this reality: the existence of two states at the heart of our continent with opposed fundamentals of society, the socialist GDR and the imperialist Federal Republic.'[105]

---

[101] *Neues Deutschland*, 2 and 4 Apr. 1965.

[102] See, for example, Alfred Kosing, *Nation in Geschichte und Gegenwart: Studie zur historisch-materialistischen Theorie der Nation* (East Berlin, 1976).

[103] Timothy Garton Ash, *In Europe's Name: Germany and the Divided Continent* (New York, 1993), 189. On this constitutional amendment see, too, *Neues Deutschland*, 28 Sept. 1974. On the 'farewell to the nation', see Dietrich Staritz, *Geschichte der DDR*, 2nd edn. (Frankfurt, 1996), 278–9.

[104] Monika Kaiser, *Machtwechsel von Ulbricht zu Honecker: Funktionsmechanismen der SED-Diktatur in Konfliktssituationen 1962 bis 1972* (Berlin, 1997), 279.

[105] *Neues Deutschland*, 19 Jan. 1971.

Shortly after the conclusion of the Basic Treaty between the Federal Republic and the GDR in 1972, the SED changed its attitude towards Prussian history yet again.[106] Under the slogan of 'heritage and tradition', the GDR regime attempted to co-opt certain aspects of Germany's historical and cultural past. In order to legitimize the existence of two German nations—one 'capitalist' and one 'socialist'—the SED appropriated 'progressive' traditions of the German past. As opposed to the 'reactionary' state of the Federal Republic (so the concept of 'heritage and tradition' suggested), the GDR had learnt from the lessons of history.[107] In 1985, shortly after the statue of Frederick the Great had been returned to Unter den Linden, the East German historian Ernst Engelberg published a relatively positive biography of Bismarck in which he praised 'how strong and rich in personality he [Bismarck] was and how able he proved himself to be in solving problems in his own way from above after the failed revolution of 1848'.[108]

None the less, however hard the SED leadership strove to reinvent traditions for their state, the idea of 'heritage and tradition' became increasingly questionable in the 1980s. As Günther Heydemann argued, the concept's basic idea, namely to establish greater historical legitimacy for the GDR, could only be persuasive if the supposed advantages of the SED state corresponded with the daily economic and social experiences of the country's citizens. For the majority of GDR citizens this was not the case.[109] From the mid-1980s onwards in particular, the SED's historical propaganda was less and less able to conceal either the growing dissatisfaction of GDR citizens with the political leadership or the country's increasing economic difficulties that would eventually bring about its collapse.[110]

Bismarck after reunification

When the Berlin Wall fell in autumn 1989, many political observers in Germany and abroad assumed that the myths of German nationalism would

---

[106] Hellmut Diwald, 'Geschichtsbild und Geschichtsbewußtsein im gegenwärtigen Deutschland', *Saeculum*, XXVIII (1978), 22–30.

[107] See Günther Heydemann, 'Geschichtsbild und Geschichtspropaganda in der ära Honecker: Die "Erbe-und-Tradition"-Konzeption der DDR', in Ute Daniel and Wolfram Siemann (eds.), *Propaganda: Meinungskampf: Verführung und politische Sinnstiftung 1789–1989* (Frankfurt, 1994), 161–71.

[108] Ernst Engelberg, *Bismarck*, 2 vols. (Berlin, 1985–1990), here vol. 1: *Urpreuße und Reichsgründer*, p. xiii.

[109] Heydemann, 'Geschichtsbild', 170–1.

[110] On the collapse of the GDR, see Mary Fulbrook, *Anatomy of a Dictatorship: Inside the GDR, 1949–1989* (Oxford, 1995), 279–83.

quickly be revived once again in a reunified Germany.[111] Even some historians feared that German reunification would lead to a 'return to the traditions of the Bismarckian Reich which belongs again to the arsenal of nationalist propaganda in Germany'.[112]

It is true that the unexpected end of German partition resulted in Bismarck's temporary return to the political arena. In late October 1989, a few days before the collapse of the GDR, Deutsche Bank's CEO Alfred Herrhausen invoked memories of Bismarck when he underlined the necessity of reconsidering German identity in the event of reunification. Herrhausen believed 'that we have good chances to experience a new Bismarckian Era, in which the German nation-state can contribute to peace and stability in Europe'.[113]

The subsequent public debate on Bismarck after reunification was not, however, dominated by discussions about the similarities between 1871 and 1990.[114] Quite the opposite was true. The editor of *Die Zeit*, Theo Sommer, for example, wrote: 'The second German unification, 120 years after the first, is not—thank God—a business of blood and tears. This unification is a democratic one. . . . Also, the difficulties involved in the unification process of 1990 are much bigger than they were in 1870: psychologically, but moreover in financial and economic respects. These difficulties would have been more demanding, if not too demanding, for Bismarck.'[115] Sommer's article reflected a widespread attitude towards the Iron Chancellor in reunified Germany. When the German Historical Museum (DHM) opened its large 1990 Bismarck exhibition in Berlin, the DHM's director, Christoph Stölzl, emphasized that no one was interested in promoting uncritical or even heroic images of Bismarck any longer.[116]

The experiences of the past ten years have proven Stölzl right. A revival of the Bismarck myth in the context of the re-emergence of a new German nationalism is not in sight. Even if a nationalist party was to play an important role in German domestic policies once again, it seems highly unlikely that Bismarck would be the reference point for that movement for two major reasons. First,

[111] See Dörner, *Hermannsmythos*. Also, Daniel Johnson, 'Blood, Iron and Champagne: The Explosive Legacy of Bismarck', *The Times*, 10 July 1998.

[112] Machtan, *Bismarck*, 192. Also Stefan Berger, *The Search for Normality: National Identity and Historical Consciousness in Germany since 1800* (Providence, RI, and Oxford, 1997), 113 ff.

[113] Herrhausen, as quoted in *Die Zeit*, 27 Oct. 1989.

[114] See Rolf Parr, 'Bismarck-Mythen—Bismarck-Analogien', *Kulturrevolution*, XXIV (1991), 12–16.

[115] *Die Zeit*, 21 Sept. 1990.

[116] See Christoph Stölzl's introductory note in *Bismarck—Preussen, Deutschland und Europa: Eine Austellung des Deutschen Historischen Museums Berlin, 26. August–25. November 1990* (Berlin, 1990), not paginated. See, too, Susanne Schreiber, 'Wider den Heroenkult', *Handelsblatt*, 31 Aug. 1990.

the political power of a myth essentially depends on its widespread appeal. Only if a mythical narrative is anchored in the collective memory of a social entity can it be used effectively as a weapon in political debates. In the collective memory of reunified Germany, however, the Bismarckian Era plays a marginal role.[117] According to a survey in 1998, most Germans (53 per cent) do not even know who Otto von Bismarck was.[118] Secondly, the political transformations of 1989 have led to a reunified German nation-state, but not to a return to Bismarck's Reich. The myth consequently lacks relevance for the problems of the present and future. In terms of its political orientation, its constitution, and its political culture, the Federal Republic is more a break with Bismarck's Reich than its continuation. For both of these reasons, it seems reasonable to assume that Bismarck's 'second life' as a political myth, 'as an emotionally charged and contested figure', is irrevocably over.[119]

---

[117] Felix P. Lutz, *Das Geschichtsbewußtsein der Deutschen: Grundlagen der politischen Kultur in Ost und West* (Cologne, 2000), 175–7. On the general de-politicization of public debates over the Prussian past after 1990, see Gavriel D. Rosenfeld, 'A Mastered Past? Prussia in Postwar German Memory', *German History* XXII (2004), 505–35.

[118] *Die Woche*, 30 Jan. 1998, 11.

[119] Jürgen Kocka, 'Otto von Bismarcks zweites Leben', *Berliner Tagesspiegel*, 26 July 1998.

10

Conclusion

Between 1918 and 1933, Germany witnessed an uncompromising clash of ideologies and invented historical traditions. Ideological conflict translated into a fierce pseudo-historical and highly political fight for the 'correct' and universal interpretation of the German past. In the course of this battle over the past, the Bismarck myth proved to be one of the most powerful weapons employed by right-wing circles in their struggle against Weimar. The myth suggested that the Republic had been founded against the 'spirit of Bismarck' by those political groups which the Iron Chancellor himself had characterized as the 'internal enemies of the Empire'. One of the prime intentions of the myth-makers was to associate the Weimar Republic with the odium of treason. In order to restore the historical legitimacy which the democratic state was allegedly lacking, the Republic would therefore have to be replaced by some form of authoritarian system dominated by a towering leader figure: a 'second Bismarck'.

To the extent that the Bismarck myth radically questioned the Weimar Republic's historical legitimacy, its character differed fundamentally in the periods before 1918 and after 1933. While the Bismarck myth served as a narrative to legitimize the political system during most of the Kaiserreich and the years after 1933, it fulfilled quite the opposite task between 1918 and 1933. Even in the Federal Republic, where Bismarck reappeared in the public debate as a 'warrant of reunification' up until the early 1970s, the myth was never used to question the democratic state's historical legitimacy.

The Bismarck myth was originally created and disseminated in the early 1890s by the political opponents of Wilhelm II and the New Course. Shortly after Bismarck's death in 1898, however, the myth was appropriated by the Kaiser and his government. The Iron Chancellor was redefined as a loyal servant of the Hohenzollern dynasty. Bismarck had completed Prussia's mission for national unity in a genuinely German way: from 'above'. In the years to follow this became *the* foundation myth of the German Empire, a narrative that was used to 'prove' the historical legitimacy of the Kaiserreich. The Bismarck myth was instrumentalized for a large variety of purposes; for example, it served to justify Germany's struggle to become a world power or to attack those groups within the Reich which were dissatisfied with the political and social order of Wilhelmine Germany. Whoever dared to call into question the existing political regime was consequently accused of the worst possible crime: committing treason against the legacy of the Iron Chancellor.

After 1914, the Bismarck myth served as a source of wartime mobilization. The Great War was interpreted as a defensive struggle over Bismarck's inheritance. Annexationist war aims were equally formulated with reference to the Iron Chancellor's policy of 'Blood and Iron'. The First World War did not, however, end with a German victory, but rather with the military defeat of Imperial Germany which was itself swept away in the wake of the November Revolution. The political events of 1918–19 and the increasing polarization of German society as a result of military defeat, revolution, and counter-revolution had repercussions upon the public perception of Bismarck. In the first weeks after the end of the Great War, it seemed as if the Bismarck myth could no longer be appropriated to meet the political needs of a fundamentally changed present. Up until early 1919, the collapse of the regime established by Bismarck was welcomed by a majority of Germans. Many people felt that the establishment of a democratic Republic would not only ensure the conclusion of a moderate peace agreement, but also pave the way to a more just political and social order.

There was another reason why it initially seemed as if Bismarck was losing his relevance: since the end of World War I, Bismarck's *kleindeutsch* solution to the German question, the main reason for his mystification, was considered to be outdated by virtually all Germans. Under the influence of the Austro-German war alliance against the Entente, leading politicians and intellectuals promoted the *Anschluß* of Austria and thus the abandonment of Bismarck's *kleindeutsch* concept of the German nation-state.

The strongest supporters of *Anschluß* came from within the republican left. The SPD in particular propagated a peaceful revision of the 1871 borders and thereby hoped to associate the democratic state with a highly popular foreign policy success. Social Democrats, such as Paul Löbe or Friedrich Ebert, argued that the establishment of a *großdeutsch* Republic would be a fulfilment of the revolutionary aims of 1848. At the same time, the idea of a democratic *Großdeutschland* was used as an argument against Bismarck's *kleindeutsch* Reich in the first months of the Republic's existence. Bismarck's Reich of 1871 was represented as a catastrophic deviation from the *großdeutsch*-democratic traditions of the early German nationalist movement. With the explicit ban on a *großdeutsch* enlargement of the Reich imposed by the Western Allies in Versailles, this argument lost its pervasiveness. Consequently, right-wing politicians argued that the Republic had betrayed 'Bismarck's legacy' without succeeding in its ultimate objective: the establishment of the *großdeutsch* Republic. This popular accusation was combined with the 'stab-in-the-back' motif, according to which Bismarck's political enemies—the Left Liberals, the Centre, and the Social Democrats—had committed treason against the 'undefeated' German army.

The Bismarck myth experienced a sudden and unexpected revival after the radicalization of the German revolution in the winter of 1918–19 and the publication of the harsh peace conditions which were to be imposed on Germany by the Allied Powers. However, it became evident that the myth had fundamentally changed both in character and function. As a symbol of the retrospectively idealized 'great' German past, Bismarck became an important political weapon in right-wing propaganda against a Republic which was allegedly unable to live up to the 'high' standards set by the followers of Bismarck. In other words, whereas between 1898 and 1918 the prime task of the myth had been the legitimization of the existing state, its main function after the revolution was to de-legitimize the new political system.

Left-Liberal and Social Democratic intellectuals countered the nationalists' Bismarck myth with the argument that Bismarck's policies had split the German people into political camps and had prevented a thorough process of democratization. Consequently, the Bismarckian era was interpreted by the left as an expression of Germany's political and moral decline after the failed revolution of 1848. According to the left, Bismarck's Reich had been a a 'feudal' state protecting the interests of the rich few and ignoring those of the working classes. The constitution of 1919, on the other hand, was represented as a deliberate abandonment of Bismarck's political system and the fulfilment of the liberal-democratic tradition of 1848.

None the less, from the start, the Republicans were in a position of disadvantage in the civil war of historical myths and invented traditions. Born out of military defeat and an unloved revolution, Weimar lacked a generally accepted foundation myth and cherished historical-political traditions upon which to build. Additionally, the Republic could not count on the support of those institutions which were essential in the process of instilling democratic principles in a younger generation. Neither German schools nor universities were strongholds of democracy. Weimar historiography in particular did little to emphasize the historical legitimacy of the Republic. In the light of the identity crisis engendered by the loss of 'national greatness' in 1918, the vast majority of

German historians came to see it as their task to remind their contemporaries of 'better times' in the past. Bismarck's policies were thereby accorded the status of a yardstick against which the increasingly despised Republic was measured.

Despite its generally anti-democratic character, the Bismarck myth was far from static. In fact, the politically motivated references to Bismarck were modified constantly according to changing practical needs. In the debates over the Law for the Protection of the Republic following the assassination of Walther Rathenau in 1922, for example, the law was compared with the legislation that Bismarck had enacted unsuccessfully against political Catholicism and the socialist movement in the late 1870s and 1880s. The DNVP, accused of stimulating the lethal ideological climate in which the assassination of Rathenau had been carried out, rejected the law as the SPD's late revenge for Bismarck's anti-socialist legislation. Although the DNVP was unable to prevent the passing of the law, the debates were evidence of the fact that Bismarck was politically useful in a variety of different contexts. The Bismarckian era was a historical quarry which the right became particularly astute at exploiting.

Only a few months later, in the context of the Battle of the Ruhr, the content of the Bismarck myth underwent another change: the myth was externalized and directed against the French occupiers of German soil. The Battle of the Ruhr gave a sharp and immediate relevance to memories of the Franco-Prussian War of 1870–1, causing the Republic's various subcultures to temporarily lay aside their internal differences. For a short while, the diametrically opposed viewpoints that marked the early Weimar period seemed noticeably blunted; even representatives and supporters of the Republic referred to Bismarck in formulating their criticism of Poincaré's policy. Nevertheless, the content of the Bismarck myth was never undisputed. While the nationalist right campaigned for active resistance to French occupation in 1923 under the banner of the Iron Chancellor, the moderate right represented Bismarck as an advocate of passive resistance.

The controversy over the 'correct' interpretation of Bismarck's lessons for the present and future outlasted even the state crisis of 1923. During the Reichstag election campaigns of 1924, both the DVP and the DNVP formulated their political goals with reference to the Iron Chancellor in order to lend historical legitimacy to their policies. Ironically, Bismarck was used both as an exponent of the German Nationalists' thirst for revenge *and* as the figurehead of Stresemann's foreign policy of international reconciliation.

In the presidential election of 1925, the DVP and the DNVP combined their efforts to instrumentalize Bismarck as a tangible resource in the battle for votes. Karl Jarres, the *Reichsblock*'s candidate for presidency in the first round of voting, campaigned with the slogan 'Back to Bismarck'. In the second round of voting, the *Reichsblock*'s campaign strategists projected 'Bismarckian qualities' onto Paul von Hindenburg in order to increase his chances of success over the Republican presidential candidate, Wilhelm Marx. Democratic parties to the left of the DVP also endorsed historical-political campaigning. As opposed to the bourgeois right, however, the republican *Volksblock* campaigned for votes by referring to the 1848 revolution.

Hindenburg's close victory over Marx strengthened those circles which had, since 1919, been trying to deprive the Republic of its legitimacy through the use of the Bismarck myth. They had assisted in placing a man at the pinnacle of power who was more sympathetic to their social and political ideals than his Social Democratic predecessor in office, Friedrich Ebert. Hindenburg was indeed prepared to support several projects of great symbolic importance to the Weimar right. The League for the Erection of a Bismarck National Monument, for example, which had taken up its work in the days of the Kaiserreich but ceased to exist after the outbreak of the First World War, was re-founded soon after Hindenburg had taken office. Hindenburg himself was very much in favour of this project. He also personally supported the two-part Bismarck film of 1925–7 which appealed to the anti-modernist sentiments and anxieties of large segments of post-war German society and succeeded in popularizing the anti-republican Bismarck myth via a modern mass medium.

The popularity of pseudo-historical and ideological films such as *Bismarck* or *Fridericus Rex* indicates that despite some political successes in the Stresemann Era, the governments' attempts to instil democratic principles in the majority of German citizens had failed. The great symbolic controversies of the 1920s (especially the long-running disagreement over the introduction of 18 January as a national holiday) demonstrated the deep divisions in German society. The fundamental lack of consensus in relation to ideology, religion, and class remained a gaping chasm even during the 'Golden Twenties', a chasm which could not be spanned either by the temporary decrease in economic pressure or by the accompanying reduction in domestic political tension.

When the economic and political situation in Germany worsened after 1929, the content of the Bismarck myth radicalized in a similar way. To be sure, the idea of overcoming parliamentary democracy in favour of a more authoritarian political system had been an essential component of the Bismarck myth ever since 1918. However, the severe and permanent crisis after 1929 intensified the perceived need for a charismatic leader of 'Bismarckian qualities' to brush aside the seemingly helpless democracy and to solve Germany's problems without parliamentary constraints.

The man who profited most from this crisis was Adolf Hitler. There can be no doubt that Hitler's astonishing success in public elections after 1929 was partly due to his demagogic use of the magical power of political myths. He was quick to exploit the connection between the Bismarck myth and the widespread desire for a politically strong charismatic leadership. Hitler suggested that he was the long-awaited 'second Bismarck', both willing and able to vigorously combat all allegedly divisive forces in a currently 'leaderless' and divided society. He also promised to launch a concerted effort to overcome the restrictions imposed on Germany by the Treaty of Versailles. This promise included the revision of the *kleindeutsch* borders. According to Hitler, German politicians after Bismarck had failed to pursue the goal of *Großdeutschland*. After the SPD's hopes for an *Anschluß* of Austria had foundered in the face of Allied opposition in 1919, and given that Brüning's attempt to achieve a *großdeutsch* enlargement via the Austro-Germans customs union in 1931 had failed on similar grounds, Hitler was able to present himself as the only politician with the necessary determination to 'complete' Bismarck's Reich.

The importance of Hitler's promise to become a 'second Bismarck' who would revise the *kleindeutsch* borders cannot be overestimated when examining the reasons for the massive support he received in the early 1930s. The widespread belief in the coming Bismarckian Führer who would lead Germany to new heights helped to bridge the gulf between Hitler's intellectually unsophisticated movement and Germany's educated classes. When Hitler was appointed as Chancellor of the German Reich on 30 January 1933, he was consequently first and foremost welcomed by vast sections of the German population as the man to continue and to complete the work of Bismarck by revising *both* Versailles: the *kleindeutsch* solution of 1871 and the peace settlement of 1919.

Hitler's 'seizure of power' marked the end of the fierce political battle over Bismarck's legacy, which had raged between 1918 and 1933. However, the outcome of this ideological struggle was not what the 'Bismarckians' had hoped for. The men who helped Hitler to power on 30 January 1933 intended to use the Nazi movement to implement their 'Bismarckian' authoritarian policies. However, even though Nazi propaganda suggested in the coming months that 'Bismarck's spirit' had triumphed with the 'seizure of power', Hitler was far from being interested in a restoration of Bismarck's Empire. Ironically, the Bismarck myth started to lose importance just at the time when its proponents thought they had achieved their aims.

The mythically exaggerated figure of the Iron Chancellor would never again leave such a clear trail in Germany's political culture as it did before 1933. Bismarck continued to appear in public debates after 1933 (and indeed after 1945), but the myth never had the same destructive power as between 1918 and Hitler's 'seizure of power'. The main reason for this is clear: one of the few common features of Wilhelmine Germany, the 'Third Reich', the GDR, and the Federal Republic, was that there was a basic consensus (either authoritarian or democratically defined) which protected the existence of the state. The Weimar Republic completely lacked this basic consensus.

In Weimar, the public debate on Bismarck's legacy was a fundamental controversy over which norms and values should constitute the German nation-state. At the very heart of this fierce and uncompromising battle over the past lay differing and irreconcilable conceptualizations of the present and future of the German state and people. The public debate on Bismarck thus mirrored the fundamental lack of any basic political and ethical consensus within Weimar's fragmented political culture. It was this lack of consensus which largely contributed to the failure of Germany's first democracy.

BIBLIOGRAPHY

ARCHIVAL SOURCES

Politisches Archiv des Auswärtigen Amtes, Berlin:

Stresemann papers
File 'Parlamentarischer Untersuchungsausschuss für die Schuldfrage des Weltkrieges'

Otto-von-Bismarck-Stiftung, Friedrichsruh:

Sammlung A ('Kanzler')
Otto (II.) von Bismarck papers
'Bild- und Fotosammlung'
File 'Bismarckfilm'

Bismarck-Museum, Schönhausen:

'Bild- und Objektsammlung'

Deutsches Historisches Museum, Berlin:

'Bild- und Objektsammlung'

Archiv für Christlich-Demokratische Politik, St Augustin:

Centre Party papers
Press clippings, 1918–33

Friedrich-Ebert-Stiftung, Bonn:

Press clippings, 1918–33

Bundesarchiv Berlin:

Hugenberg papers
Westarp papers
File 'Deutschnationale Volkspartei'
File 'Deutsch-Österreichische Arbeitsgemeinschaft'
File 'Reichskanzlei'
Pressearchiv des Deutschen Reichslandbundes

Bundesarchiv Koblenz:

Political poster collection (1918–33)

Bundesfilmarchiv Berlin:

File 'Bismarckfilm' (I and II)

Hauptstaatsarchiv Nordrhein-Westfalen, Düsseldorf:

File 'Verein zur Errichtung eines Bismarck-Nationaldenkmals e.V.'

Landesarchiv Berlin:

'Zeitgeschichtliche Sammlung'

PRINTED SOURCES

Cabinet records

Die Regierung der Volksbeauftragten 1918/19, ed. Erich Matthias and Susanne Miller, 2 vols. (Düsseldorf, 1969).

Akten der Reichskanzlei (AdR), Weimar Republic:

Das Kabinett Scheidemann, 13. Februar bis 20. Juni 1919, ed. Hagen Schulze (Boppard, 1971).

Das Kabinett Bauer, 21. Juni 1919 bis 27. März 1920, ed. Anton Golecki (Boppard, 1980).

Das Kabinett Müller I, 27. März bis 21. Juni 1920, ed. Martin Vogt (Boppard, 1971).

Das Kabinett Fehrenbach, 25. Juni 1920 bis 4. Mai 1921, ed. Peter Wulf (Boppard, 1972).

Die Kabinette Wirth I und II, 26. Oktober 1921 bis 22. November 1922, ed. Ingrid Schulze-Bidlingmaier, 2 vols. (Boppard, 1973).

Das Kabinett Cuno, 22. November 1922 bis 12. August 1923, ed. Karl-Heinz Harbeck (Boppard, 1968).

Die Kabinette Stresemann I und II, 13. August bis 30. November 1923, ed. Karl Dietrich Erdmann and Martin Vogt, 2 vols. (Boppard, 1978).

Die Kabinette Marx I und II, 30. November 1923 bis 15. Januar 1925, ed. Günter Abramowski, 2 vols. (Boppard, 1973).

Die Kabinette Luther I und II, 15. Januar 1925 bis 17. Mai 1926, ed. Karl-Heinz Minuth, 2 vols. (Boppard, 1977).

Die Kabinette Marx III und IV, 17. Mai 1926 bis 28. Juni 1928, ed. Günter Abramowski, 2 vols. (Boppard, 1988).

Das Kabinett Müller II, 28. Juni 1928 bis 27. März 1929, ed. Martin Vogt, 2 vols. (Boppard, 1970).

Die Kabinette Brüning I und II, 30. März 1930 bis 1. Juni 1932, ed. Tilmann Koops, 3 vols. (Boppard, 1982).

Das Kabinett von Papen, 1. Juni bis 3. Dezember 1932, ed. Karl-Heinz Minuth, 2 vols. (Boppard, 1989).

Das Kabinett von Schleicher, 3. Dezember 1932 bis 30. Januar 1933, ed. Anton Golecki (Boppard, 1986).

Parliamentary records

Verhandlungen der Verfassunggebenden Deutschen Nationalversammlung (NV). Stenographische Berichte und Anlagen, 1919.

Verhandlungen des Reichstags (RT). Stenographische Berichte und Anlagen, 1918–33.
Verhandlungen des Preußischen Abgeordnetenhauses (PAH). Stenographische
Berichte und Anlagen, 1918–33.

Treaties, constitutional texts, and historical calendars

Egelhaafs Historisch-politische Jahresübersicht (Stuttgart, 1918–33).
Schulthess' Europäischer Geschichtskalender (Munich, 1890–1933).
Der Staatsvertrag von St Germain (Vienna, 1919).
Deutsche Verfassungen, ed. Rudolf Schuster, 2nd edn. (Munich, 1992).
The Bonn Constitution: Basic Law for the Federal Republic of Germany (New York, 1949).
Treaty of Peace between the Allied and Associated Powers and Germany (London, 1925).
Die Verfassung des Deutschen Reiches vom 11. August 1919, ed. Gerhard Anschütz,
2nd edn. (Berlin, 1921).

Other edited source collections

Akten zur Deutschen Auswärtigen Politik 1918–1945, B series: 1925–33 (Göttingen, 1967).
BISMARCK, OTTO VON, *Die gesammelten Werke, Friedrichsruher Ausgabe*, 19 vols.
(Berlin, 1924–35).
——*Die gesammelten Werke, Neue Friedrichsruher Ausgabe* (Paderborn, Munich,
Vienna, and Zurich, 2004 ff.).
Die deutsche Revolution 1918–1919: Dokumente, ed. Gerhard A. Ritter and Susanne
Miller, 2nd edn. (Hamburg, 1975).
*Die große Politik der europäischen Kabinette 1871 bis 1890: Sammlung der diplomatischen
Akten des Auswärtigen Amtes*, ed. Johannes Lepsius, Albrecht Mendelssohn
Bartholdy, and Friedrich Thimme, 40 vols. (Berlin, 1922–7).
Hitler: Reden und Proklamationen, 1932–1945, ed. Max Domarus, 2 vols. (Wiesbaden,
1973).
Hitler: Reden, Schriften, Anordnungen, Februar 1925 bis Januar 1933, vol. 1: *Die
Wiederbegründung der NSDAP, Februar 1925–Juni 1926*, ed. Clemens Vollnhans
(Munich, 1992).
Hitler: Reden, Schriften, Anordnungen, Februar 1925 bis Januar 1933, vol. 2: *Vom
Weimarer Parteitag bis zur Reichstagswahl, Juli 1926–Mai 1928*, part 2: *August
1927–Mai 1928*, ed. Bärbel Dusik (Munich, 1996).
Hitler: Reden, Schriften, Anordnungen. Februar 1925 bis Januar 1933, vol. 2 A: *Außen-
politische Standortbestimmung nach der Reichstagswahl Juni–Juli 1928*, ed. Gerhard L.
Weinberg, Christian Hartmann, and Klaus A. Lankheit (Munich, 1995).
Hitler: Reden, Schriften, Anordnungen, Februar 1925 bis Januar 1933, vol. 4 A: *Von der
Reichstagswahl zur Reichspräsidentschaftswahl, Oktober 1930–Juni 1931*, ed. Constan-
tin Goschler (Munich, 1996).
Hitler: Reden, Schriften, Anordnungen, Februar 1925 bis Januar 1933, vol. 4 B: *Von der
Reichstagswahl bis zur Reichspräsidentenwahl*, ed. Christian Hartmann (Munich,
1996).
Hitler: Reden, Schriften, Anordnungen, Februar 1925 bis Januar 1933, vol. 5: *Von der
Reichspräsidentschaftswahl bis zur Machtergreifung, April 1932–Januar 1933*, ed. Klaus
A. Lankheit (Munich, 1996).

Der Hitler-Prozess 1924: Wortlaut der Hauptgerichtsverhandlung vor dem Volksgericht München I, ed. Lothar Gruchmann and Reinhard Weber (Munich, 1999).

Jahrbuch der öffentlichen Meinung 1965–1967, ed. Elisabeth Noelle and Erich P. Neumann (Allensbach and Bonn, 1967).

Nationalliberalismus in der Weimarer Republik: Die Führungsgremien der Deutschen Volkspartei, ed. Eberhard Kolb and Ludwig Richter, 2 vols. (Düsseldorf, 1999).

Politics and Government in the Federal Republic of Germany 1944–1994: Basic Documents, ed. Carl-Christoph Schweitzer *et al.*, 2nd edn. (Providence, RI, 1995).

Politik und Wirtschaft in der Krise von 1930–32: Quellen zur Ära Brüning, ed. Ilse Maurer, Udo Wengst, and Jürgen Heideking, 2 vols. (Düsseldorf, 1980).

Ursachen und Folgen: Vom deutschen Zusammenbruch 1918 und 1945 bis zur staatlichen Neuordnung Deutschlands in der Gegenwart, ed. Herbert Michaelis, Ernst Schräpler, and Günter Scheel, vol. 2: *Der militärische Zusammenbruch und das Ende des Kaiserreiches* (Berlin, 1958).

Newspapers and periodicals

Alldeutsche Blätter, Berliner Tageblatt, Bismarck-Blatt, Deutsches Echo, Deutsche Stimmen, Deutsche Allgemeine Zeitung, Deutsche Tageszeitung, Eiserne Blätter, Der Film, Frankfurter Illustrierte, Frankfurter Zeitung, Gelbe Hefte, Germania, Hamburger Echo, Hamburger Nachrichten, Hamburger Tageblatt, Die Hilfe, Historisch-Politische Blätter für das katholische Deutschland, Das Hochland, Jung-Bismarck Berlin, Das junge Deutschland, Kladderadatsch, Kölnische Volkszeitung, Korrespondenz der Deutschnationalen Volkspartei, Der Morgen, Münchner Illustrierte Presse, Münchener Neueste Nachrichten, Neue Preußische Zeitung, Regensburger Anzeiger, Rheinisch-Westfälische Zeitung, Rote Fahne, Simplicissimus, Sozialistische Monatshefte, Die Tat, Der Tag, Die Tradition, Völkischer Beobachter, Vorwärts, Die Weltbühne

PRINTED PRIMARY SOURCES

ABUSCH, ALEXANDER, *Der Irrweg einer Nation: Ein Beitrag zum Verständnis deutscher Geschichte* (Berlin, 1946).

AUTENRIETH, OTTO, *Bismarck der Zweite: Der Roman der deutschen Zukunft* (Munich, 1921).

BAMBERGER, LUDWIG, *Bismarck posthumus: Sonderabdruck aus der Wochenschrift 'Die Nation'* (Berlin, 1899).

BAUER, OTTO, *Die österreichische Revolution* (Vienna, 1923).

BAUMGARDT, RUDOLF, *Bismarck* (Munich and Vienna, 1951).

BARTELS, ADOLF, 'Adolf Hitlers *Mein Kampf* ', *Deutsches Schrifttum*, XIX (1927).

BEWER, MAX, *Rembrandt und Bismarck*, 10th edn. (Dresden, 1892).

BINDER, JULIUS, *Führerauslese in der Demokratie* (Langensalza, 1929).

Bismarck-Album des Kladderadatsch, 1849–1898 (Berlin, 1898).

BISMARCK, OTTO VON, *Gedanken und Erinnerungen*, 3 vols. (Berlin and Stuttgart, 1898–1919).

BLOEM, WALTER, *Unvergängliches Deutschland: Ein Buch von Volk und Heimat* (Berlin, 1933).

BRANCA, GERHARD VON, *Die Deutsch-Österreichische Arbeitsgemeinschaft* (Munich, 1927).

BRAUSEWETTER, ERNST, *Fürst Bismarcks 81. Geburtstag—Vollendung des 80. Lebensjahres: Berichte über die Ereignisse vor und an demselben* (Leipzig, 1895).

BRÜNING, HEINRICH, *Memoiren 1918–1934* (Stuttgart, 1970).

BURCKHARDT, JACOB, *Briefe*, ed. Max Burckhardt, 6 vols. (Stuttgart, 1960).

CARLYLE, THOMAS, *Friedrich der Große*, translated from English into German Kurt Linnebach (Berlin and Amsterdam, 1943).

CLAß, HEINRICH, *Wenn ich der Kaiser wär: Politische Wahrheiten und Notwendigkeiten*, 5th edn. (Leipzig 1914),

—— *Wider den Strom: Vom Werden und Wachsen der nationalen Opposition im alten Reich* (Leipzig, 1932).

CURTIUS, JULIUS, *Bemühung um Österreich: Das Scheitern des Zollunionsplans von 1931* (Heidelberg, 1951).

EGELHAAF, GOTTLOB, *Bismarck und der Weltkrieg* (Halle, 1915).

EHRLICH, EUGEN, *Bismarck und der Weltkrieg* (Zurich, 1920).

EINSIEDEL, HEINRICH, GRAF VON, *Tagebuch der Versuchung 1942–1950* (Frankfurt, Berlin, and Vienna, 1985).

ENDERES, BRUNO VON, *Die wirtschaftliche Bedeutung der Anschlußfrage* (Leipzig, 1929).

EYCK, ERICH, *Bismarck: Leben und Werk*, 3 vols. (Zurich, 1941–4).

Feier der Reichsgründung, veranstaltet am 18. Januar 1923 von der Universität Giessen (Giessen, 1923).

Feier der 50. Wiederkehr des Tages der Reichsgründung am 18. Januar 1921 an der Technischen Hochschule Darmstadt (Darmstadt, 1921).

FONTANE, THEODOR, *Briefe an Georg Friedländer*, ed. Kurt Schreinert (Heidelberg, 1954).

FRANK, HANS, *Im Angesicht des Galgens: Deutung Hitlers und seiner Zeit auf Grund eigener Erlebnisse und Erkenntnisse* (Munich, 1953).

FREYER, HANS, *Das politische Semester: Ein Vorschlag zur Universitätsreform* (Jena, 1933).

Gedenkfeier zum 150. Geburtstag des Reichskanzlers Fürst Otto von Bismarck, ed. German Foreign Office (Bonn, 1965).

GERSTENMAIER, EUGEN, *Neuer Nationalismus? Von der Wandlung der Deutschen* (Stuttgart, 1965).

GEßLER, OTTO, *Reichswehrpolitik in der Weimarer Zeit* (Stuttgart, 1958).

GLAWE, WALTHER, *Vom Zweiten und vom Dritten Reich: Rede, gehalten auf der Reichsgründungsfeier der Ernst-Moritz-Arndt-Universität Greifswald am 18. Januar 1934* (Greifswald, 1934.)

GOEBBELS, JOSEPH, *Die Tagebücher von Joseph Goebbels: Sämtliche Fragmente*, ed. Elke Froehlich, 5 vols. (Munich, 1987).

GÖRLER, CARL, *Die Weimarer Verfassung im Verhältnis zu ihrem Frankfurter Vorbild und zum Werke Bismarcks* (Annaberg, 1927).

GOETZ, WALTER, *Historiker in meiner Zeit: Gesammelte Aufsätze* (Cologne and Graz, 1957).

GRADENWITZ, OTTO (ed.), *Akten über Bismarcks großdeutsche Reise vom Jahre 1892* (Heidelberg, 1921).

—— *Bismarcks letzter Kampf 1888–1898* (Berlin, 1924).

GROUSILLIERS, AIDE, *Das Bismarck-Museum in Wort und Bild: Ein Denkmal deutscher Dankbarkeit* (Berlin, 1899).

HAFFNER, SEBASTIAN, *Defying Hitler: A Memoir*, translated from German into English Oliver Pretzel (London, 2000).

HAGEN, MAXIMILIAN VON, *Das Bismarckbild in der Literatur der Gegenwart* (Berlin, 1929).

HALLER, JOHANNES, *Epochen der deutschen Geschichte* (Stuttgart, 1922).

—— *Reden und Aufsätze zur Geschichte und Politik* (Stuttgart and Berlin, 1934).

HASSEL, ULRICH VON, *The von Hassel Diaries 1938–1944: The Story of the Forces against Hitler inside Germany as Recorded by Ambassador Ulrich von Hassel, a Leader of the Movement* (London, 1948).

HAUPTMANN, GERHART, *Seid einig! Rede gehalten auf der Reichsgründungsfeier in Hirschberg am 18. Januar 1921* (Hirschberg, Silesia, 1921).

HAUSHOFER, KARL, 'Mitteleuropa und der Anschluß', in Friedrich Kleinwächter und Heinz von Paller (eds.), *Die Anschlußfrage in ihrer kulturellen, politischen und wirtschaftlichen Bedeutung* (Vienna, 1930), 150–3.

HEINEMANN, GUSTAV W., *Zur Reichsgründung 1871: Zum hundertsten Geburtstag des ersten Deutschen Reichspräsidenten Friedrich Ebert*, ed. Bundeszentrale für politische Bildung (Bonn, 1971).

HERBIG, GUSTAV, *Hoffen und Harren: Rede zum Gedächtnis der Reichsgründung, gehalten am 18. Januar 1922* (Breslau, 1922).

HERZFELD, HANS, *Deutschland und das geschlagene Frankreich 1871–1873: Friedensschluß, Kriegsentschädigung, Besatzungszeit* (Berlin, 1924).

HITLER, ADOLF, *Mein Kampf*, translated from German into English James Murphy, 2nd edn. (London, 1939).

—— *The Speeches of Adolf Hitler, April 1922–August 1939*, ed. Max Domarus, translated from German into English Norman H. Baynes (Oxford, 1942).

—— *Hitler's Secret Book*, introd. Telford Taylor, translated from German into English Salvator Attanasio, 2nd edn. (New York, 1962).

—— *Sämtliche Aufzeichnungen, 1905–1924*, ed. Eberhard Jäckel (Stuttgart, 1980).

HOERMANN, FRANZ X., *Großdeutschlands vierhundertjähriger Niedergang zum Kleindeutschland: Die erste Ursache des heutigen politischen Zusammenbruchs* (Regensburg, 1924).

HOFMANN, HERMANN (ed.), *Fürst Bismarck 1890–1898*, 2 vols. (Stuttgart, 1918).

HOFMANN, WOLFGANG (ed.), *Hindenburg-Album des Kladderadatsch* (Berlin, 1927).

JASPERS, KARL, *Die Schuldfrage* (Heidelberg, 1946).

JASPERS, KARL, *Reden zur Verleihung des Friedenspreises des deutschen Buchhandels*, ed. Hannah Arendt (Munich, 1958).

JASPERS, KARL, *Freiheit und Wiedervereinigung: Über Aufgaben deutscher Politik* (Munich, 1960).

KADEN, RICHARD, *In der alten Armee: Lebenserinnerungen aus Frieden und Krieg* (Groitzsch, 1933).

KAHL, WILHELM, *Bismarck lebt: Gedächtnisrede bei der allgemeinen Trauerfeier in Berlin am 7. August 1898* (Freiburg im Breisgau, 1898).

KAPP, ADOLF, 'Der großdeutsche Gedanke einst und jetzt', *Kriegshefte der Süddeutschen Monatshefte* (1914/15), 46–51.

KAUFMANN, ERICH, *Bismarcks Erbe in der Reichsverfassung* (Berlin, 1917).

—— 'Grundfragen der künftigen Reichsverfassung (1919)', in *Gesammelte Schriften*, vol. I, ed. Albert Holger von Scherpenberg (Göttingen, 1960), 253–96.

KANTOROWICZ, HERMANN U., *Bismarcks Schatten* (Freiburg im Breisgau, 1921).

—— 'The German Constitution in Theory and Practice', *Economia*, VII (1927).

KEHR, ECKART, *Der Primat der Innenpolitik: Economic Interest, Militarism, and Foreign Policy: Essays on German History*, translated from German into English by Grete Heinz (Berkeley, 1977).

KESSLER, HARRY, GRAF, *Gesichter und Zeiten: Erinnerungen* (Berlin, 1962).

—— *Tagebücher 1918 bis 1937*, ed. Wolfgang Pfeiffer-Belli (Frankfurt and Leipzig, 1996).

KOHL, HORST (ed.), *Mit Bismarck daheim und im Felde: Kennworte aus seinen Briefen und Reden* (Berlin, 1915).

KUMSTELLER, BERNHARD, *Geschichtsbuch für die deutsche Jugend: Volksschulausgabe* (Leipzig, 1925).

LANGE, KARL, *Bismarcks Sturz und die öffentliche Meinung in Deutschland und im Auslande* (Berlin and Leipzig, 1927).

LE MANG, ERICH, *Die persönliche Schuld Wilhelms II: ein zeitgemäßer Rückblick* (Dresden, 1919).

LENZ, MAX, *Von Luther zu Bismarck* (Munich and Berlin, 1920).

—— *Wille, Macht und Schicksal*, 3rd edn. (Munich and Berlin, 1922).

LICHTWARK, ALFRED, and RATHENAU, WALTHER, *Der rheinische Bismarck* (Berlin, 1912).

LINDENBERG, PAUL (ed.), *Hindenburg-Denkmal für das deutsche Volk* (Berlin, 1923).

LÖWENSTEIN, HUBERTUS VON, *The Tragedy of a Nation: Germany 1918–1934* (London, 1934).

LUDWIG, EMIL, *Bismarck: Triologie eines Kämpfers* (Potsdam, 1924).

—— *Bismarck: Geschichte eines Kämpfers* (Berlin, 1926).

MANN, HEINRICH, *Der Hass: deutsche Zeitgeschichte* (Amsterdam, 1933).

MANN, THOMAS, *Tagebücher 1933–1934*, ed. Peter de Mendelssohn (Frankfurt, 1977).

MARCKS, ERICH, 'Bismarck und unser Krieg', *Süddeutsche Monatshefte*, XI (1914), 780–7.

—— *Das Deutsche Reich von 1871 bis 1921*, 6th rev. edn. (Leipzig, 1922).

—— *Bismarck: Ein Lebensbild*, 21st–23rd edn. (Stuttgart and Berlin, 1924).

——— *Geschichte und Gegenwart: Fünf historisch—politische Reden* (Stuttgart, Berlin, and Leipzig, 1925).

——— *Auf- und Niedergang im deutschen Schicksal* (Berlin, 1927).

MEINECKE, FRIEDRICH, *Nach der Revolution: Geschichtliche Betrachtungen über unsere Lage* (Munich and Berlin, 1919).

——— *The German Catastrophe: Reflections and Recollections*, translated from the German Sidney B. Fay (Cambridge, Mass., 1950).

MEISSNER, OTTO, *Staatssekretär unter Ebert-Hindenburg-Hitler: Der Schicksalsweg des deutschen Volkes von 1918–1945, wie ich ihn erlebte* (Hamburg, 1950).

MENNELL, ARTHUR, and GARLEPP, BRUNO, *Bismarck—Denkmal für das deutsche Volk* (Chicago, 1895).

MEYER, ARNOLD OSKAR, *Bismarck: Der Mensch und der Staatsmann*, 2nd edn. (Stuttgart, 1949).

MOELLER VAN DEN BRUCK, ARTHUR, *Das dritte Reich*, ed. Hans Schwarz, 3rd edn. (Hamburg, 1931).

MOLTKE, ELIZA VON (ed.), *Erinnerungen, Briefe, Dokumente: Helmuth von Moltke 1877–1916* (Stuttgart, 1922).

MOMMSEN, WILHELM, *Bismarcks Sturz und die Parteien* (Berlin, 1924).

——— *Politische Geschichte von Bismarck bis zur Gegenwart 1850–1933* (Frankfurt, 1935).

——— 'Der Kampf um das Bismarck-Bild', *Universitas*, V (1950), 273–80.

NÄF, WERNER, *Bismarcks Außenpolitik 1871–1890* (St Gallen, 1925).

NAUMANN, FRIEDRICH, *Mitteleuropa* (Berlin, 1915).

NEYEN, EMIL, *Wilhelm II: Sein Werk, 450 Milliarden neuer Schulden und 21 fliehende Könige* (Berlin, 1919).

NIEKISCH, ERNST, *Grundfragen deutscher Außenpolitik* (Berlin, 1925).

ONCKEN, HERMANN, *Lassalle: Eine politische Biographie*, 3rd edn. (Stuttgart and Berlin, 1920).

——— *Unser Reich: Rede, gehalten bei der Gedächtnisfeier der Reichsgründung* (Heidelberg, 1921).

——— *Deutsche Vergangenheit und deutsche Zukunft. Rede gehalten bei der Reichsgründungsfeier am 16.1.1926* (Munich, 1926).

——— 'Bismarck und Weimar', in Bernhard Harms (ed.), *Recht und Staat im neuen Deutschland* (Berlin, 1929), 47–67.

——— 'Die Wiedergeburt der großdeutschen Idee', in Hermann Oncken, *Nation und Geschichte: Reden und Aufsätze 1919–1935* (Berlin, 1935), 45–70.

PENZLER, JOHANNES (ed.), *Fürst Bismarck nach seiner Entlassung*, 7 vols. (Leipzig, 1897–8).

RATHENAU, WALTHER, *Der Kaiser* (Berlin, 1919).

REDSLOB, EDWIN, *Von Weimar nach Europa: Erlebtes und Durchdachtes* (Berlin, 1972).

REHBEIN, ARTHUR, *Bismarck im Sachsenwald* (Berlin, 1925).

Reichsgründungsfeiern der Friedrich-Wilhelms-Universität zu Berlin (Berlin 1921–6).

RITTER, GERHARD, *Die Legende von der verschmähten englisch-deutschen Freundschaft 1898–1901* (Freiburg, 1921).

ROLOFF, GUSTAV, *Die Bilanz des Krieges: Ursprung, Kampf, Ergebnis* (Königstein im Taunus, 1921).

ROTHFELS, HANS (ed.), 'Zur Geschichte des Rückversicherungsvertrages', *Preußische Jahrbücher*, CLXXXVII (1922), 265–92.

——(ed.), *Bismarck und der Staat: Ausgewählte Dokumente*, 2nd edn. (Stuttgart, 1953).

——'Zum 150. Geburtstag Bismarcks', *Vierteljahreshefte für Zeitgeschichte*, XVIII (1965), 225–35.

——'Otto von Bismarck—Persönlichkeit und Werk', *Das Parlament*, 7 Apr. 1965.

——(ed.), *Bismarck: Vorträge und Abhandlungen* (Stuttgart, 1970).

SAITSCHICK, ROBERT, *Bismarck und das Schicksal des deutschen Volkes: Zur Psychologie und Geschichte der deutschen Frage* (Munich, 1949).

SALIN, EDGAR, *Die deutschen Tribute: Zwölf Reden* (Berlin, 1930).

SCHAEDER, ERICH, *Reich und Volk: Festrede zur Feier der Reichsgründung, Schlesische Friedrich-Wilhelms-Universität* (Breslau, 1921).

SCHÄFER, DIETRICH, *Das Reich als Republik: Deutschland und Preußen* (Berlin, 1919).

SCHIEDER, THEODOR, 'Bismarcks Tod und die Welt: Vortrag gehalten am 40. Todestag Bismarcks im Reichssender Königsberg', *Vergangenheit und Gegenwart: Monatsschrift für Geschichtsunterricht und politische Erziehung*, XXVIII (1938), 576–83.

——'Bismarck: Zur Wiederkehr seines Geburtstages vor 150 Jahren', *Geschichte in Wissenschaft und Unterricht*, XVI (1965), 197–207.

SCHMIDT-PAULI, EDGAR VON, *Der Kaiser: das wahre Gesicht Wilhelms II.* (Berlin, 1928).

SCHMITT, CARL, *Die geistesgeschichtliche Lage des heutigen Parlamentarismus*, reprint of the 2nd edn. of 1926 (Berlin, 1961).

SCHMITTMANN, BENEDICT, *Preußen-Deutschland oder deutsches Deutschland?* (Bonn, 1920).

SCHULZE-PFÄLZER, GERHARD, *Von Spa nach Weimar: Die Geschichte der deutschen Zeitenwende* (Leipzig and Zurich, 1929).

SCHÜßLER, WILHELM, *Bismarcks Sturz* (Berlin and Leipzig, 1921).

SCHWEINITZ, LOTHAR VON, *Denkwürdigkeiten des Botschafters General von Schweinitz* (Berlin, 1927).

SEECKT, HANS VON, *Aus seinem Leben 1918–1936* (Leipzig, 1941).

SIEMERING, HERTHA (ed.), *Die deutschen Jugendverbände* (Berlin, 1923).

SPAHN, MARTIN, *Denkrede am 50: Gedenktage der Reichsgründung* (Cologne, 1921).

SPENGLER, OSWALD, *Preußentum und Sozialismus* (Munich, 1920).

STOLBERG-WERNIGERODE, ALBRECHT, GRAF ZU, *Zurück zu Bismarck* (Berlin, 1926).

STRESEMANN, GUSTAV, *Bismarck und wir* (Berlin, 1916).

——*Nationale Realpolitik: Rede des Reichsaußenministers Dr. Stresemann auf dem 6. Parteitag der Deutschen Volkspartei in Dortmund am 14. November 1924* (Berlin, 1924).

——*Essays and Speeches on Various Subjects*, with an introduction Rochus von Rheinbaben (London, 1930).

—— *Vermächtnis: Der Nachlass in drei Bänden*, ed. Henry Bernhard (Berlin, 1932).

—— *Schriften*, ed. Arnold Harttung (Berlin, 1976).

STRIEBITZ, ARNOLD, *Der Eiserne Kanzler: Ein Lebensbild für das deutsche Volk* (Leipzig, 1915).

TROELTSCH, ERNST, *Spectatorbriefe: Aufsätze über die Revolution und die Weltpolitik 1918/22* (Tübingen, 1924).

WEBER, MAX, *Gesammelte politische Schriften*, ed. Johannes Winckelmann, 2nd edn. (Tübingen, 1958).

—— *Economy and Society*, ed. G. Roth and C. Wittich (Berkeley, 1978).

WEBER, WILHELM, *Vom vergangenen und vom zukünftigen Deutschen: Eine Gedächtnisrede zur Reichsgründung für die Stuttgarter und Hohenheimer Studenten* (Tübingen, 1923).

WENTZKE, PAUL, *Ruhrkampf: Einbruch und Abwehr im rheinisch-westfälischen Industriegebiet*, 2 vols. (Berlin, 1930–2).

WESTARP, KUNO, GRAF VON, *Konservative Politik im Übergang vom Kaiserreich zur Weimarer Republik*, ed. Friedrich, Freiherr von Gaertringen (Düsseldorf, 2001).

WESTPHAL, OTTO, *Feinde Bismarcks: Geistige Grundlagen der deutschen Opposition 1848–1918* (Munich and Berlin, 1930).

—— 'Bismarck und Hitler', *Vergangenheit und Gegenwart*, XXIII (1933), 469–81.

WILDENBRUCH, ERNST VON, *Letzte Gedichte* (Berlin, 1908).

ZECHLIN, EGMONT, *Schwarz Rot Gold und Schwarz Weiß Rot in Geschichte und Gegenwart* (Berlin, 1926).

ZIEHEN, LUDWIG, *Bismarck: Geleitbuch zum Bismarck-Film* (Berlin, 1926).

ZIEKURSCH, JOHANNES, *Politische Geschichte des neuen deutschen Kaiserreiches*, vol. 1: *Die Reichsgründung* (Frankfurt, 1925).

—— 'Bismarcks Innenpolitik', *Der Eiserne Steg*, III (1926), 47–57.

SECONDARY WORKS

ALMOND, GABRIEL D., 'The Study of Political Culture', in Berg-Schlosser and Rytlewski (eds.), *Political Culture*, 13–26.

AMBROSIUS, GEROLD, 'Flüchtlinge und Vertriebene in der westdeutschen Wirtschaftsgeschichte', in Rainer Schulze (ed.), *Flüchtlinge und Vertriebene in der westdeutschen Nachkriegsgeschichte* (Hildesheim, 1987), 216–27.

ANDERSON, BENEDICT, *Imagined Communities: Reflections on the Origin and Spread of Nationalism*, 2nd rev. edn. (London and New York, 1991).

ANDERSON, MARGARET L., *Windthorst: A Political Biography* (Oxford, 1981).

ANDREWS, HERBERT D., 'Hitler, Bismarck and History', *German Studies Review*, XIV (1991), 511–36.

ASSMANN, ALEIDA, *Erinnerungsräume: Formen und Wandlungen des kulturellen Gedächtnisses* (Munich, 1999).

ASSMANN, JAN, *Kultur und Gedächtnis* (Frankfurt, 1988).

AUERBACH, HELLMUTH, 'Volksstimmung und veröffentlichte Meinung in Deutschland zwischen März und November 1938', in Franz Knipping and Klaus-Jürgen Müller (eds.), *Machtbewußtsein in Deutschland am Vorabend des Zweiten Weltkrieges* (Paderborn, 1984), 273–93.

BADIA, GILBERT, 'Rosa Luxemburg', in Etienne François and Hagen Schulze (eds.), *Deutsche Erinnerungsorte*, vol. II (Munich, 2001), 105–21.

BAECHLER, CHRISTIAN, *Gustave Stresemann (1878–1929): De l'imperialisme à la sécurité collective* (Strasbourg, 1996).

BAIRD, JAY W., *To Die for Germany: Heroes in the Nazi Pantheon* (Bloomington, Ind., 1990).

BARKAI, AVRAHAM, *Vom Boykott zur 'Entjudung': Der wirtschaftliche Existenzkampf der Juden im Dritten Reich 1933–1943* (Frankfurt, 1987).

BARTHEL, KONRAD, *Friedrich der Große in Hitlers Geschichtsbild* (Wiesbaden, 1977).

BEHRENBECK, SABINE, *Der Kult um die toten Helden: Nationalsozialistische Mythen, Riten und Symbole 1923–1945* (Vierow, 1996).

BEHRENS, REINHARD, 'Die Deutschnationalen in Hamburg 1918–1933', Ph.D. thesis (Hamburg, 1973).

BENDER, PETER, *Die 'Neue Ostpolitik' und ihre Folgen: Vom Mauerbau bis zur Vereinigung*, 3rd rev. edn. (Munich, 1995).

BENDIKAT, ELFI, and LEHNERT, DETLEF, ' "Schwarzweißrot gegen Schwarzrotgold": Identifikation und Abgrenzung parteipolitischer Teilkulturen im Reichstagswahlkampf des Frühjahres 1924', in Detlef Lehnert and Klaus Megerle (eds.), *Politische Teilkulturen zwischen Integration und Polarisierung: Zur politischen Kultur in der Weimarer Republik* (Opladen, 1990), 102–42.

BENNETT, EDWARD W., *Germany and the Diplomacy of the Financial Crisis 1931* (Cambridge, Mass., 1962).

BENZ, WOLFGANG, *Zwischen Hitler und Adenauer: Studien zur deutschen Nachkriegsgesellschaft* (Frankfurt, 1991).

BERG-SCHLOSSER, DIRK, and RYTLEWSKI, RALF (eds.), *Political Culture in Germany* (London, 1993).

BERGER, STEFAN, *The Search for Normality: National Identity and Historical Consciousness in Germany since 1800* (Providence, RI, and Oxford, 1997).

BERGHAHN, VOLKER R., *Der Stahlhelm: Bund der Frontsoldaten 1918–1935* (Düsseldorf, 1966).

—— 'Das Volksbegehren gegen den Young-Plan und die Ursprünge des Präsidialregimes 1928–1930', in Dirk Stegmann *et al.* (eds.), *Industrielle Gesellschaft und politisches System: Beiträge zur politischen Sozialgeschichte: Festschrift für Fritz Fischer zum siebzigsten Geburtstag* (Bonn, 1978), 431–48.

BIRK, GERHARD, 'Der Tag von Sedan: Intentionen, Resonanz und Widerstand (1871–1895)', *Jahrbuch für Volkskunde und Kulturgeschichte*, XXV (1982), 95–110.

BIRKENFELD, WOLFGANG, 'Der Rufmord am Reichspräsidenten: Zu Grenzformen des politischen Kampfes gegen die frühe Weimarer Republik 1919–1925', *Archiv für Sozialgeschichte*, V (1965), 453–500.

BLACKBOURN, DAVID, and ELEY, GEOFF, *The Peculiarities of German History: Bourgeois Society and Politics in Nineteeth-Century Germany* (Oxford, 1984).

BLEUEL, HANS P., and KLINNERT, ERNST, *Deutsche Studenten auf dem Weg ins Dritte Reich: Ideologien—Programme—Aktionen 1918–1933* (Gütersloh, 1967).

BLUHM, HARALD, 'Befreiungskriege und Preußenrenaissance', in Rudolf Speth and Edgar Wolfrum (eds.), *Politische Mythen und Geschichtspolitik: Konstruktion—Inszenierung—Mobilisierung* (Berlin, 1996), 71–95.

BLUMENBERG, HANS, *Arbeit am Mythos* (Frankfurt, 1996).

BOCK, PETRA, and WOLFRUM, EDGAR (eds.), *Umkämpfte Vergangenheit: Geschichtsbilder, Erinnerung und Vergangenheitspolitik im internationalen Vergleich* (Göttingen, 1999).

BOEMEKE, MANFRED F., FELDMAN, GERALD D., and GLASER, ELISABETH (eds.), *The Treaty of Versailles: A Reassessment after 75 Years* (Cambridge, 1998).

BORCHARDT, KNUT, *Wachstum, Krisen, Handlungsspielräume der Wirtschaftspolitik* (Göttingen, 1982).

BORN, KARL E., *Die deutsche Bankenkrise 1931: Finanzen und Politik* (Munich, 1967).

BRACHER, KARL DIETRICH, *The German Dictatorship: The Origins, Structure, and Effects of National Socialism*, translated from German into English by Jean Steinberg (London, 1971).

——*Die Auflösung der Weimarer Republik: Eine Studie zum Problem des Machtzerfalls in der Demokratie*, reprint of the 5th edn. (Düsseldorf, 1978).

——'Das Ende Preußens', in Karl Dietrich Erdmann (ed.), *Preußen: Seine Wirkung auf die deutsche Geschichte* (Stuttgart, 1985), 281–307.

——*et al.* (eds.), *Die Nationalsozialistische Machtergreifung: Studien zur Errichtung des totalitären Herrschaftssystems in Deutschland 1933/34*, 2nd edn. (Cologne, 1962).

BRAUER, STEFAN, *Grundpositionen der deutschen Rechten 1871–1945* (Tübingen, 1999).

BREITENBORN, KONRAD, *Bismarck: Kult und Kitsch um den Reichsgründer* (Frankfurt, 1990).

——'Das Bismarck-Museum in Schönhausen', *Museumskunde*, LVI (1991), 167–74.

BREUNING, KLAUS, *Die Vision des Reiches: Deutscher Katholizismus zwischen Demokratie und Diktatur 1929–1934* (Munich, 1969).

BROSZAT, MARTIN, 'Betrachtungen zu "Hitlers Zweitem Buch" ', *Vierteljahreshefte für Zeitgeschichte*, VI (1961), 417–30.

——'Soziale Motivation und Führerbindung des Nationalsozialismus', *Vierteljahreshefte für Zeitgeschichte*, XVIII (1970), 392–409.

BRUCH, RÜDIGER VOM, and MÜLLER, RAINER A. (eds.), *Historikerlexikon: Von der Antike bis zum 20. Jahrhundert* (Munich, 1991).

BRUDE-FIRNAU, GISELA, *Die literarische Deutung Kaiser Wilhelms II zwischen 1889 und 1989* (Heidelberg, 1997).

BURKHARDT, JOHANNES, 'Kriegsgrund Geschichte? 1870, 1813, 1756—historische Argumente und Orientierungen bei Ausbruch des Ersten Weltkrieges', in Johannes Burkhardt *et al.* (eds.), *Lange und kurze Wege in den ersten Weltkrieg: Vier Augsburger Beiträge zur Kriegsursachenforschung* (Munich, 1996), 9–86.

BUSCH, OTTO (ed.), *Das Preußenbild in der Geschichte: Protokoll eines Symposiums* (Berlin and New York, 1981).

BUSSCHE, RAIMUND VON DEM, *Konservatismus in der Weimarer Republik: Die Politisierung des Unpolitischen* (Heidelberg, 1998).

BUSSENIUS, DANIEL, 'Eine ungeliebte Tradition: Die Weimarer Linke und die 48er Revolution 1918–1925', in Heinrich August Winkler (ed.), *Griff nach der Deutungsmacht: Zur Geschichte der Geschichtspolitik in Deutschland* (Göttingen, 2004), 90–114.

CARLYLE, THOMAS, *On Heroes, Hero-Worship, and the Heroic in History* (London, 1841).

CARR, EDWARD H., *German–Soviet Relations between the Two World Wars 1919–1939* (Baltimore, 1951).

CARSTEN, FRANCIS L., *Reichswehr und Politik 1918–1933*, 3rd edn. (Cologne and Berlin, 1966).

CARY, NOEL D., 'The Making of the Reich President, 1925: German Conservatism and the Nomination of Paul von Hindenburg', *Central European History*, XXIII (1990), 179–204.

CASSIRER, ERNST, *The Myth of the State* (London, 1946).

CHICKERING, ROGER, *'We men who feel most German': A Cultural Study of the Pan-German League 1886–1914* (Boston, London, and Sydney, 1984).

CHILDERS, THOMAS C., *The Nazi Voter: The Social Foundations of Fascism in Germany, 1919–1933* (Chapel Hill and London, 1983).

—— 'The Limits of National Socialist Mobilisation: The Election of 6 November 1932 and the Fragmentation of the Nazi Constituency', in Thomas C. Childers (ed.), *The Formation of the Nazi Constituency 1919–1933* (London and Sydney, 1986), 232–59.

CLARK, CHRISTOPHER M., *Kaiser Wilhelm II* (Harlow, 2000).

DANN, OTTO, *Nation und Nationalismus in Deutschland 1770–1990*, 3rd rev. edn. (Munich, 1996).

DAVIDSON, JOHN E., 'Working for the man, whoever that may be: The Vocation of Wolfgang Liebeneiner', in Robert C. Reimer (ed.), *Cultural History through a National Socialist Lens: Essays on the Cinema of the Third Reich* (New York, 2000), 240–67.

DEMANDT, ALEXANDER, *Geschichte als Argument: Drei Formen politischen Zukunftsdenkens im Altertum* (Konstanz, 1972).

DIWALD, HELLMUT, 'Geschichtsbild und Geschichtsbewußtsein im gegenwärtigen Deutschland', *Saeculum*, XXVIII (1978), 22–30.

DOMANSKY, ELIZABETH, 'Politische Dimensionen von Jugendprotest und Generationenkonflikt in der Zwischenkriegszeit in Deutschland', in Dieter Dowe (ed.), *Jugendprotest und Generationenkonflikt in Europa im 20. Jahrhundert* (Berlin, 1986).

DÖRNER, ANDREAS, *Politischer Mythos und symbolische Politik: Der Hermannmythos*: *Zur Entstehung des Nationalbewußtseins der Deutschen* (Reinbek bei Hamburg, 1996).

DORPALEN, ANDREAS, 'The German Historians and Bismarck', *The Review of Politics*, XV (1953).

—— *Hindenburg and the Weimar Republic* (Princeton, 1964).

DÖRR, MANFRED, 'Die deutschnationale Volkspartei 1925 bis 1928', Ph.D. thesis (Marburg, 1964).

DORRMANN, MICHAEL, '"Wenn Bismarck wiederkäme": Kunst, Ideologie und Rathenaus Engagement für ein Bismarck-National-Denkmal', in Hans Wilderotter (ed.), *Die Extreme berühren sich: Walther Rathenau, 1867–1922* (Berlin, 1993), 99–108.

—— 'Das Bismarck-Nationaldenkmal am Rhein: Ein Beitrag zur Geschichtskultur des Deutschen Reiches', *Zeitschrift für Geschichtswissenschaft*, XLIV (1996), 1061–87.

DREWNIAK, BOGUSLAW, *Der deutsche Film 1938–1945* (Düsseldorf, 1987).

DÜLFFER, JOST, *Nazi Germany 1933–1945: Faith and Annihilation*, translated from the German by Dean Scott McMurry (London, 1996).

—— and HOLL, KARL (eds.), *Bereit zum Krieg: Kriegsmentalität im wilhelminischen Deutschland 1890–1914* (Göttingen, 1986).

—— and HÜBNER, HANS (eds.), *Otto von Bismarck: Person-Politik-Mythos* (Berlin, 1993).

EBERAN, BARBRO, *Luther? Friedrich 'der Große'? Wagner? Nietzsche? . . . ? . . . ? Wer war an Hitler schuld? Die Debatte um die Schuldfrage 1945–1949* (Munich, 1983).

EKSTEINS, MODRIS, *The Limits of Reason: The German Democratic Press and the Collapse of Weimar Democracy* (Oxford, 1975).

ENGELBERG, ERNST, *Bismarck*, 2 vols. (Berlin, 1985–90).

EPKENHANS, MICHAEL, *Die Otto-von-Bismarck-Stiftung 1996–2000* (Friedrichsruh, 2000).

ERDMANN, KARL D., 'Gustav Stresemann: Sein Bild in der Geschichte', *Historische Zeitschrift*, CCXXVII (1978), 599–616.

—— *Gustav Stresemann: The Revision of Versailles and the Weimar Parliamentary System*, Speech delivered at the German Historical Institute, London (London and Ashford, 1980).

—— (ed.), *Preußen: Seine Wirkung auf die deutsche Geschichte* (Stuttgart, 1985).

—— and SCHULZE, HAGEN (eds.), *Weimar: Selbstpreisgabe einer Demokratie* (Düsseldorf, 1980).

ERGER, JOHANNES, *Der Kapp-Lüttwitz-Putsch: Ein Beitrag zur deutschen Innenpolitik 1919/20* (Düsseldorf, 1967).

FABER, KARL-GEORG, 'Johannes Ziekursch', in Hans-Ulrich Wehler (ed.), *Deutsche Historiker*, vol. 3 (Göttingen, 1972), 109–23.

FALLOIS, IMMO VON, *Kalkül und Illusion: Der Machtkampf zwischen Reichswehr und SA während der Röhm-Krise 1934* (Berlin, 1994).

FALTER, JÜRGEN, 'Unemployment and the Radicalization of the German Electorate 1928–33', in Peter Stachura (ed.), *Unemployment and the Great Depression in Weimar Germany* (London, 1986), 187–207.

FALTER, JÜRGEN, 'The Two Hindenburg Elections of 1925 and 1932: A Total Reversal of Voter Coalitions', *Central European History*, XXIII (1990), 225–41.

——*Hitlers Wähler* (Munich, 1991).

——*et al.* (eds.), *Wahlen und Abstimmungen in der Weimarer Republik: Materialien zum Wahlverhalten 1919–1933* (Munich, 1986).

FARQUHARSON, JOHN E., *The Plough and the Swastika: The NSDAP and Agriculture in Germany 1928–1945* (London and Beverly Hills, Cal., 1976).

FAULENBACH, BERND (ed.), *Geschichtswissenschaft in Deutschland: Traditionelle Positionen und gegenwärtige Aufgaben* (Munich, 1974).

——*Ideologie des deutschen Weges: Die deutsche Geschichte in der Historiographie zwischen Kaiserreich und Nationalsozialismus* (Munich, 1980).

——' "Deutscher Sonderweg": Zur Geschichte und Problematik einer zentralen Kategorie des deutschen geschichtlichen Bewußtseins', *Aus Politik und Zeitgeschichte*, XXXIII (1981), 3–21.

——'Die "nationale Revolution" und die deutsche Geschichte: Zum zeitgenössischen Urteil der Historiker', in Wolfgang Michalka (ed.), *Die nationalsozialistische Machtergreifung* (Paderborn, Munich, Vienna, and Zurich, 1984), 357–71.

——'Nach der Niederlage: Zeitgeschichtliche Fragen und apologetische Tendenzen in der Historiographie der Weimarer Zeit', in Peter Schöttler (ed.), *Geschichte als Legitimationswissenschaft 1918–1945* (Frankfurt, 1997), 31–51.

FEHRENBACH, ELISABETH, 'Die Reichsgründung in der deutschen Geschichtsschreibung', in Theodor Schieder and Ernst Deuerlein (eds.), *Reichsgründung 1870/71: Tatsachen, Kontroversen, Interpretationen* (Stuttgart, 1970), 259–90.

——'Über die Bedeutung der politischen Symbole im Nationalstaat', *Historische Zeitschrift*, CCXIII (1971), 296–357.

FELDMAN, GERALD D., and STEINISCH, IRMGARD, *Industrie und Gewerkschaften 1918–1924: die überforderte Zentralarbeitsgemeinschaft* (Stuttgart, 1985).

FENSKE, HANS, 'Das "Dritte Reich": Die Perversion der Reichsidee', in Bernd Martin (ed.), *Deutschland in Europa: Ein historischer Rückblick* (Munich, 1992), 210–30.

FEST, JOACHIM C., *Hitler*, translated from German into English by Richard and Clara Winston (London, 1974).

——*Plotting Hitler's Death: The German Resistance to Hitler 1933–1945*, trans. Bruce Little (London, 1997).

——*Der Untergang: Hitler und das Ende des Dritten Reiches* (Berlin, 2002).

FINK, CAROLE, FROHN, AXEL, and HEIDEKING, JÜRGEN (eds.), *Genoa, Rapallo, and European Reconstruction in 1922* (Washington, DC, 1991).

FISCHER, CONAN, *The German Communists and the Rise of Nazism* (New York, 1991).

FISCHER, FRITZ, *Griff nach der Weltmacht: Die Kriegszielpolitik des kaiserlichen Deutschland 1914/18* (Düsseldorf, 1961).

FISCHER, HEINZ-DIETRICH (ed.), *Deutsche Zeitschriften des 17. bis 20. Jahrhunderts* (Pullach, 1973).

FLACKE, MONIKA (ed.), *Mythen der Nationen* (Berlin, 1998).

FLEURY, ANTOINE (ed.), *Le Plan d'Union fédérale européenne: Perspectives nationales, avec documents* (Frankfurt, 1998).

FRANÇOIS, ETIENNE, and SCHULZE, HAGEN (eds.), *Deutsche Erinnerungsorte*, 3 vols. (Munich, 2001).

FRANKEL, RICHARD, 'From the Beer Halls to the Halls of Power: The Cult of Bismarck and the Legitimization of a New German Right', *German Studies Review*, XXVI (2003), 543–60.

FRANZEN, EMIL, 'Das Bismarck-Bild in unserer Zeit', *Neues Abendland*, V (1950), 223–30.

FREISEL, LUDWIG, 'Das Bismarckbild der Alldeutschen: Bismarck im Bewußtsein und in der Politik des Alldeutschen Verbandes von 1890 bis 1933: Ein Beitrag zum Bismarckverständnis des deutschen Nationalismus', Ph.D. thesis (University of Würzburg, 1964).

FREITAG, WERNER, 'Nationale Mythen und kirchliches Heil: Der "Tag von Potsdam"', *Westfälische Forschungen*, XLI (1991), 379–430.

FRICKE, DIETER, et al. (eds.), *Lexikon zur Parteiengeschichte: Die bürgerlichen und kleinbürgerlichen Parteien und Verbände in Deutschland (1789–1945)*, 4 vols. (Leipzig, 1983–6).

FRIEDEL, ALOIS, *Deutsche Staatssymbole: Herkunft und Bedeutung der politischen Symbolik in Deutschland* (Frankfurt and Bonn, 1968).

FRIEDLÄNDER, SAUL, *Nazi Germany and the Jews: The Years of Persecution 1933–39* (London, 1997).

FRITZSCHE, PETER, 'Presidential Victory and Popular Festivity in Weimar Germany: Hindenburg's 1925 Election', *Central European History*, 23 (1990), 205–24.

FULBROOK, MARY, *Anatomy of a Dictatorship: Inside the GDR 1949–1989* (Oxford, 1995).

GALL, LOTHAR (ed.), *Das Bismarck-Problem in der Geschichtsschreibung nach 1945* (Cologne and Berlin, 1971).

——*Bismarck: The White Revolutionary*, translated from the German by J. A. Underwood, 2 vols. (London, 1986).

—— 'Die Deutschen und Bismarck', in Ralph Melville et al. (eds.), *Deutschland und Europa in der Neuzeit: Festschrift für Karl Otmar von Arentin zum 65. Geburtstag*, 2 vols. (Stuttgart, 1988), 2. 525–36.

—— (ed.), *Aufbruch zur Freiheit* (Frankfurt, 1998).

GARMAN, SEBASTIAN P., 'Foundation Myths and Political Identities: Ancient Rome and Anglo-Saxon England Compared', Ph.D. thesis (London School of Economics, 1994).

GARTON ASH, TIMOTHY, *In Europe's Name: Germany and the Divided Continent* (New York, 1993).

GÄRTRINGEN, FRIEDRICH FREIHERR VON, 'Die Deutschnationale Volkspartei', in Erich Mathias and Rudolf Morsey (eds.), *Das Ende der Parteien 1933* (Düsseldorf, 1960), 543–652.

—— '"Dolchstoß"—Diskussion und "Dolchstoßlegende" im Wandel von vier Jahrzehnten', in Friedrich, Freiherr von Gärtringen and Waldemar Besson (eds.), *Geschichte und Geschichtsbewußtsein* (Göttingen, 1963), 122–60.

GAY, PETER, *Weimar Culture: The Outsider as Insider*, 4th edn. (London, 1992).

GEBHARDT, JÜRGEN, 'Messianische Politik und ideologische Massenbewegung', in Joachim Knoll and Julius Schoeps (eds.), *Von kommenden Zeiten: Geschichtsprophetien im 19. und 20. Jahrhundert* (Stuttgart and Bonn, 1984), 44–56.

GEISS, IMMANUEL, 'Die Fischer-Kontroverse: Ein kritischer Beitrag zum Verhältnis zwischen Historiographie und Politik in der Bundesrepublik', in Immanuel Geiss, *Studien über Geschichte und Geschichtswissenschaft* (Frankfurt, 1972), 108–98.

GEMEIN, GISBERT J., 'Die DNVP in Düsseldorf', Ph.D. thesis (Cologne, 1969).

GERWARTH, ROBERT, 'Republik und Reichsgründung: Bismarcks kleindeutsche Lösung im Meinungsstreit der ersten deutschen Demokratie 1918–1933', in Winkler (ed.), *Griff nach der Deutungsmacht*, 115–33.

GIES, HORST, *Geschichtsunterricht unter der Diktatur Hitlers* (Cologne, Weimar, and Vienna, 1992).

GILDEA, ROBERT, *The Past in French History* (New Haven and London, 1994).

GÖTZ, NORBERT, 'Ungleiche Geschwister: Die Konstruktion von nationalsozialistischer Volksgemeinschaft und schwedischem Volksheim', Ph.D. thesis (Berlin, 1999).

GÖTZ VON OLENHAUSEN, IRMTRAUD, 'Die Krise der jungen Generation und der Aufstieg des Nationalsozialismus: Eine Analyse der Jugendorganisationen der Weimarer Zeit', *Jahrbuch des Archivs der Deutschen Jugendbewegung*, XII (1980).

GRADMANN, CHRISTOPH, *Historische Belletristik: Populäre historische Biographien in der Weimarer Republik* (Frankfurt and New York, 1993).

GRAML, HERMANN, *et al.* (eds.), *The German Resistance to Hitler* (London, 1970).

GRATHWOL, ROBERT P., *Stresemann and the DNVP: Reconciliation or Revenge in German Foreign Policy 1924–1928* (Lawrence, Kan., 1980).

GROH, DIETER, *Negative Integration und revolutionärer Attentismus: Die deutsche Sozialdemokratie am Vorabend des ersten Weltkrieges* (Frankfurt, 1973).

——and BRANDT, PETER, *'Vaterlandslose Gesellen': Sozialdemokratie und Nation 1860–1990* (Munich, 1992).

GRÖPPEL, PETER-ARNDT, and WEBER, KARSTEN, *Heldenverehrung als politische Gefahr: Der Bismarck-Kult des deutschen Bürgertums im 2. Reich* (Grünwald, 1973).

GROSSER, DIETER (ed.), *German Unification: The Unexpected Challenge* (Oxford, 1990).

GUSY, CHRISTOPH, *Weimar—die wehrlose Republik? Verfassungsschutzrecht und Verfassungsschutz in der Weimarer Republik* (Tübingen, 1991).

HAGEMANN, THOMAS, 'Das Bismarck-Bild in der deutschen Öffentlichkeit nach 1890: Mythen-Strukturen, Inhalte, Ausdrucksformen des Bismarck-Kultes und das Beispiel der Verehrerpost aus den Beständen des Archivs der Otto-von-Bismarck-Stiftung in Friedrichsruh', state exam thesis (University of Paderborn, 1999).

HAGENLÜCKE, HEINZ, *Deutsche Vaterlandspartei: Die nationale Rechte am Ende des Kaiserreiches* (Düsseldorf, 1997).

HAGENOW, ELISABETH VON, *Politik und Bild: Die Postkarte als Medium der Propaganda* (Hamburg, 1994).

HALBWACHS, MAURICE, *Les Cadres sociaux de la mémoire* (Paris, 1925).

——*La Mémoire collective* (Paris, 1950).

HALLMANN, HANS (ed.), *Revision des Bismarck-Bildes: Die Diskussion der deutschen Fachhistoriker 1945–1955* (Darmstadt, 1972).

HAMEROW, THEODORE S., *On the Road to the Wolf's Lair: German Resistance to Hitler* (Cambridge, Mass., 1997).

HAMILTON, RICHARD, *Who Voted for Hitler?* (Princeton, 1982).

HANK, MANFRED, *Kanzler ohne Amt: Fürst Bismarck nach seiner Entlassung 1890–1898* (Munich, 1980).

HARDTWIG, WOLFGANG, 'Erinnerung, Wissenschaft, Mythos: Nationale Geschichtsbilder und politische Symbole in der Reichsgründungszeit und im Kaiserreich', in Wolfgang Hardtwig, *Geschichtskultur und Wissenschaft* (Munich, 1990), 224–63.

—— 'Der bezweifelte Patriotismus—nationales Bewußtsein und Denkmal 1786 bis 1933', *Geschichte in Wissenschaft und Unterricht*, XLIV (1993), 773–85.

—— 'Bürgertum, Staatssymbolik und Staatsbewußtsein im Deutschen Kaiserreich 1871–1914', in Wolfgang Hardtwig, *Nationalismus und Bürgerkultur in Deutschland 1500–1914: Ausgewählte Aufsätze* (Göttingen, 1994), 191–218.

—— 'Der Bismarck-Mythos: Gestalt und Funktionen zwischen politischer Öffentlichkeit und Wissenschaft', in Wolfgang Hardtwig, *Hochkultur des bürgerlichen Zeitalters: Ausgewählte Aufsätze* (Göttingen, forthcoming).

HEDINGER, HANS-WALTER, 'Der Bismarckkult. Ein Umriß', in Gunter Stephenson (ed.), *Der Religionswandel in unserer Zeit im Spiegel der Religionswissenschaften* (Darmstadt, 1976), 201–15.

—— 'Bismarck-Denkmäler und Bismarck-Verehrung', in Ekkehard Mai and Stephan Waetzold (eds.), *Kunstverwaltung, Bau- und Denkmalpolitik im Kaiserreich* (Berlin, 1981), 277–314.

HEFFEN, ANNEGRET, *Der Reichskunstwart—Kunstpolitik in den Jahren 1920–1933: Zu den Bemühungen um eine offizielle Reichskunstpolitik in der Weimarer Republik* (Essen, 1986).

HEIBER, HELMUT, *Joseph Goebbels*, 3rd edn. (Munich, 1988).

HEINEMANN, ULRICH, *Die verdrängte Niederlage: Politische Öffentlichkeit und Kriegsschuldfrage in der Weimarer Republik* (Göttingen, 1983).

HERFF, JEFFREY, *Divided Memory: The Nazi Past in the Two Germanys* (Cambridge, Mass., 1997).

HERTZMANN, LEWIS, *DNVP: Right-Wing Opposition in the Weimar Republic 1918–1924* (Lincoln, Neb., 1963).

HERZ, RUDOLF, *Hoffmann & Hitler: Fotografie als Medium des Führer-Mythos* (Munich, 1994).

HERZ, THOMAS, and SCHWAB-TAPP, MICHAEL, *Umkämpfte Vergangenheit: Diskurse über den Nationalsozialismus seit 1945* (Opladen, 1997).

HERZFELD, HANS, 'Staat und Nation in der deutschen Geschichtsschreibung der Weimarer Zeit', in *Veritas-Iustitia-Libertas: Festschrift zur 200-Jahrfeier der Columbia-University, New York, überreicht von der Freien Universität Berlin und der Deutschen Hochschule für Politik* (Berlin, 1954), 129–43.

HESS, JÜRGEN C., *'Das ganze Deutschland soll es sein': Demokratischer Nationalismus in der Weimarer Republik am Beispiel der Deutschen Demokratischen Partei* (Stuttgart, 1978).

HEUSS, THEODOR, *Friedrich Naumann: Der Mann, das Werk, die Zeit*, 3rd rev. edn. (Munich and Hamburg, 1968).

HEYDE, PHILIPP, *Das Ende der Reparationen: Deutschland, Frankreich und der Youngplan 1929–1932* (Paderborn, 1998).

HEYDEMANN, GÜNTHER, 'Geschichtsbild und Geschichtspropaganda in der Ära Honecker: Die "Erbe-und-Tradition"-Konzeption der DDR', in Ute Daniel and Wolfram Siemann (eds.), *Propaganda: Meinungskampf: Verführung und politische Sinnstiftung 1789–1989* (Frankfurt, 1994), 161–71.

HILDEBRAND, KLAUS, *Das vergangene Reich: Deutsche Außenpolitik von Bismarck bis Hitler 1871–1945* (Stuttgart, 1995).

HILLGRUBER, ANDREAS, *Großmachtpolitik und Militarismus im 20. Jahrhundert* (Düsseldorf, 1974).

HOBSBAWM, ERIC, and RANGER, TERENCE (eds.), *The Invention of Tradition*, 2nd edn. (Cambridge, 1996).

HOFFMANN, DIERK, 'Die Integration von Flüchtlingen und Vertriebenen nach 1945: Interdisziplinäre Ergebnisse und Forschungsperspektiven: Ein Forschungskolloquium des Instituts für Zeitgeschichte', *Vierteljahreshefte für Zeitgeschichte*, XLVI (1998), 551–4.

HOLZBACH, HEIDRUN, *Das 'System Hugenberg': Die Organisation bürgerlicher Sammlungs-politik vor dem Aufstieg der NSDAP* (Stuttgart, 1981).

HORT, JAKOB, *Bismarck in München: Formen und Funktionen der Bismarckrezeption (1885–1934)* (Frankfurt, 2004).

HUBER, ERNST R., *Deutsche Verfassungsgeschichte seit 1789*, vol. 5: *Weltkrieg, Revolution und Reichserneuerung 1914–1919* (Stuttgart, 1978).

——*Deutsche Verfassungsgeschichte seit 1789*, vol. 6: *Die Weimarer Reichsverfassung* (Stuttgart, 1981).

——*Deutsche Verfassungsgeschichte seit 1789*, vol. 7: *Ausbau, Schutz und Untergang der Weimarer Republik* (Stuttgart, 1984).

——*Deutsche Verfassungsgeschichte seit 1789*, vol. 3: *Bismarck und das Reich*, 3rd edn. (Stuttgart, 1988).

HÜRTER, JOHANNES, *Wilhelm Groener: Reichswehrminister am Ende der Weimarer Republik (1928–1932)* (Munich, 1993).

HUTTON, PATRICK H., *History as an Art of Memory* (Hanover and London, 1993).

IGGERS, GEORGE G., *The German Conception of History: The National Tradition of Historical Thought from Herder to the Present*, 2nd rev. edn. (Middletown, Conn., 1983).

ISNENGHI, MARIO (ed.), *I luoghi della memoria*, 3 vols. (Rome and Bari, 1987–8).

JÄCKEL, EBERHARD, *Hitlers Weltanschauung: Entwurf einer Herrschaft*, 4th rev. edn. (Stuttgart, 1991).

JACOBSON, JON, *Locarno Diplomacy: Germany and the West 1925–1929* (Princeton, 1972).

JÄGER, WOLFGANG, *Historische Forschung und politische Kultur in Deutschland: die Debatte über den Ausbruch des Ersten Weltkrieges* (Göttingen, 1984).

JAMES, HAROLD, *The German Slump: Politics and Economics 1924–1936* (Oxford, 1986).

—— 'Economic Reasons for the Collapse of the Weimar Republic', in Ian Kershaw (ed.), *Weimar: Why did German Democracy Fail?* (London, 1990), 30–57.

JARAUSCH, KONRAD H., *Deutsche Studenten 1800–1970* (Frankfurt, 1984).

—— *After Unity: Reconfiguring German Identities* (Providence, RI, and Oxford, 1997).

JASPER, GOTTHARD, *Der Schutz der Republik: Studien zur staatlichen Sicherung der Demokratie in der Weimarer Republik 1922–1930* (Tübingen, 1963).

JOCHMANN, WERNER, 'Brünings Deflationspolitik und der Untergang der Weimarer Republik', in Dirk Stegmann *et al.* (eds.), *Industrielle Gesellschaft und politisches System: Beiträge zur politischen Sozialgeschichte: Festschrift für Fritz Fischer zum 70. Geburtstag* (Bonn 1978), 97–112.

JONES, LARRY E., 'Generational Conflict and the Problems of Political Mobilization in the Weimar Republic', in Larry E. Jones and James Retallack (eds.), *Elections, Mass Politics, and Social Change in Modern Germany* (Washington, DC, and Cambridge, 1992), 347–69.

—— 'Stabilisierung von Rechts: Gustav Stresemann und das Streben nach politischer Stabilität 1923–1929', in Karl H. Pohl (ed.), *Politiker und Bürger: Gustav Stresemann und seine Zeit* (Göttingen, 2002), 162–93.

KAEHLER, SIEGFRIED A., 'Der 1. April 1895 und sein zeitgeschichtlicher Hintergrund', *Nachrichten von der Akademie der Wissenschaften in Göttingen: Philologisch-Historische Klasse*, III (1948), 30–41.

KAELBLE, HARTMUT, *Der Boom 1948–1973* (Opladen, 1992).

KAISER, MONIKA, *Machtwechsel von Ulbricht zu Honecker: Funktionsmechanismen der SED-Diktatur in Konfliktssituationen 1962 bis 1972* (Berlin, 1997).

KAUFMANN, WALTER H., *Monarchism in the Weimar Republic* (New York, 1953).

KEETON, EDWARD D., *Briand's Locarno Policy: French Economics, Politics and Diplomacy 1925–1929* (New York and London, 1987).

KERSHAW, IAN, *The 'Hitler Myth': Image and Reality in the Third Reich* (Oxford and New York, 1987).

—— (ed.), *Weimar: Why did German Democracy Fail?* (London, 1990).

—— 'Der 30. Januar 1933: Ausweg aus der Staatskrise und Anfang des Staatsverfalls', in Heinrich August Winkler (ed.), *Die deutsche Staatskrise 1930–1933: Handlungsspielräume und Alternativen* (Munich, 1992), 277–84.

—— *Hitler: 1889–1936: Hubris* (London, 1999).

—— *Hitler: 1936–45: Nemesis* (London, 2000).

KETTENACKER, LOTHAR, 'Sozialpsychologische Aspekte der Führer-Herrschaft', in Lothar Kettenacker and Gerhard Hirschfeld (eds.), *Der 'Führerstaat': Mythos und Realität: Studien zur Struktur und Politik des Dritten Reiches* (Stuttgart, 1981), 98–132.

—— 'Der Mythos vom Reich', in Karl H. Bohrer (ed.), *Mythos und Moderne: Begriff und Bild einer Rekonstruktion* (Frankfurt, 1983), 261–89.

KLEIN, FRITZ, 'Between Compiègne and Versailles: The Germans on the Way from a Misunderstood Defeat to an Unwanted Peace', in Boemeke *et al.* (eds.), *Treaty of Versailles*, 203–20.

KLEßMANN, CHRISTOPH, *Die doppelte Staatsgründung: Deutsche Geschichte 1945–1955*, 5th rev. edn. (Göttingen, 1991).

KLÖNNE, ARNO, *Jugend im Dritten Reich* (Munich, 1990).

KLOSS, GÜNTER, and SEELE, SIEGLINDE, *Bismarck-Türme and Bismarck-Säulen: Eine Bestandsaufnahme* (Petersberg, 1997).

KNOCK, THOMAS J., *Woodrow Wilson and the Quest for a New World Order* (New York, 1992).

KOGAN, ARTHUR G., 'Genesis of the Anschluss Problem: Germany and the Germans of the Hapsburg Monarchy in the Autumn of 1918', *Journal of Central European Affairs*, XX (1960), 24–50.

KOLB, EBERHARD (ed.), *Vom Kaiserreich zur Weimarer Republik* (Cologne, 1972).

—— (ed.), *Europa und die Reichsgründung: Preußen-Deutschland in der Sicht der großen europäischen Mächte 1860–1880* (Munich, 1980).

—— *The Weimar Republic*, translated from the German by P. S. Falla (London, 1988).

——and RICHTER, LUDWIG (eds.), *Nationalliberalismus in der Weimarer Republik: Die Führungsgremien der Deutschen Volkspartei*, 2 vols. (Düsseldorf, 1999).

KÖNNEMANN, ERWIN (ed.), *Der Kapp-Lüttwitz-Ludendorff-Putsch* (Berlin, 1996).

KOSCHNIK, LEONORE, 'Mythos zu Lebzeiten—Bismarck als nationale Kultfigur', in *Bismarck-Preussen, Deutschland und Europa: Eine Ausstellung des Deutschen Historischen Museums Berlin, 26. August–25. November 1990*, 3rd edn. (Berlin, 1990), 455–8.

KOSELLEK, REINHART, 'Revolution, Rebellion, Aufruhr, Bürgerkrieg', in Otto Brunner *et al.* (eds.), *Geschichtliche Grundbegriffe: Historisches Lexikon der politisch-sozialen Sprache*, vol. 5 (Stuttgart, 1984), 689–788.

KOSING, ALFRED, *Nation in Geschichte und Gegenwart: Studie zur historisch-materialistischen Theorie der Nation* (East Berlin, 1976).

KOSZYK, KURT, *Deutsche Presse im 19. und 20. Jahrhundert: Geschichte der Presse Teil II* (Berlin, 1966).

KRABBE, WOLFGANG R. (ed.), *Politische Jugend in der Weimarer Republik* (Bochum, 1993).

——'Die Bismarckjugend der Deutschnationalen Volkspartei', *German Studies Review*, XVII (1994), 9–32.

——*Die gescheiterte Zukunft der Ersten Republik: Jugendorganisationen bürgerlicher Parteien im Weimarer Staat 1918–1933* (Opladen, 1995).

KRACAUER, SIEGFRIED, *Von Caligari zu Hitler* (Frankfurt, 1984).

KREGEL, BERND, *Außenpolitik und Systemstabilisierung in der DDR* (Opladen, 1979).

KREUZ, LEO, *Das Kuratorium Unteilbares Deutschland: Aufbau, Programmatik: Wirkung* (Opladen, 1980).

KRÖGER, MARTIN, and THIMME, ROLAND, *Die Geschichtsbilder des Historikers Karl Dietrich Erdmann: Vom Dritten Reich zur Bundesrepublik* (Munich, 1996).

KROLL, FRANK-LOTHAR, *Utopie als Ideologie: Geschichtsdenken im Dritten Reich* (Paderborn, 1998).

KRUCK, ALFRED, *Geschichte des Alldeutschen Verbandes: 1890–1939* (Wiesbaden, 1954).

KRUEDENER, JÜRGEN, BARON VON (ed.), *Economic Crisis and Political Collapse: The Weimar Republic 1924–1933* (New York, Oxford, and Munich, 1990).

Krüger, Peter, 'A Rainy Day, April 16 1922: The Rapallo Treaty and Cloudy Perspectives for German Foreign Policy', in Carole Fink, Axel Frohn, and Jürgen Heideking (eds.), *Genoa, Rapallo, and European Reconstruction in 1922* (Washington, DC, 1991), 49–64.

—— *Die Außenpolitik der Republik von Weimar*, 2nd edn. (Darmstadt, 1993).

Kuhrt, Eberhard, and Löwis, Henning von der, *Griff nach der deutschen Geschichte: Erbaneignung und Traditionspflege in der DDR* (Paderborn, 1988).

Lang, Karen, 'The Hamburg Bismarck Monument as "Lighthouse of National Thought"', in Wessel Reinink and Jeroen Stumpel (eds.), *Memory and Oblivion* (Dordrecht, 1999), 567–79.

Lange, Karl, 'Der Terminus Lebensraum in Hitler's Mein Kampf', *Vierteljahreshefte für Zeitgeschichte*, XIII (1965), 426–37.

Le Goff, Jacques, *Histoire et mémoire* (Paris, 1985).

Lehnert, Detlef, and Megerle, Klaus (eds.), *Politische Identität und nationale Gedenktage: Zur politischen Kultur in der Weimarer Republik* (Opladen, 1989).

—— and —— (eds.), *Politische Teilkulturen zwischen Integration und Polarisierung: Zur politischen Kultur in der Weimarer Republik* (Opladen, 1990).

——, ——, Lehnert, Detlef, and Megerle, Klaus, 'Problems of Identity and Consensus in a Fragmented Society: The Weimar Republic', in Dirk Berg-Schlosser and Ralf Rytlewski (eds.), *Political Culture in Germany* (London, 1993), 80–95.

Leopold, John A., *Alfred Hugenberg: The Radical Nationalist Campaign against the Weimar Republic* (New Haven and London, 1977).

Lepp, Claudia, 'Protestanten feiern ihre Nation: Die kulturprotestantischen Ursprünge des Sedantages', *Historisches Jahrbuch*, CXVIII (1998), 201–22.

Lepsius, Rainer M., 'Parteiensystem und Sozialstruktur: Zum Problem der Demokratisierung der deutschen Gesellschaft', in Gerhard A. Ritter (ed.), *Deutsche Parteien vor 1918* (Cologne, 1973), 56–80.

—— 'Das Erbe des Nationalsozialismus und die politische Kultur der Nachfolgestaaten des "Großdeutschen Reiches"', in Rainer M. Lepsius, *Demokratie in Deutschland: Soziologisch-historische Konstellationsanalysen* (Göttingen, 1993), 229–45.

Lerman, Katharine A., *The Chancellor as Courtier: Bernhard von Bülow and the Governance of Germany 1900–1909* (Cambridge, 1990).

Liebe, Werner, *Die Deutschnationale Volkspartei 1918–1924* (Düsseldorf, 1966).

Lobinski-Demedts, Maja, *Die Fortschreibung des Bismarck-Mythos in der Weimarer Republik: Analyse der Spielfilme 1925/27*, MA thesis (Bremen, 1997).

—— 'Bismarck im Film', in Machtan (ed.), *National-Mythos*, 156–79.

Low, Alfred D., *The Anschluss Movement 1918–19 and the Paris Peace Conference* (Philadelphia, 1974).

Luckau, Alma, *The German Delegation at the Paris Peace Conference* (New York, 1971).

Lutz, Felix P., *Das Geschichtsbewußtsein der Deutschen: Grundlagen der politischen Kultur in Ost und West* (Cologne, 2000).

Lutz, Heinrich, *Zwischen Habsburg und Preußen: Deutschland 1815–1866* (Berlin, 1994).

McGuire, Michael C. Q., 'Bismarck in Walhalla: The Cult of Bismarck and the Politics of National Identity in Imperial Germany 1890–1915', Ph.D. thesis (University of Pennsylvania, 1993).

Machtan, Lothar, 'Der inszenierte Mythos: Bismarck im Film', in Jost Dülffer and Hans Hübner (eds.), *Otto von Bismarck: Person—Politik—Mythos* (Berlin, 1993), 247–58.

—— (ed.), *Bismarck und der deutsche National-Mythos* (Bremen, 1994).

—— *Bismarcks Tod und Deutschlands Tränen: Reportage einer Tragödie* (Munich, 1998).

Malinowski, Stephan, *Von König zum Führer: Sozialer Niedergang und politische Radikalisierung im deutschen Adel zwischen Kaiserreich und NS-Staat* (Berlin, 2003).

Marks, Sally, 'Smoke and Mirrors: In Smoke-Filled Rooms and the Galerie des Glaces', in Boemeke *et al.* (eds.), *Treaty of Versailles*, 337–70.

Marquardt, Axel, and Rathsack, Heinz (eds.), *Preußen im Film* (Hamburg, 1981).

Mathias, Erich, and Morsey, Rudolf (eds.), *Das Ende der Parteien 1933* (Düsseldorf, 1960).

Maurer, Michael, 'Feste und Feiern als historischer Forschungsgegenstand. Ernst Walter Zeeden zum 75. Geburtstag', *Historische Zeitschrift*, CCLIII (1991), 101–30.

Meister, Rainer, *Die grosse Depression: Zwangslagen und Handlungsspielräume der Wirtschafts- und Finanzpolitik in Deutschland 1929–1932* (Regensburg, 1991).

Meyer, Christoph, *Die deutschlandpolitische Doppelstrategie: Wilhelm Wolfgang Schütz und das Kuratorium Unteilbares Deutschland* (Landsberg, 1997).

Miller, Susanne, 'Das Ringen um "die einzige großdeutsche Republik": Die Sozialdemokratie in österreich und im Deutschen Reich zur Anschlußfrage 1918/19', *Archiv für Sozialgeschichte*, XI (1971), 1–68.

Mommsen, Hans, 'Der Reichstagsbrand und seine politischen Folgen', *Vierteljahreshefte für Zeitgeschichte*, XII (1964), 351–413.

—— *The Rise and Fall of Weimar Democracy 1918–1933*, trans. Elberg Foster and Larry E. Jones (London, 1996).

—— 'Das Jahr 1930 als Zäsur in der deutschen Entwicklung der Zwischenkriegszeit', in Lothar Ehrlich and Jürgen John (eds.), *Weimar 1930: Politik und Kultur im Vorfeld der NS-Diktatur* (Cologne, Weimar, and Vienna, 1998), 1–13.

Mommsen, Wolfgang J., *Max Weber and German Politics 1890–1920* (Chicago and London, 1984).

—— *Das Ringen um den nationalen Staat: Die Gründung und der innere Ausbau des deutschen Reiches unter Otto von Bismarck 1850–1890* (Berlin, 1993).

—— 'The Spirit of 1914 and the Ideology of a German "Sonderweg"', in Wolfgang J. Mommsen, *Imperial Germany 1867–1918: Politics, Culture and Society in an Authoritarian State*, trans. Richard Deveson (London and New York, 1995), 205–16.

—— 'Der Vertrag von Versailles: Eine Bilanz', in Gerd Krumeich (ed.), *Versailles 1919—Ziele—Wirkung—Wahrnehmung* (Essen, 2001), 351–60.

Morsey, Rudolf, *Die Deutsche Zentrumspartei 1917–1923* (Düsseldorf, 1966).

—— *Bismarck und die deutschen Katholiken* (Friedrichsruh, 2000).

MOSSE, GEORGE L., *Ein Volk, ein Reich, ein Führer: Die völkischen Ursprünge des Nationalsozialismus* (Königstein, 1979).

MÜLLER-KOPPE, JENS, 'Die deutsche Sozialdemokratie und der Bismarck-Mythos', in Machtan (ed.), *National-Mythos*, 181–207.

MÜNKLER, HERFRIED, 'Nationalsozialismus und Preußen/Preußentum: Bericht über ein Forschungsprojekt', in Otto Busch (ed.), *Das Preußenbild in der Geschichte: Protokoll eines Symposiums* (Berlin and New York, 1981), 247–64.

—— 'Das kollektive Gedächtnis der DDR', in Dieter Vorsteher (ed.), *Parteiauftrag: Ein neues Deutschland: Bilder, Rituale und Symbole der frühen DDR* (Berlin, 1996), 458–68.

—— 'Das Reich als politische Macht und politischer Mythos', in Herfried Münkler, *Reich-Nation-Europa: Modelle politischer Ordnung* (Weinheim, 1996), 11–59.

MUSCHELER, KARLHEINZ, *Hermann Ulrich Kantorowicz: Eine Biographie* (Berlin, 1984).

MYERS, DUANE P., *Germany and the Question of Austrian Anschluss 1918–1922* (New Haven and London, 1968).

NEEBE, REINHARD, *Grossindustrie, Staat und NSDAP 1930–1933: Paul Silverberg und Reichsverband der Deutschen Industrie in der Krise der Weimarer Republik* (Göttingen, 1981).

NICHOLLS, ANTHONY J., *Weimar and the Rise of Hitler*, 3rd edn. (London, 1991).

—— *The Bonn Republic: West German Democracy, 1945–1990* (London, 1997).

NIEWYK, DONALD L., *The Jews in Weimar Germany* (Manchester, 1980).

NIPPERDEY, THOMAS, 'Nationalidee und Nationaldenkmal in Deutschland im 19. Jahrhundert', *Historische Zeitschrift*, CCVI (1968), 529–85.

NORA, PIERRE, *et al.* (eds.), *Les Lieux de mémoire*, 3 vols. (Paris, 1984–92).

NORDALM, JENS, *Historismus und moderne Welt: Erich Marcks, 1861–1938, in der deutschen Geschichtswissenschaft* (Berlin, 2003).

NYORMARKAY, JOSEPH, *Charisma and Factionalism in the Nazi Party* (Minneapolis, 1967).

OLDEN, RUDOLF, *Gustav Stresemann* (Berlin, 1929).

OLENHAUSEN, IRMTRAUD, GÖTZ VON, 'Die Krise der jungen Generation und der Aufstieg des Nationalsozialismus: Eine Analyse der Jugendorganisationen der Weimarer Zeit', *Jahrbuch des Archivs der Deutschen Jugendbewegung*, XII (1980), 53–82.

ORLOW, DIETRICH, *The History of the Nazi Party*, vol. I: *1919–1933* (Pittsburgh, 1969).

—— *Weimar Prussia 1918–1925: The Unlikely Rock of Democracy* (Pittsburgh, 1986).

PARR, ROLF, 'Bismarck-Mythen—Bismarck-Analogien', *Kulturrevolution*, XXIV (1991), 12–16.

—— *'Zwei Seelen wohnen, ach! In meiner Brust!': Strukturen und Funktionen der Mythisierung Bismarcks 1860–1918* (Munich, 1992).

PATCH, WILLIAM L., *Heinrich Brüning and the Dissolution of the Weimar Republic* (Cambridge, 1998).

PECK, ABRAHAM J., *Radicals and Reactionaries: The Crisis of Conservatism in Wilhelmine Germany* (Washington, DC, 1978).

PERRY, HANS-JÜRGEN, '*Nirgends ist ihm ganz zu trauen': Bismarck im Urteil Theodor Fontanes* (Friedrichsruh, 2002).

PEUKERT, DETLEF J. K., *The Weimar Republic: The Crisis of Classical Modernity*, trans. by Richard Deveson (London, 1991).

PFLANZE, OTTO, *Bismarck and the Development of Germany*, 3 vols., 2nd edn. (Princeton, 1990).

——'Bismarck's "Gedanken und Erinnerungen"', in George Egerton (ed.), *Political Memoir: Essays on the Politics of Memoir* (London, 1994), 28–61.

PLAGEMANN, VOLKER, 'Bismarck-Denkmäler', in Hans-Ernst Mittig and Volker Plagemann (eds.), *Denkmäler im 19. Jahrhundert: Deutung und Kritik* (Munich, 1972), 217–52.

POGGE VON STRANDMANN, HARTMUT: 'Rapallo—Strategy in Preventive Diplomacy: New Sources and New Interpretations', in Volker R. Berghahn and Martin Kitchen (eds.), *Germany in the Age of Total War: Essays in Honour of Francis Carsten* (London and Totowa, NJ, 1981), 123–46.

——(ed.), *Walther Rathenau: Industrialist, Banker, Intellectual and Politician: Notes and Diaries 1907–1922*, 2nd edn. (Oxford, 1988).

——'The Role of British and German Historians in Mobilizing Public Opinion in 1914', in Benedikt Stuchtey and Peter Wende (eds.), *British and German Historiography 1750–1950* (Oxford, 2000), 335–71.

PÖLS, WERNER, 'Bismarckverehrung und Bismarcklegende als innenpolitisches Problem der Wilhelminischen Zeit', *Jahrbuch für die Geschichte Mittel- und Ostdeutschlands XX* (1971), 183–201.

POMMIER, ÉDOUARD, 'Versailles: The Image of the Sovereign', in Pierre Nora and Lawrence D. Kritzman (eds.), *Realms of Memory: The Construction of the French Past*, vol. 3: *Symbolism*, trans. Arthur Goldhammer (New York and Chichester, 1998), 293–324.

PUHLE, HANS-JÜRGEN, *Agrarische Interessenpolitik und preußischer Konservatismus im wilhelminischen Reich 1893–1914: Ein Beitrag zur Analyse des Nationalismus in Deutschland am Beispiel des Bundes der Landwirte und der Deutsch-Konservativen Partei* (Hanover, 1966).

REBENTISCH, DIETER, *Friedrich Ebert und die Paulskirche: Die Weimarer Demokratie und die 75-Jahrfeier der 1848er Revolution* (Heidelberg, 1998).

REGEL, HELMUT, 'Die Friedericus-Filme der Weimarer Republik', in Marquardt and Rathsack (eds.), *Preussen im Film*, 124–34.

REINHARDT, DIRK, '"Kollektive Erinnerung" und "kollektives Gedächtnis": Zur Frage der übertragbarkeit individualpsychologischer Begriffe auf gesellschaftliche Phänomene', in Clemens Wischermann (ed.), *Die Legitimität der Erinnerung und die Geschichtswissenschaft* (Stuttgart, 1996), 87–100.

RENAN, ERNEST, 'Das Plebiszit der Vergeßlichen: über Nationen und den Dämon des Nationalismus—Ein Vortrag aus dem Jahre 1882', reprinted in *Frankfurter Allgemeine Zeitung*, 27 Mar. 1993.

RENSING, MATTHIAS, *Geschichte und Politik in den Reden der deutschen Bundespräsidenten 1949–1984* (Münster and New York, 1996).

RETALLACK, JAMES N., *Notables of the Right: The Conservative Party and Political Mobilization in Germany 1876–1918* (Boston, 1988).

REUTER, HERMANN, *Bismarck: Spuren und Wirkungen: die Bismarcks in der Altmark, das Phänomen der Bismarck-Türme und -Denkmäler, Bismarck'sche Kultur- und Wirkungs-geschichte* (Lingen, 1996).

RIBBE, WOLFGANG, 'Flaggenstreit und Heiliger Hain: Bemerkungen zur nationalen Symbolik in der Weimarer Republik', in Dietrich Kurze (ed.), *Aus Theorie und Praxis: Festschrift für Hans Herzfeld zum 80. Geburtstag* (Berlin and New York, 1972), 175–88.

RIESBERG, KLAUS E., 'Die SPD in der "Locarno-Krise" Oktober/November 1925', *Vierteljahreshefte für Zeitgeschichte*, XXX (1982), 130–61.

RINGER, FRITZ K., *The Decline of the German Mandarins: The German Academic Community 1890–1933* (Cambridge, Mass., 1969).

RÖDDER, ANDREAS, *Stresemanns Erbe: Julius Curtius und die deutsche Außenpolitik 1929–1931* (Paderborn and Munich, 1996).

—— 'Dichtung und Wahrheit: Der Quellenwert von Heinrich Brünings Memoiren und seine Kanzlerschaft', *Historische Zeitschrift*, CCLXV (1997), 77–116.

ROHE, KARL, *Das Reichsbanner Schwarz Rot Gold: Ein Beitrag zur Geschichte und Struktur der politischen Kampfverbände zur Zeit der Weimarer Republik* (Düsseldorf, 1966).

—— *Wahlen und Wählertraditionen in Deutschland: Kulturelle Grundlagen deutscher Parteien und Parteiensysteme im 19. und 20. Jahrhundert* (Frankfurt, 1992).

RÖHL, JOHN C. G., *Germany without Bismarck: The Crisis of Government in the Second Reich 1890–1900* (London, 1967).

—— *Wilhelm II.: Der Aufbau der Persönlichen Monarchie 1888–1900* (Munich, 2001).

ROPER, KATHERINE, 'Friedericus Films in Weimar Society: Potsdamismus in a Democracy', *German Studies Review*, XXVI (2003), 493–514.

ROSENFELD, GAVRIEL D., *Munich and Memory: Architecture, Monuments and the Legacy of the Third Reich* (Berkeley, Los Angeles, and London, 2000).

—— 'A Mastered Past? Prussia in Postwar German Memory', *German History* XXII (2004), 505–35.

ROSENHAFT, EVE, *Beating the Fascists? The German Communists and Political Violence 1929–1933* (Cambridge, 1983).

ROSENSTONE, ROBERT A., *Revising History-Film and the Construction of a New Past* (Princeton, 1995).

ROUSSO, HENRY, *Vichy, un passé qui ne passe pas* (Paris, 1996).

SABROW, MARTIN, *Verwaltete Vergangenheit: Geschichtskultur und Herrschaftslegitimation in der DDR* (Leipzig, 1997).

—— *Der Rathenaumord: Rekonstruktion einer Verschwörung gegen die Republik von Weimar* (Frankfurt, 1999).

SAUER, WOLFGANG, 'Das Problem des deutschen Nationalstaates', in Hans-Ulrich Wehler (ed.), *Moderne deutsche Sozialgeschichte* (Cologne, 1966), 407–36.

Schaefer, Rainer, *SPD in der Ära Brüning: Tolerierung oder Mobilisierung? Handlungsspielräume und Strategien sozialdemokratischer Politik 1930–1932* (Frankfurt, 1990).

Scharrer, Manfred, *'Freiheit is immer . . .': Die Legende von Rosa & Karl* (Berlin, 2002).

Schellack, Fritz, *Nationalfeiertage in Deutschland von 1871–1945* (Frankfurt, 1990).

Schieder, Theodor, *Das Deutsche Kaiserreich von 1871 als Nationalstaat*, 2nd edn. (Göttingen, 1991).

Schildt, Axel, *Konservatismus in Deutschland: Von den Anfängen im 18. Jahrhundert bis zur Gegenwart* (Munich, 1998).

Schirmer, Dietmar, 'Politisch-kulturelle Deutungsmuster: Vorstellungen von der Welt der Politik in der Weimarer Republik', in Detlef Lehnert and Klaus Megerle (eds.), *Politische Identität und nationale Gedenktage: Zur politischen Kultur in der Weimarer Republik* (Opladen, 1989), 31–60.

——*Mythos—Heilshoffnung—Modernität: Politisch-kulturelle Deutungscodes in der Weimarer Republik* (Opladen, 1992).

Schlenke, Manfred, 'Nationalsozialismus und Preußen/Preußentum', in Otto Büsch (ed.), *Das Preußenbild in der Geschichte* (Berlin and New York, 1981), 247–64.

——'Nationalsozialismus und Preußen: Legitimation durch Tradition', in Manfred Schleuke (ed.), *Preußische Geschichte: Eine Bilanz in Daten und Deutungen*, 2nd edn. (Freiburg and Würzburg, 1991), 262–7.

Schmädeke, Jürgen, and Steinbach, Peter (eds.), *Der Widerstand gegen den Nationalsozialismus: Die deutsche Gesellschaft und der Widerstand gegen Hitler* (Munich, 1994).

Schmitt, Carl, *Political Romanticism*, reprint of the 1st edn. of 1925 (Cambridge, Mass., 1986).

Schoch, Rainer (ed.), *Politische Plakate der Weimarer Republik 1918–1933* (Darmstadt, 1980).

Schoenberger, Gerhard, 'Das Preußenbild im deutschen Film: Geschichte und Ideologie', in Marquardt and Rathsack (eds.), *Preußen im Film*, 9–38.

Schönhoven, Klaus, 'Aufbruch in die sozialliberale Ära: Zur Bedeutung der 60er Jahre in der Geschichte der Bundesrepublik', *Geschichte und Gesellschaft*, XXV (1999), 123–45.

——*Geschichtspolitik: Über den öffentlichen Umgang mit Geschichte und Erinnerung* (Bonn, 2003).

Schönwälder, Karen, *Historiker und Politik: Geschichtswissenschaft im Nationalsozialismus* (Frankfurt and New York, 1992).

Schöttler, Peter (ed.), *Geschichte als Legitimationswissenschaft 1918–1945* (Frankfurt, 1997).

Schreiner, Klaus, '"Wann kommt der Retter Deutschlands?" Formen und Funktionen von politischem Messianismus in der Weimarer Republik', *Saeculum*, XLIX (1998), 107–60.

Schridde, Rudolf, *Zum Bismarckbild im Geschichtsunterricht: Eine historisch-didaktische Analyse deutscher Geschichtsbücher* (Düsseldorf, 1974).

SCHROEDER, KLAUS, *Der SED-Staat: Geschichte und Strukturen der DDR* (Munich, 1998).

SCHUBERT, SEBASTIAN, 'Abschied vom Nationalstaat? Die deutsche Reichsgründung 1871 in der Geschichtspolitik des geteilten Deutschlands von 1965 bis 1974', in Winkler (ed.), *Griff nach der Deutungsmacht*, 230–65.

SCHULZE, HAGEN, *Weimar: Deutschland 1917–1933*, 4th rev. edn. (Berlin, 1994).

SCHULZE, RAINER (ed.), *Flüchtlinge und Vertriebene in der westdeutschen Nachkriegsgeschichte* (Hildesheim, 1987).

SEE, KLAUS VON, *Deutsche Germanen-Ideologie: Vom Humanismus bis zur Gegenwart* (Frankfurt, 1970).

SEIER, HELLMUT, 'Bismarck und die Anfänge des Kaiserreiches im Urteil der deutschen Historiographie vor 1914', in Johannes Kunisch (ed.), *Bismarck und seine Zeit* (Berlin, 1992), 359–95.

SHAMIR, HAIM, *Economic Crisis and French Foreign Policy 1930–1936* (Leiden, 1989).

SMITH, WOODRUFF D., *The Ideological Origins of Nazi Imperialism* (New York and Oxford, 1986).

SONTHEIMER, KURT, *Antidemokratisches Denken in der Weimarer Republik: Die politischen Ideen des deutschen Nationalismus zwischen 1918 und 1933*, 4th edn. (Munich, 1994).

SPETH, RUDOLF, and WOLFRUM, EDGAR, (eds.), *Politische Mythen und Geschichtspolitik: Konstruktion—Inszenierung—Mobilisierung* (Berlin, 1996).

STAMBROOK, F. G., 'The German-Austrian Customs Union Project of 1931: A Study of German Methods and Motives', in Hans W. Gatzke (ed.), *European Diplomacy Between the Two Wars* (Chicago, 1972).

STARITZ, DIETRICH, *Geschichte der DDR*, 2nd edn. (Frankfurt, 1996).

STEGMANN, DIRK, *Die Erben Bismarcks: Parteien und Verbände in der Spätphase des Wilhelminischen Deutschlands* (Cologne and Berlin, 1970).

STÖBER, RUDOLF, 'Bismarcks geheime Presseorganisation', *Historische Zeitschrift*, CCLXII (1996), 423–51.

STRATH, BO (ed.), *Myth and Memory in the Construction of Community: Historical Patterns in Europe and Beyond* (Brussels, 2000).

STUDT, CHRISTOPH, *Das Bismarckbild der deutschen Öffentlichkeit* (Friedrichsruh, 1999).

STÜRMER, MICHAEL, 'Bismarck-Mythos und Historie', *Aus Politik und Zeitgeschichte*, XVI (1971), 1–30.

SUVAL, STANLEY, 'Overcoming Kleindeutschland: The Politics of Historical Mythmaking in the Weimar Republik', *Central European History*, II (1969), 312–30.

—— *The Anschluß Question in Germany and Austria in the Weimar Era: A Study of Nationalism in Germany and Austria 1918–1932* (Baltimore and London, 1974).

SYNOTTEK, ARNOLD, 'Die Fischer Kontroverse. Ein Beitrag zur Entwicklung historisch-politischen Bewußtseins in der Bundesrepublik', in Immanuel Geiss and Bernd Jürgen Wendt (eds.), *Deutschland in der Weltpolitik des 19. Jahrhunderts* (Düsseldorf, 1973), 19–47.

THAMER, HANS-ULRICH, 'Geschichte und Propaganda: Kulturhistorische Ausstellungen in der NS-Zeit', *Geschichte und Gesellschaft*, XXIV (1998), 349–81.

THIMME, ANNELIESE, *Gustav Stresemann: Eine politische Biographie zur Geschichte der Weimarer Republik* (Hanover and Frankfurt, 1957).

——— *Flucht in den Mythos: Die Deutschnationale Volkspartei und die Niederlage von 1918* (Göttingen, 1969).

THIMME, ROLAND, *Stresemann und die Deutsche Volkspartei 1923–1925* (Lübeck and Hamburg, 1961).

THORNSETT, MICHAEL C., *The German Opposition to Hitler: The Resistance, the Underground, and Assassination Plots 1938–1945* (London, 1997).

TIRRELL, SARAH R., *German Agrarian Politics after Bismarck's Fall: The Formation of the Farmers' League* (New York, 1951).

TRIPPE, CHRISTIAN F., *Konservative Verfassungspolitik 1918–1923: Die DNVP als Opposition in Reich und Ländern* (Düsseldorf, 1995).

TURNER, HENRY ASHBY, Jr., *German Big Business and the Rise of Hitler* (New York and Oxford, 1985).

——— *Hitler's Thirty Days to Power: January 1933* (Reading, Mass., 1996).

TYRELL, ALBRECHT, *Vom 'Trommler' zum 'Führer': Der Wandel von Hitlers Selbstverständnis zwischen 1919 und 1924 und die Entwicklung der NSDAP* (Munich, 1975).

UFFELMANN, UWE (ed.), *Identitätsbildung und Geschichtsbewußtsein nach der Vereinigung Deutschlands* (Weinheim, 1993).

ULLRICH, VOLKER, *Die nervöse Großmacht: Aufstieg und Untergang des deutschen Kaiserreiches 1871–1918* (Frankfurt, 1997).

URBANITSCH, PETER, 'Großbritannien und die Verträge von Locarno', Ph.D. thesis (Vienna, 1968).

VALLENTIN, ANTONIA, *Gustav Stresemann: Vom Werden einer Staatsidee* (Leipzig, 1929).

VASCIK, GEORGE, 'Agrarian Conservatism in Wilhelmine Germany: Diederich Hahn and the Agrarian League', in Larry Eugene Jones and James Retallack (eds.), *Between Reform, Reaction, and Resistance: Studies in the History of German Conservatism from 1789 to 1945* (Providence, RI, and Oxford, 1993), 229–60.

VERHEY, JEFFREY, *The Spirit of 1914: Militarism, Myth, and Mobilization in Germany* (Cambridge, 2000).

VOIGT, GERD, *Otto Hoetzsch 1876–1946: Wissenschaft und Politik im Leben eines deutschen Historikers* (East Berlin, 1978).

WALDMAN, ERIC, *The Spartacist Uprising of 1919 and the Crisis of the German Socialist Movement: A Study of the Relation of Political Theory and Party Practice* (Milwaukee, 1958).

WALSDORFF, MARTIN, *Westorientierung und Ostpolitik: Stresemanns Rußlandpolitik in der Locarno-Ära* (Bremen, 1971).

WATT, RICHARD M., *The Kings Depart: The Tragedy of Germany: Versailles and the German Revolution* (London, 1968).

WEBER, HERMANN, *Die Wandlung des deutschen Kommunismus: Die Stalinisierung der KPD in der Weimarer Republik*, 2 vols. (Frankfurt, 1969).

WEGNER-KORFES, SIGRID, *Otto von Bismarck und Rußland: Des Reichskanzlers Rußlandpolitik und sein realpolitisches Erbe in der Interpretation bürgerlicher Politiker 1918–1945* (Berlin, 1990).

WEHLER, HANS-ULRICH (ed.), *Deutsche Historiker*, vols. I–III (Göttingen, 1971–3).

——*Deutsche Gesellschaftsgeschichte*, vol. 3: *Von der 'Deutschen Doppelrevolution' bis zum Beginn des Ersten Weltkrieges 1849–1914* (Munich, 1995).

WEISZ, CHRISTOPH, *Geschichtsauffassung und politisches Denken Münchener Historiker der Weimarer Republik: Konrad Beyerle, Max Buchner, Michael Doeberl, Erich Marcks, Karl Alexander von Müller, Hermann Oncken* (Berlin, 1970).

WELCH, DAVID, *Propaganda and the German Cinema 1933–1945*, 2nd rev. edn. (Oxford, 2001).

WINKLER, HEINRICH AUGUST, *Von der Revolution zur Stabilisierung: Arbeiter und Arbeiterbewegung in der Weimarer Republik 1918–1924*, 2nd rev. edn. (Berlin and Bonn, 1985).

——*Der Schein der Normalität: Arbeiter und Arbeiterbewegung in der Weimarer Republik 1924–1930*, 2nd rev. edn. (Berlin and Bonn, 1988).

——*Der Weg in die Katastrophe: Arbeiter und Arbeiterbewegung in der Weimarer Republik*, 2nd rev. edn. (Berlin and Bonn, 1990).

——'Die Revolution von 1918/19 und das Problem der Kontinuität in der deutschen Geschichte', *Historische Zeitschrift*, CCL (1990), 303–19.

——(ed.), *Die deutsche Staatskrise 1930–1933: Handlungsspielräume und Alternativen* (Munich, 1992).

——*Weimar 1918–1933: Die Geschichte der ersten deutschen Demokratie*, 2nd rev. edn. (Munich, 1994).

——*Der lange Weg nach Westen*, vol. 1: *Deutsche Geschichte vom Ende des Alten Reiches bis zum Untergang der Weimarer Republik* (Munich, 2000).

——*Der lange Weg nach Westen*, vol. 2: *Deutsche Geschichte vom 'Dritten Reich' bis zur Wiedervereinigung* (Munich, 2000).

——(ed.), *Griff nach der Deutungsmacht: Zur Geschichte der Geschichtspolitik in Deutschland* (Göttingen, 2004).

WITT, PETER-CHRISTIAN, 'Die Gründung des Deutschen Reiches oder dreimal Kaiserfest', in Uwe Schultz (ed.), *Das Fest: Eine Kulturgeschichte von der Antike bis zur Gegenwart* (Munich, 1988), 306–17.

WITTENBERG, ERICH, *Bismarcks politische Persönlichkeit im Bilde der Weimar-Republik: Eine ideengeschichtliche Beleuchtung einer politischen Tradition* (Lund, 1969).

WOLFRUM, EDGAR, 'Geschichte als Politikum—Geschichtspolitik: Internationale Forschungen zum 19. und 20. Jahrhundert', *Neue Politische Literatur*, XLI (1996), 376–401.

——'Der Kult um den verlorenen Nationalstaat in der Bundesrepublik Deutschland bis Mitte der 60er Jahre', *Historische Anthropologie*, V (1997), 83–114.

——'Geschichtspolitik und deutsche Frage', *Geschichte und Gesellschaft*, XXIV (1998), 382–411.

——*Geschichtspolitik in der Bundesrepublik Deutschland. Der Weg zur bundesrepublikanischen Erinnerung 1948–1990* (Darmstadt, 1999).

WOLFRUM, EDGAR, *Geschichte als Waffe: vom Kaiserreich bis zur Wiedervereinigung* (Göttingen, 2001).

WRIGHT, JONATHAN D., 'Stresemann and Locarno', *Contemporary European History*, IV (1995), 109–31.

—— *Gustav Stresemann: Weimar's Greatest Statesman* (Oxford, 2002).

WÜLFING, WULF, BRUNS, KARIN, and PARR, ROLF, *Historische Mythologie der Deutschen 1789–1918* (Munich, 1991).

ZECHLIN, EGMONT, 'Der Inbegriff des germanischen Menschen: Das Bismarck-Bild 1915: Eine Mischung aus Sage und Mythos', *Die Zeit*, 2 Apr. 1965.

ZMARZLIK, HANS-GÜNTER, *Das Bismarckbild der Deutschen—gestern und heute* (Freiburg im Breisgau, 1965).

INDEX